Empath, Narcissists and Codependency Cycle Recovery:

Learn How to Deal with a Narcissistic Personality and Escape from a Codependent Relationship Even if You are a Highly Sensitive Person

DANIEL ANDERSON

EMPATH

How to live in an insensitive world
when you're too sensitive

By

DANIEL ANDERSON

TABLE OF CONTENT

CHAPTER 1

UNDERSTANDING AN EMPATH

Who Is an Empath?

What does it mean to be an "empath"? Does it mean I'm psychic? Or does it simply mean that I'm incredibly sensitive to the emotional feelings of others? Are empaths more likely to be really "good" people? Do they have any other natural gifts or sensitivities that are noteworthy? And how do empaths USE their gifts in the real world to make a difference or an impact in the places that they live?

Describing what an empath IS...is quite simple:

An empath is someone who has an unusually strong sense of connection, sensitivity and "simpatico' with the emotions and feelings of other people. The word sensitive is probably the word that conveys the essence of what an empath IS, better than any other word...however, it doesn't mean they are emotionally sensitive themselves.

In other words, many empaths are very practical and pragmatic with their own emotions but are highly sensitive to YOURS.

Are all empaths naturally really good people?

It's a funny question and one that probably can't be answered with 100% carte blanche certainty as a result. BUT, in my own experience, empaths tend to be highly caring, nurturing and emotionally available people by nature, and tend to be givers, rather than takers as a general rule as well.

What kind of work do empaths do?

The most common is service work that incorporates their gifts in a way that "serves" the people who need them most.

For example?

Many empaths have tremendous psychic and intuitive gifts, simply because they are far more naturally connected to the emotions and needs of other people. Many social scientists describe empaths as having a very REAL "6th sense" which is the ability to identify, understand and ultimately bond with people and their problems in the way that most of us can't. This leads to an astounding amount of insight and intuition that can border on being unexplained.

Some recent studies seem to suggest that the 6th sense that emotional empaths have is quite literally, a more highly developed brain in 2 specific areas.

What are they?

The area in the brain that modulates a feeling of "connection" to others, (well known to be triggered through meditation) and another area deep in the brain thought to trigger synesthesia, a little known but proven phenomena where people can hear colours and see sounds. (it's also thought by many to be a possible scientific explanation for everything from psychic abilities to spirit communication to seeing and sensing auras)

Are all empaths psychic?

Not. But MANY, inexplicably... are. And when you combine these two little-understood abilities, you get people who not only are incredibly attuned to the energetic frequencies of others; they are ALSO able to see future events and make powerful predictions about how where you are NOW will impact where you're going to end up. (and what you MAY need to do to avoid a catastrophe before you get there!)

The power of an empath is not always seen as important as it should be. Those with the skills of an empath maintain psychic abilities which could prove enormously helpful to those dealing with serious psychological issues. How is this so? An empath has the potential to perform emotional healing which can be considered a tremendous benefit to those suffering from depression and other related mental issues.

The reason this is so is that an empath is an individual that can "feel" the emotions of another person. This does not just refer to the ability to be perceptive to someone's emotional state. Such talents can be considered a skill, but it would hardly rise to the level of psychic ability. No, with an empath, the sensitivity to a person's emotional state will be far deeper and far more impactful. An empath can tap into the emotional aura of a person and outright experience what the other person is feeling.

In essence, the empath will extract a duplication of the other person's emotions and absorb them into his/her being. Once these emotions have been absorbed, the empath becomes the other person at least from an emotionally perceptive state. In many ways, this can be one of the most difficult of all psychic abilities to endure. It can be a sincerely troubling thing to deal with one's emotional state much less that of another person. The empath will do so and experience exactly what another is experiencing.

Questions will arise regarding why an empath would do this. Different empaths have different reason and motivations for their actions. One reason that people cultivate their abilities to serve as an empath would be to act as an emotional healer. Yes, it is possible to enter into the mind and psyche of the person whose emotions are being fused with and reducing the negative energy and replacing it with positive energy. This can yield a unique response in the form of eradicating the negative psychological holds poor energy can have on a person. And in some cases, the negative psychological consequences can be reversed or outright eliminated. That is certainly a good thing and the results of which could free a person of problematic psychic hindrances forever more.

This is not to suggest that meeting with an empath will automatically replace the need for seeking the help of a legitimate psychotherapist. The level of one's psychological dysfunction must always be addressed when discussing whether or not an empath should be the primary caregiver. In some instances, serious psychiatric help may be required. However, there is no reason why an empath cannot offer secondary help to those in dire need of it. The secondary help offered by the empath could prove to be a tremendous support to even the most serious of all psychological conditions.

A discussion about the psychic abilities of an empath is far more complex than more people realize. An empath is more than just a perceptive person. Rather, the empath can be considered an emotional chameleon that is capable of delving deep into the emotional state of another. In some cases, the empath may even determine the process for healing even the most afflicted emotional energy.

Are You An Empath?

Empathic people are emotionally sensitive. In these changing times, people who have always been sensitive may find they are even more sensitive now. And people who were not that sensitive may find they are becoming more so.

According to Dr Kyra Mesich, sensitivity is an issue of our times. And for the reasons stated above I agree. It impacts all types of personalities, ages, cultures. It is especially prevalent in people who try to impact other people positively.

It is more often activated in situations with people who mirror our subconscious feelings and beliefs.

Why should you care about this? Well first of all, if you are not aware of it, it can explain certain phenomena happening in your life that you may not have understood before such as unexplained mood swings such as crying for no apparent reason or very angry about something that might normally just be an irritant, increased fatigue, insomnia, body aches and tension, and illness... also could be buoyantly happy..

From a business or career perspective, it can impact your ability to be productive, interact with others, make a contribution in the world and have the energy to make a good living doing it. From a personal standpoint, it can impact your ability to have fun, partake in physical activity, your relationships and your well-being. And that's just a start.

What are the signs that you are an empath?

(emotionally sensitive)

1. Emotionally sensitive people feel emotions often and deeply. They may feel as if they "wear their emotions on their sleeves but not necessarily. Men may feel things but not show it as much due to cultural training that it is not okay to do so.

2. They are keenly aware of the emotions of people around them.

3. Sensitive people are easily hurt or upset. An insult or unkind remark will affect them deeply.

4. In a similar vein, sensitive people may strive to avoid conflicts because the negativity affects them so much.

5. Sensitive people are not able to shake off emotions easily. Once they are saddened or upset by something, they cannot just switch gears and forget it. (this appears to be changing)

6. Sensitive people are greatly affected by emotions they witness. They feel deeply for others' suffering. They may cry at Hallmark commercials or when others cry or when they connect deeply with someone.

7. Sensitive people may suffer from recurrent depression, anxiety or other psychological disorders.

8. On the positive side, sensitive people, are also keenly aware of and affected by beauty in art, music and nature. They are the world's greatest artists and art appreciators.

9. Sensitive people are prone to stimulus overload. That is, they can't stand large crowds, loud noise, or hectic environments. They feel overwhelmed and depleted by too many stimuli.

10. Sensitive people are born that way. They were sensitive children. I think this is not as true as it once was. As I said before, people are becoming more sensitive than they ever were.

11. A truly sensitive person sometimes feels animosity toward his sensitive nature. Most sensitive people whole-heartedly wish they were tougher and more thick-skinned. They feel like their sensitivity is a weakness. Therefore some sensitive adults have learned how to hide their sensitivity from others.

How to Tell If You Are An Empath

Are you an Empath? If you answer yes to some of the following questions, you probably are:

• I can tell when someone says one thing but means another.

• I can often see through other peoples' eyes.

• I get compliments like: "You understand me better than others do."

• If I have to give the same speech to three different strangers, it comes out differently every time. Somehow I sense the way they need to hear the information.

• I can easily feel the negative emotions and physical symptoms of another.

• I feel particularly free when outside in nature.

• I can easily connect with my pet's world.

• Watching TV shows with highly dramatic emotional confrontations like Jerry Springer makes me feel sick and cry.

• My friendships are much more intense than others' friendships.

• My need to connect with others like myself is strong, to know I'm not alone.

Empaths can be people pleasers. It is so easy for them to know what others want to hear and to have. They tend to be kind people who only want to help. Often they are found in the helping professions like healers and caregivers. They volunteer their time and energy and think nothing of giving all they have, sometimes to their detriment.

It is important for Empaths to take time for themselves. Because they give away so much of their energy or it is drawn from them, they need to find a quiet place to recharge. Consider using some protection images every day to keep others from draining your energy, particularly in crowded places like buses, subways and stores. The elderly and young mothers will draw energy from you without meaning to.

Being an Empath is not a choice. Either you were born that way or not. That means that you may have been receiving other people's energies from day one. Like when my father was in the hospital having his gall bladder removed, I could feel my mother's worry about him for days afterwards. And when my dear grandfather died when I was eight years old, I have memories of my mother's overwhelming grief and sadness that I thought were my emotions.

Most of the clients I see have some empathic ability and don't know it. When they feel bad, which is often, they believe it is their own emotions causing this. A lot of the time they have picked up a negative emotion like fear, anger or sadness from someone close to them and cannot tell that it is not their own. That is quite understandable if you don't know that is something you could do.

Here is a little exercise to recognize which emotions are yours. When you get comfortable doing this, you will be able to tell when you have picked up emotions that are not yours.

Is This Mine?

1. Take three slow deep breaths;

2. One at a time, pay attention:

- To your breath

- To your physical body

- To your conscious mind

- To your emotions right now

3. Notice how the above four feel right now.

 When you notice something different happening in one of the above four through your day, try the following ways to Release:

1. Say, "All that does not belong to me, be gone;"

2. In your mind cut the cord between you and the other person;

3. In your mind draw a circle of protection and step into it, taking it with you;

4. Tap the 9 EFT points repeating, "Release others' energies;"

5. Shower off other's energies; or

6. Strong physical exercise.

Then pay attention to the above four to see if you feel like you again.

You need to be willing to be who you are. That means learning to ground so that your life is in balance with the time you spend using your Empath abilities. You can use sex, aerobic exercise, sleep, walking outdoors, massage, stretching, sitting or standing in direct contact with the earth, looking after your pet, cleaning your home, gardening or concentrating on your paying job.

It is important to learn to pay attention to your own emotions, compared to what you pick up. This takes practice, but over time, you will learn how to separate yourself from others' emotions. Empaths are needed now more than ever in these changing times. Learn to enjoy your abilities and find balance in your life.

Characteristics of an Empath

Empaths are loving, caring, kind people who want to help others. They are often found doing volunteer work and may serve others through emotionally-demanding careers as childcare givers, medical professionals, hospice workers, midwives, and such. Most empaths came in with a mission to heal people, animals, plants, and the planet. As healers, many have taken on so much external energy that they spend most of their time trying to clear unwanted energy and recuperate from the last episode that "blew their doors off."

Here are a few characteristics of empaths who have not learned to filter out other people's emotions or manage their energy:

You constantly feel overwhelmed with emotions, and you may cry a lot, feel sad, angry, or depressed for no good reason. You may be tempted to think you are crazy for having random mood swings and bouts of unexplained fatigue. If you are a woman, it's like having PMS all the time! Unrestrained empathy can cause a person to manifest symptoms similar to bipolar (manic-depressive) disorder.

You drop by the store feeling great, but once you get in a crowd, you start feeling down, angry, sad or overwhelmed. You feel you must be coming down with something, so you decide to go home and rest.

If you've found that you can't be in public without becoming overwhelmed you may start to live the life of a hermit. But, even at home, you get depressed when you watch the news, and you cry while watching a movie. You feel horrible when a commercial for the Humane Society shows animals that need a home. You may rescue more animals than you can care for.

You feel sorry for people no matter who they are or what they have done. You feel the need to stop and help anyone in your path. You can't pass by a homeless person without giving him money-even if you don't have it to spare.

Many empaths are overweight. When they absorb stressful emotions, it can trigger panic attacks, depression as well as food, sex, and drug binges. Some may overeat to cope with emotional stress or use their body weight as a shield or buffer. In Chapter 9 of Yvonne Perry's book, she shows how to use light as protection.

Most empaths can physically and emotionally heal others by drawing the pain or ailment out of the sick person and into their bodies. For obvious reasons, this is not recommended unless you know how to keep from becoming ill in the process.

From chest pains and stomach cramps to migraines and fever, you manifest symptoms without contracting an actual illness. Later, you learn that your "ailment" coincided with the onset of a friend or family member's illness.

No one can lie to you because you can see through their facade and know what they mean. You may even know why they lied.

People-even strangers-open up and start volunteering their personal information. You may be sitting in the waiting room minding your own business and waiting for your turn when the person next to you starts sharing all kinds of personal information. You didn't ask them to, and they never considered that you might not want to hear about their drama. People may feel better after speaking with you, but you end up feeling worse because they have transferred their emotional pain to you.

Some empaths don't do well with intimate relationships. Constantly taking on their partner's pain and emotions, they may easily get their feelings hurt, desire to spend time alone rather than with the partner, feel vulnerable when having sex, and feel that they have to continually retrieve their energy when it gets jumbled with that of their partner. They may be so afraid of becoming engulfed by another person that they close up emotionally just to survive.

The ill, the suffering, and those with weak boundaries are drawn to the unconditional understanding and compassion an empath emits without even being aware of it. Until you learn how to shut out the energy of others, you may have a pretty miserable existence in which you feel like you have to be entirely alone to survive.

It's easy to see why being an empath is often very draining. No wonder that over time, some folks shut down their empathic ability. And, with that, they also shut down a vital part of their divine guidance system. Learn how to manage the amount of info-energy you receive and hear more of what is important.

20 Things That Might Mean You Are an Empath

Being an empathic person can be challenging. Many Empaths have no idea why they feel overwhelmed by life. Their families are critical and call them too sensitive or recluse. This gift of sensitivity isn't a bad trait but something that can be controlled and should be celebrated.

An Empath receives more information about the world and activities than those who scoff at them. While it may be hard to process all the energetic information being received, an Empath can do wondrous things with this way of sensing life. Here are 20 things commonly experienced by Empaths. If your life is like this, you just might be an Empath too.

You can walk past a crowd of people and start to feel strange. You may suddenly feel angry or sad. The emotion overwhelms you, and you just have to get away. You have no explanation for your sudden changes in emotions. You just FEEL it.

You try to ignore all the rush of energy that you absorb, but you are so overwhelmed that you just want to be alone. I avoid malls for this reason and only shop at individual stores where I can dash in and back out, or I shop in open air pedestrian malls. You've been called overly sensitive all your life and usually in a negative connotation, but you know it isn't you, it's the surroundings.

You experience other physical ailments. Someone in the room has a headache, and after entering the room, you do too. You were fine before entering the room. This frequently happens to people you have relationships with, but it can occur with anyone.

You feel so lethargic that you just stay in bed. It isn't depression, but you would just rather be alone. You aren't a loner; you just need to be alone to recharge your battery. When the company leaves, you need a nap.

Your fatigue coincides with a family member's illness, but you live in another state, and there has been no communication between the two of you before your fatigue.

You experience the same symptoms as a relative's illness, but not the actual illness. For example, I was driving when my father had a stroke. I suddenly got dizzy and felt air bubbles going up through my head. I had to pull over and figure out if it was me or someone else. Later that night, I found out he had had the stroke just as I felt it.

You are overwhelmed when watching horrible thing that happen in real life or on television. Do you experience the feelings of the people involved as though you've been punched in the gut or burst into tears, shaking etc.?

You can drive over a place where there has been an accident and suddenly crumple in physical or emotional pain.

You aren't able to watch the news.

You always know what someone really means and what they meant to say.

You always know when someone is lying. I've always called this my BS Meter.

You have a knowing about situations that are more than intuition, hunches or statistical probability.

You feel compelled to care for someone even if they are unkind to you.

You feel compelled to care for someone on the spot and generally that help is accepted.

People tell you their life story and wonder why they are telling you all about it.

You can't stand In Your Face people and just want to stay away from them and generally be alone. You are very sensitive to smells, excessive talking or loud sounds. You may be so overwhelmed that you develop physical symptoms like headaches or instant colds.

You can heal instinctively by drawing pain or ailments into your own body.

You would rather drive in your car so that you can get out quickly when you start to feel overloaded.

You often feel spacey and clumsy because all the incoming energies unground you.

This list of list of possible behaviours can help you decide if you are an Empath or not. If you do feel like you are an Empath, you probably need help working with all the energy and information coming at you. Look for ways to deal with it all, and you'll find like a kinder place to be.

Empaths - The Sensitive Ones

Empaths are people whose sensitivity is much greater than that of the average Joe or Josie.

Empaths are people who:

• often get confused between their feelings and other peoples,

• can look at a person and tell what they are feeling and experiencing,

• often have difficulty being in crowded places like shopping centres or pubs,

• attract energy vampires to them (people who drain your energy) and

• can sometimes feel natural and man-made disasters before they happen,

If you are an Empath, you probably struggle with many aspects of daily life. One of the major problems with Empaths is that they tend to take on other people's emotions and issues as though they were their own. When you feel other people's feelings, you often don't realise that the emotions are coming from outside of yourself. They all tend to feel as though they are your emotions which can be very confusing and often overwhelming. After a while of accumulating emotions both yours and others, you can get very sick. To move beyond these difficulties, some new Life Skills need to be introduced and implemented.

There are some ways to counteract the problems of being an Empath. Many of them have to do with defining and clarifying who you are and what you believe. The first and most important action to take is to get focused on your thoughts and beliefs. As you come to a much clearer, more conscious awareness about who you are and what you believe compared to what others believe, you will widen the gap between yourse lf and other's emotions. Even if you do take on another's feelings, it will be easier to recognise them as not belonging to you. Once the recognition is made, you can easily let go of the other persons 'stuff'.

Another set of activities that is very important in clearing up the empathic difficulties is that of cleansing and protecting your energy field. There are many, many ways in which to do this, and I will offer just a few.

For cleansing the energy field, I recommend with every shower that you take; you imagine that the water is super powerful, sparkling, cleansing energy that flushes all over and through your body, easily washing away any build up of negative energy. At the same time while having the shower, in your mind, call out to Archangel Michael (the defender and protector) to come and use his powerful sword to swipe through any cords all over your body, that are draining your energy. These two activities will easily release great amounts of negative energy.

For protecting the energy, I recommend that every morning you call upon Archangel Michael and ask him to wrap his wings around you, sealing and protecting you from any negative energy throughout the day. I also suggest that using your imagination, you surround yourself with a beautiful sparkly mirrorball, that instantly reflects all negative energy away from you.

Simply by performing these four exercises daily and working on defining who you are and what you believe, you can make a real difference to your experiences in this life. After a while of doing that, you can even start to open up to the gifts of being an empath, such as having a greater level of insight into people's behaviour and their intentions. Being an Empath truly is a wonderful gift, and you can experience it as such with a bit of healing work.

CHAPTER 2

HIGHLY SENSITIVE PEOPLE

Highly Sensitive People

Just imagine what the world might be like if the highly sensitive people were in charge. Shopping malls, if they existed, would play soothing music at low volumes and eliminate the flashing lights. Restaurants would be designed such that you could talk in a normal tone and be heard by your dinner mates; shouting to be heard over the din of the other diners, the kitchen, and the wait staff a thing of the past. Television would stop emphasizing violence and focus more on the good stuff of life. Oh, those could be the days...

What is a highly sensitive person, you may be asking. I can't recall the first time I heard the term, but I do know it was shortly after the book, "The Highly Sensitive Person," by Elaine Aron, was released. It's best to read the book to get a full view, and in the spirit of

explanation I'll give a few bullet points here:

20% of the population is "wired" differently. They take in more information that the other 80%, and process it on a much deeper level. It's common for something they've experienced to stay with them twice as long as it would the others.

They may hear they are "too sensitive" from those around them, that they need tougher skin. They tend to be emotional and feel things deeply.

They notice the little things in their environment. This makes them attentive to what fabrics they wear, what type of food they eat (and how often), how well they sleep if one small thing around them changes, and what perfume the person next to them is wearing.

Why am I bringing this up? Because Leslie and I are highly sensitive people and we spent our lives up until we heard the term wondering what was wrong with us. In light of this new information we understand that there are many like us; in fact, a quick poll of those we enjoy being with shows that many of them are highly sensitive, too - who knew! Oprah always says when you know better you do better.

Applying that to this newfound knowledge about being highly sensitive, ponder these questions:

Many may feel that there is something wrong with them because of their sensitivity. Reframing this thought, how could you view your sensitivity as a good thing?

Highly sensitive people are frequently connected to others, animals and the planet on a deep level. How can this be used to make you and those around you live a better life?

What is the best way you can take care of yourself? Perhaps it is eating more frequently, visiting spas, meeting with a group of supportive friends that share your trait, or giving yourself permission to stay in the house all day.

Learning about and living as a highly sensitive person can at once be challenging and the most rewarding thing you'll ever do. Owning our businesses, running workshops and teaching classes, developing a business alliance with a day spa, coaching one on one clients, and being part of a supportive community - our partnership first and foremost - have been terrific ways for Leslie and I to take care of our sensitivity. We encourage you to find the support you need to discover the true contribution that you are, just as you are. What first step will you take today to embrace your

Highly Sensitive People -- An Introduction to the Trait of High Sensitivity

Here is an overview and some of what I've learned during the last 9 years of intense study about the trait of high sensitivity. Also included, are some tips, tools, and strategies we've discovered on how to successfully navigate through life when you or someone important to you has the trait of high sensitivity. My goal is that I want HSPs not just to cope with their trait, but to excel with it!

I've learned highly sensitive persons or "HSPs" make up 15% to 20% of the population. (People with the trait of high sensitivity are also sometimes referred to as ultra-sensitive people, or super sensitive people.) HSP's nervous systems are different and are more sensitive to subtleties in their environment, which can be a good or bad thing. And because they process and reflect upon incoming information so deeply, they are more likely to become over stimulated and overwhelmed than Non-HSP.

Highly sensitive individuals have often said they feel they are "different" and just don't fit in; we've even heard some HSPs say they sometimes feel like they're from a different planet.

Being highly sensitive is an inherited trait and is described brilliantly in Dr Elaine Aron's book The Highly Sensitive Person: How to Thrive When the World Overwhelms You. This is a book I highly recommend.

I've also learned a great deal from Psychologist Carl G. Jung's "Psychological Types," Dr John M. Oldham's "Sensitive Personality Style," and Dr Kazimierz Dabrowski's "Theory of

Positive Disintegration" and "Overexcitabilities."

It is in highly sensitive person's nature to "pause-to-check" and not to rush into new or different situations, but rather to proceed much more cautiously than their Non-HSP counterparts. The trait of high sensitivity causes them to process and reflect upon incoming information very deeply. It is not that they are "fearful" or "afraid," but that it's in their nature to process incoming information so deeply. Highly sensitive persons may even sometimes need until the next day to have had enough time to process the information fully, reflect upon it, and formulate their response.

The trait of high sensitivity can be viewed as having both positive as well as negative characteristics, and it is a valid and normal trait and is not a character flaw or disorder.

On the positive side, and there is a big positive side, we have learned highly sensitive people have wonderful imaginations, are often very intelligent, creative, curious, and are known for being very hard workers, great organizers and problem solvers. They are known for being extremely conscientious and meticulous. HSP are blessed with being exceptionally intuitive, caring, compassionate and spiritual. They are also blessed with incredible aesthetic awareness and appreciation for nature, music and the arts.

Pearl S. Buck, (1892-1973), recipient of the Pulitzer Prize in 1932 and the Nobel Prize in Literature in 1938, once said about highly sensitive people:

"The truly creative mind in any field is no more than this:

A human creature born abnormally, inhumanly sensitive.

To him...

- touch is a blow,

- a sound is a noise,

- misfortune is a tragedy,

- joy is an ecstasy,

- a friend is a lover,

- a lover is a god,

- and failure is death.

Add to this cruelly delicate organism the overpowering necessity to create, create, create - so that without the creating of music or poetry or books or buildings or something of meaning, his very breath is cut off from him. He must create, must pour out creation. By some strange, unknown, inward urgency he is not alive unless he is creating." -Pearl S. Buck

There is also a strong correlation between the trait of high sensitivity and being "Gifted." It is probably accurate to say that although not all gifted people are highly sensitive, all highly sensitive people are gifted. And, Dr Dabroski's "OE" theory is that people born with overexcitabilities have a higher level of "development potential" than others and that their overexcitabilities feed, enrich, empower and amplify their talents.

Some of the diverse group of individuals that might belong on the list of those who exhibit the characteristics of the trait of high sensitivity would include: Albert Einstein, Carl Jung,

Emily Dickinson, Charles Darwin, Abraham Lincoln, Katharine Hepburn, Woody Allen, Queen Elizabeth II, Orson Welles, Walt Disney, Ansel Adams, Nicole Kidman, Nicolas Cage, Steven Spielberg, Jane Goodall, Warren Buffett, Barbara Streisand, Michael Jordan, Elton John, Bob Dylan, Jim Morrison, Jewel, John Denver, Alanis Morissette, and Princess Diana, to name a few. And, a couple of possible HSPs from TV that comes to mind include Radar O'Reilly on the classic sitcom M*A*S*H and currently Adrain Monk, the detective with OCD, on the series MONK. Some feature films portraying characters that may give some insight into the trait of high sensitivity include: "The Hours," "The Green Mile," "Amelie," "Hannibal," and "Adaptation."

We hope you'll recognise that the trait of high sensitivity is a gift and blessing, albeit a gift that can come with a hefty price tag. But, a gift we hope you'll come to realize is worth every penny of the price.

As we have come to know, the highly sensitive person's systems are very porous, that is external stimuli seems to be more directly absorbed into their bodies. (It has been said that it is as if HSP hardly have any "skin" at all to protect them from these outside stimuli.) Non-HSP is generally less porous and have natural defences which defuse external stimuli thereby not directly impacting and overloading their nervous systems.

Another way to think about this is to visualize the curve on a chart: At the point where the Non-HSP would have little or no stimulation, the HSP would be somewhat stimulated. Where Non-HSP would be somewhat stimulated, the HSP would be pretty well stimulated. And, where the Non-HSP is well stimulated, the HSP may be reaching, or might have already reached, a state of being over stimulated, over-aroused and overwhelmed, which may manifest itself in highly sensitive people as getting upset, frazzled or even angry, needing to get away, or possibly "shutting down" and becoming unable to function.

We have also learned that although many highly sensitive people are introverts, reserved, quiet or shy, there is a percentage that is high sensation seekers or extroverts. And, although they seek adventure they also get overloaded and become over stimulated with the same results as the rest of the HSP.

So, if you've ever felt you were all alone in having these overwhelming feelings and the need to seek solitude and sanctuary, we hope you find comfort in knowing that you are not alone and that you will benefit from some of the suggestions presented here.

Highly Sensitive People - Sounds, Smells and Sentiments

The first modern psychological discussion of the problems of hypersensitive and hyper-responsive people appeared in the 1930s when psychologist Carl Jung was elaborating his ideas on personality types. He speculated that approximately 25 % of his therapeutic clients were individuals who were inordinately sensitive to the stimulation coming from their surroundings. This sensitivity included, responses to sound and light and smells, as well as heightened emotional attunedness... being both easily affected by, and also very aware of, other people's feelings. He noted as well heightened attention to details of all sorts. He proposed that this sensitivity was related to a character trait which he called "introversion" and that it was also connected to the quality of "intuition".

High Sensitivity and Introversion: Introversion is no longer "low sociability."

Modern personality researchers have done hundreds of studies on the personality traits of introversion-extraversion. Early research treated it as a measure of sociability; later research looked it more generally as a physiological measure. The studies concur that introverts are:

- More physically sensitive

- More sensitive to stimuli and stimulants

- They process information more thoroughly

- They prefer to reflect before acting

- More reflective when given feedback

- More vigilant in discrimination tasks

Slower to acquire and forget information due to their deeper processing into memory

Greater sensitivity is found at all levels of the nervous system from sensitivity to pinpricks, to skin conductivity to faster reaction times

High sensitivity is innate.

You are born with it. Infant research shows that this sensitivity seems to be present from birth. Carl Jung was not far off the mark in his sense of its prevalence since current studies suggest that 15-20 % of all humans (and even animals) show the trait of high sensitivity and that it is equally divided between men and women. This non-trivial rate of appearance in the population suggests that it offered an evolutionary advantage. Individuals who are sensitive or reactive will "look before they leap" and survive to reproduce.

Hypersensitivity and PTSD

The exception to the "born with it" rule is extreme sensitivity that is associated with the after-effects of trauma.

Effects of high sensitivity on social and emotional development

Loud, busy or emotionally over-stimulating environments are harder on highly sensitive individuals. They may withdraw or minimize their exposure to these situations and develop an introverted social style.

Some highly sensitive individuals are still extroverts!

Usually, these are people who have grown up in supportive extended families where social interaction was a source of comfort, and the family "ran interference" protecting them from over-stimulation and anxiety until they had the skills to manage the world themselves. They still typically report needing a lot of "down time" to recuperate after social encounters.

Negative family environments

Highly sensitive children born into less supportive families who do not recognize their special vulnerability and protect them often grow up to be anxious, withdrawn or emotionally avoidant.

- Highly sensitive people are highly sensitive to their internal bodily processes too.

- Chronic over-arousal is a common source of stress for sensitive individuals.

Highly sensitive people often present medically with stress-related illnesses and environmental sensitivities.

These illnesses may sometimes be dismissed by others as "psychosomatic" especially since their less sensitive fellows would not be so easily overwhelmed.

Psychosomatic symptoms may indeed be produced as the individual unconsciously seeks socially acceptable ways to reduce their activity and over-stimulation.

Highly sensitive people are often accused of indecisiveness and slow decision making.

Their deep and detailed processing of information and ideas takes longer than other peoples.

Human empathy is based on our ability to read subtle emotional signals.

Individuals who are more sensitive and more vigilant naturally become better readers of these signals. Some sensitive persons have problems in intimate relationships since:

They respond so strongly to criticism.

Their detailed consideration of all aspects of life makes them prone to spot flaws in others and become irritated by their loved one's minor annoying habits.

They try to control and tune their environment to a level that they find tolerable.

With prevalence in the population of 15 to 20% that makes almost one in five of our friends and relatives "highly sensitive."

High sensitivity then is both a blessing and a curse and a normal part of the colourful spectrum of human character.

Highly Sensitive People Traits and Characteristics

Being highly sensitive is just one variety of the different personalities all of us possess. Highly sensitive people have been branded as the ones who react in a very expressive way than most people do. They can be intimidated by the slightest stimuli they receive, may it be from a beeping clock to a talkative coworker. But these people are not basing their actions solely on their emotions; on the contrary, they are very intellectual and tend to analyze things better than the others. They have negative and positive traits which can be used to their advantage or disadvantage.

Let us try to understand the various traits and characteristics of highly sensitive people by exploring every aspect of their lives. Emotionally, these people are often seen as shy or socially inhibited. They are not commonly seen interacting with people in hallways or chatting in restrooms. Most of them are introverted and like keeping to themselves. Since they were young, they have learned not to show awareness of other people's emotions.

If you are going to observe an HSP physically, you will note that most of them do not like being exposed to glaring light or in places with loud noises. Even strong odours are unappealing to these people. They think more of themselves and how they feel, and they know when they do not belong to an environment.

The introverted HSP's often feel like they do not belong in social gatherings, they are satisfied with their own company and are very much comfortable when left alone. After being forced to interact with people, they usually take time off to cool down and relax, as if relating to others is a very stressful situation.

The psychological characteristic of HSPs is extreme protectiveness of themselves and their personal spaces. Even their workspace does not allow intruders. There are also some who are trying to hide this protective nature by being all out, showing the opposite. After which, they get stressed too much which results in overstimulation even anxiety.

In terms of personal relationships, they tend to be difficult to handle. Personal issues often get in their way of relating to their partners. But the best thing that they can offer their partners is their intuitive thought and deep analogies.

Work and career is the most challenging aspect in the lives of HSP's. This is because most workplaces require you to relate with other people to do your work. But since HSP's are very creative, they have found many jobs where they feel comfortable such as one-on-one jobs and doing solo work. They are the best writers, programmers, web designers and excel on tasks which are handled alone.

In the cultural aspect, HSP's are not into the outgoing ideals of modern trends. But most of them can tolerate the changes in culture as long as they are not forced to portray such expressions.

Family problems tend to overwhelm HSP's. If they had a bad childhood, chances are they go on with their lives in denial because they find it difficult to forget situations where their emotions are challenged. But since they practice being tough, these scars do not show on their faces.

Spiritually, HSP's are blessed to be far more intuitive; they are into deep soul searching in search for the inner warmth. In their quiet times, they always find time to connect with the Supreme Being.

One in every twenty people is considered to be a highly sensitive person (HSP). This means that either you may be sensitive or someone you know is. 42% of the population is not highly sensitive, meaning that most things don't bother them the way they will an HSP. Everyone else falls somewhere in between, with the odd few being completely unemotional about anything. (By the way - 20% of the entire animal kingdom is highly-sensitive as well).

Who are HSP's and What Are They Like?

We're the thinkers, the cautious ones, the conservative people; the ones that say "Hey, wait a minute. Let's think this through before doing something rash."

Every society needs highly sensitive people, just as we need the warriors, the leaders who are ready to take risks. However, we're the ones that help to temper the not-so-sensitive types, the ones who can be bold, rash and impulsive and may not have thought things through to the consequences of their actions. Highly sensitive people are most often the people found in the roles of advisors, counsellors and advocators for restraint.

Unfortunately, in western society, we've also been labelled as somewhat "defective", according to the way non-HSP's see us. We're considered "too sensitive, too cautious, too shy, too timid, too introverted, too fearful." What needs to be realized is that these are not "problems" that need to be corrected and fixed with sensitive people. It's the labels that are attached to us that cause the problems. Many non-sensitive people are also shy, timid, introverted and fearful, while there are many highly sensitive people who are out-going, super-friendly, extroverted, and risk-takers. We just tend to think things through first and weigh all the factors that our senses pick up on before forging ahead.

Traits and Characteristics Misinterpreted

So, what are some of the traits and characteristics of a highly sensitive person? Let's look at some of the facts and the mythical labels that have been attached to this special group.

Shyness

- You'll probably find a larger portion of shy people in the HSP group. That does not mean that everyone is shy. That's a myth. A lot of non-sensitive people are also shy. Sometimes, what's mistaken as shyness is a sizing up of the situation and the people that we have just met. We're cautious. If our senses are saying something isn't right about the person, we won't be so open to them. First impressions count. It's not just the way the person is dressed, but their whole demeanour, aura, attitude and other little subtleties that we absorb with all of our senses. We process the thoughts, feelings and sensations that we receive in each new situation. This may make some of us appear "shy", when we're not.

Introverted

- Somewhat of a myth. You'll find many HSP's can be extroverted, out-going and fun-loving. You'll also find many non-sensitive people as being introverted. Don't mistake deep-thinking and inner-reflection as introversion. We do require much more alone time. This is because our nervous systems can go into overload in a situation that a non-sensitive person would find somewhat stimulating. If we become frazzled and over-stimulated, we need to find a quiet spot as soon as possible to settle back down. This is why many HSP's tend to stay at home more often than not, rather than go out to party. It's not that we don't want to... we just know our systems can't handle the overload for too long a time. If we can't get away, we'll pull into ourselves, as a sort of protective shield, to try to reduce the noise, sights, sounds and smells that are bombarding us to calm down.

Fearfulness

Unless you're completely unemotional and have a lack of conscious consideration toward others, who can say that they've never been fearful at times? This is not an exclusive trait of sensitive people. New experiences often · cause butterflies, fearful thoughts and inner-turmoil in most people. HSP's just tend to feel those emotions more deeply.

Timidness

- Caution, careful evaluation of the situation, needing the see the "entire picture", and the possible resulting consequences of our actions is just in our nature. If everyone heedlessly rushed into everything, we'd have even more chaos in our world than we do now.

Too-Sensitive

Yes, this is our major trait. We assimilate everything around us at once. Lights, noises, smells, energy vibrations, they all get absorbed, processed and evaluated. Unfortunately, when there are too much activity and noise around us, we can't handle it for a great length of time. For example, what may be low to moderate level of music for a non-sensitive person could sound like the level of a rock concert to us. Emotionally, we're affected by much of the disharmony in the world. We feel another person's heartache; we are aware of low levels of anger or resentment in a room, we empathize with other people's problems, and feel great sorrow over horrific tragedies.

What Does All This Mean?

A highly sensitive person will pick up on subtleties in the surroundings that many non-sensitive people can't see or feel. This can give us some great advantages. It can save us in many situations where there's trouble brewing. Our abilities can keep us from making disastrous business or personal decisions if we follow our instincts. And because of our deep sense of the environment around us, we're often the ones that make others aware of potential environmental problems that unscrupulous companies ignore for their benefits. HSP's are often the ones that push for reforms and changes in government law for the better good of everyone.

As with anything, it's good to know that you're not alone, that there are others out there that have to deal with the same types of situations and "labels" as you do. True, it doesn't hurt any less, but you know there are similar types that you can seek out and talk to...and they'll understand. Yes, we do tend to exhibit more of the above traits and characteristics than non-sensitive people do, but we're not exclusive owners of them either. Sometimes, it's a misinterpretation of what's going on in the mind of an HSP by non-HSP's. Only another highly sensitive person could understand. The good news is that highly sensitive people have been around for as long as man has walked the earth and we'll always be here, working to make the world a more understanding, considerate and peaceful haven for everyone.

Ten Ways to Tell If You Are an Extra Sensitive Person

It wasn't until I was back in the quiet of my own house that I felt the drain of energy. I had been at a very pleasant party and didn't exert any "out of the ordinary" energy. But as soon as I returned to my environment, I felt it. I was exhausted, tired beyond measure, like I could go to bed and sleep for a week. And it was only 9:00 p.m.! It was in that moment I finally accepted that I am one of those extra sensitive people (ESP) that I so often work within my practice. If you have ever felt the type of energy drain that I did, simply from being in a crowded room, you too may be an extra sensitive person. Here are some other clues that your sensitivity may be getting the best of you.

• You go through phases of crying or being defensive at the drop of a hat.

• You experience unexplained mood swings, especially after being around others.

• Your friends tell you, or you know yourself, that you're very intuitive.

• You will often lose yourself in a good book, tv, video game or some other solitary behaviour.

• You insulate yourself from your feelings with food, alcohol or any of the above behaviours.

• You are easily overwhelmed when you are presented with a lot of information at once.

• You have unexplained aches and pains or health issues.

• You are most comfortable in serene, soothing surroundings. Loud or harsh environments are like poison to you.

• You get overwhelmed when thinking about the pain and suffering in the world.

• You will often pick up on the needs of others and help them before they even ask.

There are many gifts which come with being an ESP, such as the ability to help others and heightened intuition. Unfortunately, your sensitivity may be getting in the way of realizing them. If you saw yourself on this list, it is most important for you to first accept your sensitivity and then take healthy measures to take care of yourself. Start with the basics, plenty of rest, hydration, healthy food, and exercise to ground you. Self-reflection is a must, and a good self-care plan will help you get a handle on your extra sensitivity. Extra sensitivity (ESP), when you managed it effectively, can be thoroughly enjoyed.

The Emotional Rollercoaster of Empaths and Highly Sensitive People

There is much more information on the traits of Highly Sensitive People (HSP's) which I won't go into here. If you are one, you know it!

I haven't, however, been able to find much information on one particular trait of HSP's, the ability to sense and feel other peoples' emotions. This empathic ability alone can have a devastating effect on the way that the HSP experiences the world.

To experience feelings that aren't your own can cause havoc, especially when it is not understood. This is not just a logical thought process or something that you 'think' is happening to someone but a 'taking on board' of that emotion ourselves. To the point that we feel it, live it out and process it just as though it were our own.

When emotions are occurring within ourselves without an apparent cause it generates confusion, upset and a gradual lowering of self-esteem. If there are no reasons for this constant emotional rollercoaster, then we can only assume that we are emotionally unstable, feeling things that we don't understand and with no apparent way out of it. This is particularly true of the negative emotions that can tend to stick like glue.

Suddenly finding yourself depressed, angry or irritable when you were feeling perfectly OK a few minutes before can become so normal that it becomes a way of life. A constant sense of 'not feeling right' within, anxious, tense and on edge can be a sign that you are living in an energy that is not yours, almost like wearing someone else's clothes that just don't fit.

I believe that we are all unconsciously affected by other people's energies. Being empathic, however, with this depth of feeling in everyday life takes it to a new level. Being called 'moody', 'too sensitive', 'emotionally unstable' or worse 'mad' does little to help an already confused state as to why you feel as much as you do.

So every person that you come into contact with, everyone that you think of (or who is thinking about you) can affect your energy and how you are feeling. Deep joy? Not! This can be an extremely difficult thing to live with when there is no understanding of what is occurring.

The majority of people do not experience this level of empathy and are therefore not going to understand it. Because it is not considered normal or widely understood, it can cause further confusion and constant questioning of 'what's wrong with me?'

The most traumatic part of this experience, for me, is that you are unlikely to ever get confirmation from others that it is their emotion and not yours. Even when you are with someone who understands this ability, they may not be aware of their depths of emotion and the constant shifts that occur. Sometimes people do not know themselves at this level and the emotion they experience, they are unaware of the thoughts and beliefs they carry and the subsequent emotional reactions.

It is empathic means that you feel the emotion from others even when they are unaware of it themselves. It means that you feel subtle shifts that are not perceivable to anyone else. It is not only strong emotional energies that are sensed; it could be a fleeting sense of irritation, fear, nervousness or any other emotion.

I spent many years trying to get confirmation from other people that it wasn't my emotion that I was experiencing. This doesn't work! To be met with a general response of 'no, it's not me' confuses you even more as others can be adamant they are not feeling something, they are genuinely unaware of it.

So what can you do about this? It takes time to realise that all you are experiencing may not be yours, to consider that you may be empathic. Its useful to start being very aware of your emotional state, to notice when you are at ease and when you are not. To note how you feel before you are with other people and then to note any changes that occur.

This is difficult at first when you have spent a lifetime just accepting the emotional shifts as normal. Difficult because you can find yourself in the throes of an emotional reaction without even being aware of it starting, or of where it came from.

It is a case of getting to know yourself, your emotional reactions and thought processes so that then, you know without a doubt that you are experiencing something that is not your own. You find a place where you have your 'normal' and anything outside of that might not be yours.

Our thoughts will create emotional shifts in ourselves, as they do with everyone, but you can generally be aware of your own 'stuff' that can cause emotional reactions.

I have come to realise that the vague sense of unease I often experience comes from not being in my energy and from living in someone else's. This means that I am taking away that persons experience and processing something that doesn't belong to me.

Understanding Highly Sensitive People

Sometimes they are called wimps, shy, nerds, neurotics, and at other times, like in the ancient past, they were known as intuitives, sages, and wise people.

Who are these interesting people?

They are the 20 per cent of the population that psychologist Dr Elaine Aron PhD calls Highly Sensitive People (HSP). Dr Aron, a self-described Highly Sensitive Person, has written several books that explain the sensitivity phenomenon and offer helpful tips for living a healthy life, fully, and happily as a sensitive person. She has helped many to understand that:

* Sensitive people are more aware of the subtleties in other people, places and things in their environment and therefore observe, reflect upon and experience more than non-sensitive people.

* Sensitivity is related to a survival strategy that inspires humans and other creatures to observe and assess situations before they proceed into them.

* The brains of sensitive beings are more active and work differently than non-sensitives.

* Different cultures value or devalue sensitivity in different ways. Low self-esteem issues are common among sensitive people because of this.

* Sensitivity is still misunderstood and was once thought to be a disorder to be treated.

With 20 per cent of the population being sensitive you probably know at least one sensitive or maybe even live with one. Perhaps it is time to consider these people in a new light and value them for the gifts that they bring into our lives. Highly Sensitive People tend to be very intelligent, conscientious and pay attention to the smallest details, so they make great employees. Because they are intuitive to other people's needs, they make great counsellors, massage therapists, coaches and tutors. Their observance of details and nuances in their environment make them ideal visual artists and musicians, and if you want someone to guide you with money management, choose an HSP because they are usually three steps ahead of the stock market and your personal needs.

Living with acute sensitivity can be a gift as it leads to great personal awareness, compassion for others and the development of skills that can assist others. The challenges of living with your sensory skills constantly registering information can be devastating if one does not realize that they are sensitive. Before developing awareness and management skills for their sensitivity, many HSP work extra hard at trying to be "normal".

They will accompany their family or friends into settings that they find uncomfortable (loud, cluttered, crowded, overstimulating), and endure a horrible experience, to avoid loneliness or just to be like the others. Many HSP tries to keep the pace of non-sensitive people and end up experiencing burn out. Because they experience so much more sensory experience, HSP needs more sleep and downtime than other people.

It is almost like they live three days condensed into a single day. Mental health days are a priority for HSP. Unfortunately, many adults are unaware that they are HSP, and they try to live their lives like the other 80 per cent and begin self-medicating with alcohol or drugs just to get through a day.

My theory is that most people with serious addiction issues are HSP and they use their drug of choice to muffle their sensory reception.

As children, many HSP is labelled as shy, fussy, inhibited, fearful, or challenged in some way. If we could change places with that child for a few minutes, we would realize that they are indeed wise, thoughtful, creative, intuitive and quite caring for others. Unfortunately, these children are easily overwhelmed, especially in a school setting where noise, visual stimulation, and topic shuffling are normal (a Feng Shui nightmare if you ask me!), and they sometimes express their discomfort through uncooperative behaviour.

Instead of implementing behaviour management techniques that are designed for the other 80 per cent of the population perhaps the offering of a quieter space, the ability to leave the classroom for sensory breaks and adopting a better understanding of their experience by teachers and caregivers could be considered. Instead of sending your child to their room as punishment, suggest that they go to their special space for some relaxing or creative time.

When you empower a Highly Sensitive Child to learn how to care for themselves at an early age, you are giving them a gift of self-respect and self-acceptance that may remain with them throughout their life. This can help them to create healthy and fulfilling lives as adults and avoid a life of suffering like many unaware HSP.

5 Myths about Highly Sensitive People

A highly sensitive person is someone who tends to be attuned to their surroundings. They are often intuitive and empathic, have a keen imagination and may feel very overwhelmed by noise, chaos and crowds. They can have trouble fitting in and have been perceived as "too shy" or "too sensitive."

Many people object to the term 'highly sensitive' because it is often thought of as being a bad thing. Some prefer terms like highly attuned or highly aware since those terms don't carry the negative connotation of being 'overly sensitive.'

It can be difficult to understand or relate to highly sensitive people. I think that's mostly because we don't understand ourselves. I certainly didn't for most of my life. Because we were seen as being different from everyone else when we were growing up, other people, particularly our parents and family, didn't know how to relate to us. A highly sensitive person often tries very hard to fit in but is unable to do so, and so they conclude that there must be something wrong with them. We're often told things like "you're too sensitive;" "get over it;" "you're childish, grow up;" and, my personal favourite "don't be so stupid." As if when we say that we are uncomfortable in certain situations or don't want to do certain things, we're just difficult.

If you are highly sensitive or know someone who is, these tips might help you have a better understanding of what it means:

We're not delicate. Being sensitive simply means that we are more tuned in to the environment and the people around us.

We pick up on things that most others do not. We notice things. It doesn't mean that we will fall apart if you are direct and honest with us (in fact we prefer it because then we know where we stand with you).

There's nothing wrong with us. We are not broken. We do not need fixing. We are just different. We don't often enjoy the same things that many others enjoy - and this isn't just in our heads, it's a physical thing. We feel physical symptoms that are uncomfortable in response to things like noise, fluorescent lighting, smoke, perfumes, chemical smells, crowds, chaotic environments, and so on.

We are not unsociable, nor do we think that we're better than everyone else. Those who are highly sensitive and also introverts can respond to over-stimulation by withdrawing and becoming quiet. We may decline to join you at a bar or an event where there are lots of people, not because we're unsociable, but because we know we wouldn't enjoy it, and we would suffer afterwards. We know, from experience, that it can take us days to recover from such over-stimulation.

Not all highly sensitive people are introverts and vice versa. There are people who are extroverted and yet also highly sensitive. The difference is that an introverted HSP will tend to withdraw when experiencing over-stimulation, while an extrovert may lash out and become aggressive or angry. Although again, this depends on the person, not all extroverted HSP's will act this way.

It's easy to think that HSP's might not thrive in leadership positions. The opposite is true. They can thrive (although they may not always want to). HSP's make great leaders because they can be more in-tune with the other members of their team and have a wider perspective. They also tend to pick up on things that others might miss - such as emotions, body language, facial expressions - because they are so highly aware.

There's no doubt about it, being highly sensitive can be difficult. But those difficulties are greatly reduced, and your sensitivities can be turned into great strengths once you fully understand and own who you are. It's easy to think there must be something wrong with you when you are not the same as the majority of other people. But being different is not a problem, it's a gift. Learn who you are and when challenging situations come up, help others to understand. Don't expect them to automatically know; you must help them - and know how to help yourself

CHAPTER 3

EMPHATIC ABILITIES

Empathic Psychic Abilities - Do You Possess This Type of Psychic Ability?

An empath or empathic person refers to someone that can sense or feel another's emotions. Empaths, are also known as highly sensitive people or sensitives and have the natural ability to connect with another's true emotions and can relate to a person on a much deeper level than the emotions the persona is displaying. Empaths experience empathy as is to family, friends, co-workers, pets, nature and inanimate objects. The gift of empathy is not restricted to time or space. Therefore, an empathic person can feel the emotions of people from a distance.

My Wife's Empathic Experience

As a young girl, I remember getting feelings about things. Back then,

I was completely convinced that I struggled with anxiety issues or some other form of mental health issue. I would have physical reactions of panic or stress on days when I was having a perfectly good day, and my thoughts were unrelated to emotions I was feeling. I have always been easily tearful when watching sad movies, and seeing or hearing someone going through difficult times is hard for me to be around without being emotional. At one point, I was so stressed by all of this "anxiety" that I saw several doctors and was successful with obtaining perceptions for anxiety medication only to realize that it did nothing for the emotions I was experiencing. Over time, I came to connect with this "issue" as I referred to it and realized I could predict things based on how I felt. It was less confusing to me when I could attach the feeling to a particular person. Once that happened, I was able to convince myself that it was normal because I mostly connected these feelings to my family and my closest friends. I rationalized that it must be an extension of our closeness or love by being able to feel what they were feeling. As ridiculous as that may seem to some, I was even forced to throw out that theory after a strange expe rience while in college.

It was my last class of the day in a packed auditorium with a lecture on finance on the menu. The auditorium was completely silent while students listened to the instructor and took notes. I was taking notes as well and suddenly began to feel so uncomfortable. I became restless and nervous. I shrugged it off and then felt as if someone had put a pillow over my face. The realization hit me, I was having one of my "anxiety attacks", and I didn't want to have it in the middle of my class. Feeling completely embarrassed that I was going to have to disturb the lecture, I began to squeeze off out my desk and grab my belongings, I took a deep breath and just got up and left. Immediately upon exiting the auditorium, I saw a close friend waiting outside for me. She was visibly upset and all at once the feelings of anxiety I had subsided. After she calmed down a bit, she told me that she had just left the apartment of a friend of the guy she was dating. While waiting on her boyfriend to arrive, his friend attacked her, put a pillow over her face, and attempted to sexually assault her. I didn't know if I was more shocked to hear the story or the fact that I was sitting through the class experiencing the emotions of what she was going through. From that day, I began to accept that for whatever reason, I had this "issue", and I wasn't as bothered by it.

It wouldn't be until many years later and frequent experiences of dealing with my "issue," that I reached out to a psychic for relationship questions. The first thing she said was that " you know you are very psychic" and at that moment, I answered her "yes." I didn't quite resonate with her style of reading, so I connected with another empathic psychic medium about a week later from my hometown, again for relationship issues. Very early in this reading, this psychic said, " You know you are very empathic." That along with her style, accuracy, and personality kept me coming back for readings, and she finally talked me into helping me develop my gift. The biggest lessons I learned during my psychic development was that it was no reason to fear the gift of empathy, and also that this gift was a huge part of my life purpose-rescue. Not to mention, I was finally able to stop calling it my "issue" and embrace it as a gift that is to be utilized in the service of others. Acknowledging and accepting my gift has allowed me to help people and has helped me to feel more connected to my spirituality.

Empathic Traits

Empathic traits and characteristics will vary with each. As with any metaphysical gift, no two people or two psychics will interpret messages the same way or sense and feel them the same way. The gift of empathy never comes alone; it is always accompanied by other metaphysical gifts and with creative gifts such as art, writing, or music. Empaths tend to express high levels of creativity and are full of imagination. Best described as great listeners or listeners of life. Empaths are natural healers and are often here on the life theme of rescue. They often find themselves helping others while putting aside their personal needs and desires. Empathic people are often great problem solvers and great thinkers. Most empaths do not discover that they are empathic until later in life.

The unique thing I have found about being empathic is the knowledge that I chose to bring this gift with me to be a part of my physical experience. It is this very knowledge that has allowed me to accept this gift and ignore the scrutiny of people that do not understand this gift or refuse to accept it as a part of their experience. Releasing my fears and being more aware of how to best use my gift is serving me well and has allowed me to truly embrace myself.

Empathic Psychic Abilities - Psychic Guide

What are Empathic Psychic Abilities?

An empathic psychic is also known as an "empath". Empaths can sense and experience the feelings of others, similar to the way telepaths can sense the thoughts of others. Empathy and telepathy are closely related to psychic abilities.

Usually, clairsentient psychics, (psychics with "clear feeling"), possess empathic psychic abilities. Empathic abilities are rare, but not unheard of.

Characteristics of an Empath

Empaths display these characteristics:

- Extreme sensitivity to the feelings of others

- An acute awareness of their surroundings

- Clear understanding of body language

- Strong knowledge of human emotion

- The ability to feel deeper than others

- The Empathic Spectrum

Not all psychics have the same amount of empathic power. Some psychics have only basic empathic abilities, while others have extremely advanced empathic powers. Most empaths fall somewhere in the middle.

Psychics with the most basic empathic abilities can sense what another is feeling, and can sometimes feel their emotions. These psychics can only understand some of what others are feeling.

Psychics with the most advanced empathic abilities can feel everything that other's are feeling. When engaged in empathic practice, these psychics often become so engaged people's feelings, that they momentarily lose sight of their own identity. Psychics such as these may be able to send emotional signals and project their feelings onto others.

Empathic Healing

Many empaths choose to use their abilities to heal others. Empaths usually place their hands on someone, to understand what they are feeling. This way, an empath can focus directly on what the patient needs.

Powerful empathic psychics can share the feelings of others, to relieve their pain. Loss and grief are two common feelings that a powerful empath can share and lessen. To reverse this method, a psychic can also share their feelings to spread joy and happiness.

A Gift or a Curse?

Because empaths spend so much time worrying about the feelings of others, they can forget to worry about themselves. Empaths may experience poor health as a result of self-neglect, emotional stress, and physical fatigue.

On the other hand, healing and spreading feelings of joy is a rare and wonderful gift!

Hopefully, you've learned something about empaths and empathic psychic abilities.

What does this mean?

If you think you might have empathic psychic abilities, you must develop your skills to uncover your true psychic power. Otherwise, your empathic power will never amount to anything useful! What a waste!

It is sometimes hard to tell whether or not someone is an empath, (a psychic who possesses empathic abilities). The problem is, you don't always know if someone possesses these psychic powers, or if they are just sensitive, understanding people. How do you know if you're empathic?

Empaths are extremely sensitive to the feelings of those around them. Often, an empath will be able to sense what someone is experiencing, even if they can't see or hear that person. Someone with this kind of ability simply "knows." Many psychics with empathic abilities report experiencing someone else's feelings as though they were their own, though this is not always the case.

A psychic with this kind of ability will be able to sense the feelings of others, especially if those feelings are very strong. Common feelings that an empath will experience include fear, joy, loneliness, excitement, love, and foreboding. The stronger the feeling, the easier it will be for the empath to sense, understand, and feel.

The thing that sets empaths apart from other, "normal" people, is that they have a deeper, more sensitive understanding of what they are feeling. This intuition comes from within and is far greater than what most people experience. For example, a "normal" person might realize that someone they love is upset by little things they say or do. However, an empath would sense this even without seeing or talking to that person, and an empath could sense if that loved one was feeling betrayed, jealous, angry, or hurt. This psychic intuition would come from within, not from the visual or audible clues of the physical world.

Empaths can tell when something is wrong, even if that something hasn't happened yet. They are overcome with a deep sense of foreboding that warns them that everything is not as it should be. A "normal" person, on the other hand, would not be able to tell when something unexpected or dangerous was going to happen.

These things all sound great, but not everyone realizes that it can also be very difficult to be an empath. This is because empaths are not able to "shut off" their abilities whenever they want. That is, they cannot choose whether or not to feel something. Instead, they must feel whatever their psychic intuition senses, even if they would rather not. This is a huge burden for empaths, and it is also why empathic psychics can get sick from exhaustion.

Although many people have heard of empaths, (psychics who can sense or feel the emotions of others), few people fully understand what it means to possess empathic psychic abilities. People naively assume that this ability is a great and wonderful gift and that it does not come at a cost to the psychic who possesses it. The truth is, this rare talent can also be a deadly burden to bear.

These psychics come wide ranges of sensitivity. On one end of the spectrum are the empathic psychics who can only vaguely recognize other people's feelings, while on the other end there are the powerful psychics who feel people's emotions as though they were their own.

Admittedly, it can be wonderful to be able to understand another person's feelings, and to be able to understand them and to help them cope with their feelings if they need help; empathic psychics are often skilled at emotional healing therapy. This is a process in which the psychic can share the burden of extreme emotion, thereby lessening the pain that it is causing the patient. Alternatively, a psychic can guide a patient through difficult emotional distress by using their sensitive, intimate understanding of a patient's emotional state of mind.

However, people don't realize that an empathic psychic doesn't necessarily choose whether or not to experience another person's feelings. Instead, they simply must accept the feelings that come to them. They constantly suffer invasions of their emotional self. They may become confused as to which feelings are their own, and which feelings come from outside sources.

What's worse, an empath usually senses extreme emotions before they experience subtle emotions. As a result, psychics must share the feelings of people in extreme emotional states, rather than the feelings of people in normal emotional states of mind. For an empathic psychic, even something as simple as walking down the street, or going to the grocery store, can be extremely emotionally taxing.

Think about it-having to constantly feel the emotions of others all the time, and without choosing to can have crippling effects on someone's psyche. Often, empathic psychics "lose themselves" in the feelings of others, and this can lead to self-doubt, confusion, loneliness, and depression.

Psychics who see their ability more as a burden than as a gift should find help by counselling with other empathic psychics who are in similar situations. Having a support network can make a living with this ability much more bearable, and can significantly improve a psychic's quality of life.

Yes, empaths possess a rare, wonderful gift that has the power to heal and help others, but it comes at an enormous cost. Is it worth it?

Empathic Abilities - What Are They and How to Tell If You Have Them

Empaths are rather intuitive beings, more adept at reading people than "signs" or tarot cards. There are people of an empathic nature that have those abilities, but that is just a small part of what is an Empath.

Interest in the empathic person has only emerged in recent times following the work of Jad Alexander. A student of psychology, Jad began to recognize certain types of people that had unique and elevated levels of sensitivity. They were very intuitive, being able to sense things at a level unknown and unavailable to the average person. He came to the conclusion after 30 years of studying such types, that they were in fact gifted, possessing the ability to "know" things intuitively such as; when someone wanted them to call, when someone was in trouble and needed help, or even how to get somewhere without ever having been there or following directions.

He concluded that these people had unique alterations to their central nervous systems (CNS). The interaction between the CNS and the brain was unique to the point that it created a "sixth sense", one that received messages at a much deeper level than "ordinary" individuals, and processed all those messages in an unconventional way. Those this phenomenon has not yet been evaluated by science, many individuals have invested time and resources into investigating exactly what is an Empath.

Through these studies, it has been determined that those with empathic natures posses particular common qualities. The most common denominator is a heightened sense of sensitivity. Often these people are labelled as over-sensitive individuals, but perhaps ultra-sensitive is a more appropriate definition. They are extremely receptive to smells, noise, and light, their sensory organs having a low threshold which amplifies the degree to which their senses react.

In addition to these heightened levels of sensitivity, Empaths are often bombarded with a constant flow of random, seemingly irrational thoughts and emotions. This is because they often "pick up" the thoughts and feelings of others, not just those in their immediate vicinity, but often of people who are miles, if not oceans away. This is the psychic make-up of what is an Empath, a condition that those unaware of their gift struggle with. Because of the huge amounts of information they are receiving, and not understanding its nature, many become overwhelmed and confused, often seeking psychological counselling, or even medication.

You may wonder, What is an Empath as opposed to a psychic . The simple explanation is; while a psychic "sees," an empathic person "feels." The hunches and gut-feelings the empathic personality experiences are psychic messages. The problem is that these messages are communicated in a type of psychic language that is both foreign and complex. Understanding this language, known as Dreamtongue, is critical to fully grasping exactly what is an Empath.

Becoming the Ultimate Empathizer

Empathy is the ability to identify with and the vicarious experiencing the feelings, thoughts, or attitudes of another person. Empathy is the capacity to understand and respond to the other's experiences.

Can you see any advantage of that in terms of persuasion? I sure can. I've been using it as a secret weapon for years in my persuasion, and I'll now share it with you.

Here's an exercise to help you get into the affluent mindset of your clients...

It's all about understanding and responding to their experiences. You may have heard of another powerful technique like this where you metaphorically 'jump' into them. Here, we are instead going to experience them.

When someone feels that kind of trust - where you are experiencing what they are going through - rapport is never far behind.

With loved ones whose patterns we know and understand, this comes naturally. This exercise you will give you an insight into people you don't know that well (if at all).

For this exercise, you'll need a partner. Here's the set up:

Ask your partner to think of anything. Call it 'A'. Notice how their body is arranged - facial features, breathing, muscle tension, gestures, etc. - and take a mental snapshot. This is how they represent thought 'A'.

Next, have them break state by looking around the room and naming three things they see. (This is just to get their mind off of 'A' and to revert to their normal state.)

Now, have them think of something qualitatively different, though not necessarily opposite. Call it 'B'.

[NOTE: When you first do this exercise thinking of the opposite may make it easier, but I encourage you to develop your skills and not use something opposite once you've got the hang of it.]

Okay, now have them break state again.

Next, have them think about either the A or B thought, without telling you which. Your job is to tell which one they're thinking about, just by looking at them. Which snapshot do they resemble the most?

Once you've done this enough times, switch roles and let them enjoy the experience of being able to tell what you're thinking. You can begin to know the people you deal with regularly.

Now you don't practice this with your prospects. You're not going to sit down with them and say, "okay, now let's practice a persuasion technique..." You practice this with the people you know well so that you can fine-tune your observation skills.

After a while, you will begin to recognize the smallest state changes in others as you converse with them. When they speak about certain topics, give you certain answers, you will experience them, and they will feel it too.

Although they will not be able to pinpoint the feeling they get, they will feel connected to you.

So what's the value in this? Certainly, it's a fast and effective way to gain rapport. It also puts the person in a state of feeling understood.

Another way this can be valuable is in determining whether or not a client is lying. Not that you need to interrogate a client, but knowing if someone's fibbing is always useful.

If a prospect, for instance, explains that their finances are "great" but their body language belies this, then these verbal and nonverbal cues can be a dead give away that this prospect doesn't have a steady hold on his finances - and this information can be used to your persuasive advantage.

You can use other persuasive strategies to get this prospect to open up about their financial situation. And once you do that, you gain even more rapport, you get to the heart of their problem, and you can immediately introduce yourself and your service as the solution to their problem.

How to Empathize with Your Partner Better

We might not be aware of it, but we are an extremely narcissistic society. This is becoming a problem that could undermine our civilization. Certainly, there are parts of this "individualism" which help society prosper and grow. The ability to think out of strict group restrictions helps people achieve and create amazing things. However, in the midst of our pursuits-we have to be careful that the focus of our lives has not become reduced to selfish ambition and blind individualism.

The first step in really cultivating kindness in our lives is choosing to try to think in terms of the other. Taking times to think and empathize with other individuals. If we are not able to empathize than we are not ever going to be able to be kind people. If we cannot learn to "walk in the shoes of another" it will be impossible to seek the good of the other. To some, empathy is natural, while it may be more difficult for other people. For those with whom empathy is not easy, perhaps a simply psychological activity could go a long way. Right now, close your eyes and think of someone in your life who is going through a rough time- it could be because of a sickness, financial problem, family or relational issues, etc. Now picture this person in your mind, see them, and imagine their thoughts, fears, sorrows, hopes, and dreams. Perhaps this may feel strange or even intrusive at first, but I guarantee as you continue with this visualization, you will start thinking outside of yourself and experiencing life from the other individual's perspective. This, in turn, will help soften your being, as you turn your focus away from yourself.

Another practice you can do is just start focusing your thoughts and prayers on the other individual. One way I like to do this is put on some calming music, close my eyes, and simply bring individuals to the forefront of my mind. As I am slowly breathing in and out, I simply wish blessing, peace, and grace on them. I find through this experience, that I grow more empathetic towards these individuals, and actually, grow in my kindness towards them. For example, if I am visualizing a family member I have not talked to in a while, I feel more compelled to call them and see how there is life going. Perhaps, if it is a friend that I know is having a hard time, I see a new perspective on how I could be a blessing to them. You can also practice doing this with basic yoga positions. Perhaps, our prayers and wishes for others have less to do with them being directly blessed from God and more to do with God changing us so that we can become more of a blessing to them. To become kind people, we have to change our whole way of viewing the world and remove the narcissistic perspective by seeing life from a different point of view

Accept them for who they are

To empathize with your partner starts with loving them and accepting them as they are despite their flaws and things that annoy you. This is what it means to love and accept someone. When you do this, it is easier to take on board what they are saying and to try and see things from how they are experiencing them. Unconditional love is probably the most valued of all the types of love as it requires you to love your partner despite their failings and faults. People crave to be loved as they are.

Talk through things with them

To empathize with your partner is the capability to share in the feelings and emotions that they have. Talk and listen to them, taking the time to take in what they are saying and respond positively and actively. Give them time and space to share what is going on and cut out any distractions making them your absolute focus, and so you can listen attentively to them. This will mean so much to your partner that you care enough to give your whole attention to them. Listening to your partner in this way is one of the key things that enhances a relationship for the better.

Put yourself in their shoes

Try and think what they are going through, imagine what you would do in their circumstances and think about how you would act if you were in their shoes. Try not to give advice but have the priority of being a listening ear first and foremost. Advise if they ask for it though in a kind and sensitive manner and look to be attentive to them as much as possible. Spend time listening to what they are going through and look to be as encouraging as you can in as positive a way as possible.

How to Empathize with Others in 3 Simple Steps

Some people are natural born empathizers. But if you're not, and you want to know how to empathize with others, then this article will put you on the right track.

If you want to learn how to identify with what other people are feeling, then follow these three simple steps on how to empathize with others:

Step 1: Look Inside Yourself.

To be able to successfully empathize with another person, you need to look inside yourself and dig up that old trunk of emotions. No matter how cold-hearted someone may be, there is a small part in each of us that still understands basic human emotion.

This is easy for others, but might be a little confusing for those who have locked their feelings away. If you belong to the latter, then this might be a meaningful experience for you too.

Stop distracting yourself from your emotions and face them head-on. This enables you to have a deeper understanding of yourself as well as of others.

Step 2: Listen To What They're Not Saying.

Feelings are tricky, and people don't always mean what they say. If you want to know how to empathize with others, be a good listener.

Don't just listen to the words that are coming out of their mouth; be observant of non-verbal expressions as well.

Are their eyes tearing up even when they say they don't care? Are they fidgety even if they claim that they're not worried? These things alone can help you identify with what's going on in their hearts.

Step 3: It's Not About You.

While understanding your own emotions is a part of learning how to empathize with others, it's not all about you.

Don't go on a tirade of how you felt this and that. Be sensitive to what the other person is feeling and allow said person to express himself.

Don't butt in or make assumptions. Instead, focus your attention on the who, why, what, where and how of that other person's feelings. It's tempting to steal the limelight; but if you do so, you will have failed your basic mission.

Learning how to empathize with others is very important because it allows you to make better and informed decisions. It gives you an in-depth perspective of why people are the way they are.

The Power of Empathic Listening

Empathic Listening can be a powerful tool to build trust and rapport with those in your care. By listening to individuals, you demonstrate your commitment to them and communicate the message that they are people of value and worth. Empathic Listening can also help you positively influence the behavioural choices of the individuals in your care.

The process of Empathic Listening is not automatic. Being a good listener is a skill that takes time and effort to develop.

The Benefits of Empathic Listening

Empathic Listening is an approach to listening that allows an individual to talk through a problem and feel understood. It has some benefits.

It takes the burden off of you. You don't need to have answers or provide advice, which can sometimes be interpreted as a lecture. Also, when you listen to empathically, you don't tell the person what to do.

You can uncover the real issues. The person you are talking with is the one who leads the conversation, not you. You will gain insight into his issues without the need for prying questions.

It allows the other person to vent. The other individual can release his feelings without having to hear advice or be judged by his behaviour.

It's an excellent tool to let someone know you understand his concern. The need to feel understood is important to us all.

Five Steps to Empathic Listening

There are five key points to listening emphatically.

Give the person your undivided attention. Move away from distractions and focus your attention on the other person. Don't try and do two things at once. Make sure your nonverbal communication sends the message that you are ready to listen. Make eye contact, lean slightly forward, and nod your head periodically to let the person know you understand what he is saying.

Be nonjudgmental. If you lecture or make statements that trivialize someone's problems, it can drive him away.

Focus on feelings, not just facts. Listen carefully to understand the person's message. Some individuals can describe their problems but have a hard time identifying their feelings.

Allow silence for reflection. Before you speak, allow the other person time to reflect on what he said. Often, he will be the first one to break the silence with further information.

Use restatement to clarify messages. Put the words the person has said into your own and restated them back to him. Allow the individual to clarify your interpretation. By offering your interpretation, you give the person the opportunity to clarify and possibly expand his message.

Learn to Develop Empathic Listening

Empathic listening is also called reflective listening or active listening. This is a way of listening and then responding, in a way that will improve trust and understanding. It is an essential skill for people in disputes, and also in listening to people, we are trying to understand. This type of listening allows you to receive and interpret correctly the message the speaker is trying to impart, and then give him a response that is appropriate. The response is an important and integral facet of the listening process. It can be critical to the positive outcome of any mediation or negotiation.

Empathic listening can list among its benefits building respect and trust, and enabling you and the speaker to release your emotions. It can also reduce tension, encourage information surfacing, and create an environment that is well able to help everyone in problem-solving. This type of listening is quite useful for anyone that is involved in a conflict, and your ability to listen can set you apart from others as a strong listener and a good problem solver.

The proper use of a listening process can profoundly impact the parties involved. Especially useful in conflicts, if you utilize empathic listening, you will be judged as a helpful mediator. When you appear to be the only person who cares about what is being said, you become more credible.

Understanding what is being said in conversation, lectures or discussions is of limited use unless you can let the others involved know that you understand what is being talked about. You will not win respect and confidence in mediation until the participants realize that you understand the problem. Sometimes, if the subject is emotionally charged, empathic listening is needed to remain objective and hear all sides of the discussion.

Empathy is defined as the ability to put yourself within another person's personality so that you can understand their feelings and emotions. You let the speaker know, through empathic listening, that you understand what they're talking about, and that you don't judge them. As a listener, you need to convey this message through non-verbal ways, which include your body language. By doing this, you encourage the speaker to express whatever he wants to say without fear of being interrupted or criticized. You don't need to agree with the speaker to utilize empathic listening, but standard feedback phrases such as "I see" and "I understand" let them know that you are listening to what they're saying without judging them.

Listening with empathy is a skill that can strengthen relationships as well as your ability to assist in disputes, and contribute to discussions. It can help to strengthen your effectiveness in both your personal and professional life. Skilled listening can increase your effectiveness, and can demonstrate your willingness to let the other parties discuss while you listen.

Empathic Shielding

You know you're empathic if you find yourself picking up other people's issues. When they're sad, you're sad, when they're happy, you're happy, when they're in pain, so are you.

Sorting out your issues from theirs can be very confusing and makes living life as an empath rather challenging. I would like to offer a very useful and effective technique I intuitively discovered many years ago to block out all those invading ene rgies. Though I am empathic myself, I have developed the ability to choose to experience the energies of others or not.

Empaths naturally fluctuate their energetic vibrations to match those of other people. When someone is sad, angry, hurt, or happy, you match your energy to theirs to feel what they're feeling. Very often, this is done as an attempt to take away that person's pain; to carry their burden for them. Sometimes it stems from a belief that to understand a person's pain, you must experience it. Whatever the reason, however, a very important lesson all empaths must learn is that it is not necessary to feel or experience another's pain to ease it.

How can you stop matching the energies of those around you? By using the principle of entrainment. Entrainment is defined as the tendency for two vibrating bodies to lock into phase and vibrate in harmony; also, as the synchronization of two or more rhythmic cycles. This principle is universal and can be seen in many everyday situations. For example, two beating heart muscle cells will, in time, synchronize. The pendulums of grandfather clocks lined against a wall will begin to swing together. Women who live together for more than a month will have their menstrual cycles at the same time frame. A guitar string tuned to a particular note, when plucked, will cause another guitar string, tuned to the same note but held a distance away, to vibrate.

We can also see examples of this in emotions. Have you ever been around someone who was in a really good mood and you found yourself feeling good as well? Or how about the opposite where you were around someone who was sad or angry, and you started feeling the same way. We tend to refer to this as "infectious".

Well, you can use this same "infectious" energy to help keep you from picking up everyone else's issues. If you keep your energies higher than those of the people around you, you will find that you aren't dipping down to pick up the sadness, anger, pain, frustration, etc. You will notice that, if you spend enough time around these individuals, they will begin to match your energy and feel better! So how can you keep your energies high? By doing everything you can to stay in a good, upbeat, happy mood when someone with lower energy is near. Think of someone or something you love, count your blessings, imagine holding a kitten or a puppy or a baby, or just realize that the best thing you can do for that person is to keep your energies high instead of dropping them down to their level. Misery might love company but it isn't very helpful to have a room full of miserable people. Be the beacon, the shining light during the storm, and help raise that person's spirits. You'll both feel much, much better and you'll begin to learn that meeting a person at the level of their pain isn't the best way to help them through it.

CHAPTER 4

GUIDE ON HOW TO OVERCOME FEAR

Fear Factor

What is Fear?

So you've analyzed your ambitions and have determined the life you want to have. You can envision it, but something seems to get in the way. Could it be fear?

Fear has a way of injecting psychological toxins into our subconscious that acts like a handcuff, restraining our ability to achieve our goals. Although the fear may be perceived, it seems so real. This perceived fear plays games with our minds, robbing us of any rational thoughts we need to cherish to move ahead.

When fear is perceived, the portion of the brain involved in fear automatically reacts. It triggers behaviours such as a racing heart, anxiety, or sweaty palms. If the fear is related to doubts about your ability, the fear will allow you to come up with an excuse why you cannot accomplish your task.

The process of fear is entirely subconscious. You are driven to think, belief, and act based upon the fear you initially perceived. If the perceived fear is funnelled through unfavourable past experiences, the subconscious mind injects even more doubt, and eventually, you feel immobile, paralyzed, unable to make it past the first step.

Because we as humans do everything to avoid pain or discomfort in our lives, we give in to the fears we are fed by our subconscious. This fear prevents you from even attempting the first move. There may be times that your ambition pulsates within you and motivates you to get it past the first step, but the discomforts and doubts created by fear can be so much more powerful than your ambitions that you cannot follow through.

Over time, this fear eats away at your self-confidence. You begin to come up with excuses why things can't get done. You play the victim role. You feel sorry for yourself. You become depressed. Your self-esteem takes a plunge - all in the name of fear.

Fear Destroys Self Confidence

Ever notice that you have no problems coming up with great, profitable ideas? You are convinced that this is the big one, the idea of all ideas. The moment you conceive your idea, the level of excitement surges within you. You can't wait to share it with your friends and family. But as the days go by the enthusiasm tapers off.

Unfortunately, this is idea number 49. The people in your life have heard it so many times that they just listen to your hype to be polite. You begin to develop a reputation for "all talk and no action". Your self-confidence slowly becomes eroded. How many times has this happened to you? What do you think contributes to this syndrome? Could it be fear?

To make the bridge from ambition to achieving your plans, you must deal with the fear factor in your life. You may feel fearless in other areas of life, but in this area of goal attainment, there is something sabotaging you every time. That something is fear.

When fear intercepts your plan, your ability to execute is jeopardized. Your enthusiasm eventually disappears, and everything is at a standstill. You once again feel disappointment in yourself, wondering what happened. You level of confidence takes a serious plunge. You withdraw for the embarrassment you feel. Your self-esteem bottoms out. You remain in hibernation until you once again feel comforta ble to emerge, hoping that no one remembers to ask about your once again failed project.

Fear of Success

Once fear is allowed to erode your self-confidence it remains in control of your life, lurking within the subconscious. Each failed attempt, or each time something is avoided due to fear, this fearful behaviour is reinforced even more. That fear is then transferred to all areas of your life. The erosion of your self-confidence simultaneously affects your self-esteem. The self-critic dominates your thought process, and self-doubt inevitably moves in as one begins to experience what many terms "fear of success". If the fear is not addressed, it continues to sabotage your every move.

Let's examine the real meaning of fear of success.

Your perception of self undergoes a transformation. You believe you are unworthy of any positive outcomes or recognition you will receive as a result of your achievements, so why even try?

You feel afraid of failing or making mistakes that you refuse to even make the first attempt.

Because your self-confidence is undermined you doubt your own abilities to execute a task. There is very little effort made to attempt a project.

You compare yourself with others and feel inferior, believing that no matter how much success you achieve, it will never stack up.

You begin to rationalize that even though you achieve all your goals, you still won't be able to find happiness and true contentment in your life. So what's the point?

Does any one of these apply to you? Try to examine your fears to determine if you fall into the above category.

Fear Conditioning

Fear is a normal, innate survival tool we all possess. It serves as a means of protecting us from harm. However, that same fear that protects us can also hinder our progress in life.

Let is examine what causes fear of success or any forms of fear that tend to hold us back.

The fear many of you experience that holds you back may be triggered by our culture, social structure, and values. Modern culture defines success in terms of wealth, fame, or prestige. We are compared to these norms and judged accordingly. If your level of confidence in your abilities are not sufficiently developed to feel comparatively capable a feeling of fear takes over. This results in anxiety. Here is where the conditioning begins. Over time, as this fear is experienced, this learned behaviour becomes ingrained in the psyche.

This form of fear conditioning allows you to become very intimidated. It causes you to put off doing something of great importance that can benefit your life in significant ways. Each time it gets put off the fear is reinforced even more, and the conditioning continues. Because fear is an automatic, physiological reaction, you find yourself doing or acting in ways that are so unlike you.

Fear conditioning destroys your self-image. It places you under enormous stress because you feel you cannot live up to your expectations or even worse the increased expectations that are dictated by our culture.

Overcoming Fear, Fear Not!

You are now aware of the power fear can have over you. You may have attributed your inability to gain your success momentum to fear. You must learn to overcome fear and discard this albatross that sabotages your ability to achieve your goals. But how?

You must first make that decision for CHANGE. You must choose whether to allow your fears to ruin any plans you have for the future or to break free of them. It is a choice, yes a choice you must make. Spend some time alone to look way down into the recesses of your heart and decide what fears are holding you back. Make a list of them. You are the only one who truly knows the fear that binds you. You are the only one who can free yourself from your fear. Decide to let go of the victim role that fear has you living in and make an effort to let it disappear from your life. This is the first step towards overcoming fear.

The next step to overcoming fear is awareness. Be able to recognize when fear has control of you and assess that fear. Acknowledge it out loud and ask "what am I afraid would happen to me"? What do I have to lose for trying? What am I really afraid of? Write them down. Stop and try to imagine how your life would be if you resisted the fear. Think about how great it would feel. Think about the opportunities missed by allowing the fear to stay in control.

Now that you know what you are truly afraid of try to address the fears. If it is lack of knowledge, find ways to educate yourself about the subject matter. Take a course, research on the web, find a mentor, a life coach. Associate with people who will encourage and guide you. Address all the reasons why you feel fearful and diffuse fear. As you gain more knowledge, your level of confidence will grow simultaneously. High self-confidence will replace doubts and fear.

Positive self-talk is another way to reinforce confidence and diminish fear. Giving positive self-affirmations is a form of self-conditioning that replaces the doubts lodged in the subconscious. Remind yourself that "you can" achieve.

Alternative tools for dealing with the anxiety caused by fear are neurofeedback and biofeedback therapies. These modalities help to reduce the effects of fear conditioning, restore clearer objectives, and create more focus on the goals at hand. To this end, the individual can progress at a faster pace.

Most importantly, take action. Don't just sit around hoping, thinking and planning forever, or waiting for the right time to act. The best time to start is today. Jump in! Figure out what you're good at and make that move right now. The best way to overcome fear is by being proactive. With each effort your level of confidence increases.

Above all, believe through faith that you can overcome your fears and achieve your goals. Believe that you can accomplish great things in your life.

Remember having fears is a normal part of what makes us human. It is an emotion just like love, happiness, or sadness. The problem arises when fear has so much control over your life that it hinders your ability to succeed in achieving your goals. The most successful people have fears. They just NEVER let their fears hold them back. So how badly do you want to overcome your fears? That is the question of significance.

Overcome Fear and Overcome Your Fate

Is "Fate" your genetic blueprint? A "habit pattern" you attract into your life without realizing it?

Overcoming fear is a "one quick step" process: Stop it! Fear is an emotional rush, limbic brain response to perceived danger...real or not. It's of no benefit.

"The only thing we have to fear is fear itself- nameless, unreasoning, unjustified terror which paralyzes needed efforts to convert retreat into advance." Franklin D. Roosevelt

You cannot get rid of fear - but you can create a "NO" habit response that turns your attention to solutions and inspiration. Repeat that - and you open the door to your "destiny" and leave your old genetic "fate" behind.

Do you have to overcome fear?

Nope. Many motivate themselves with fear - especially recently. The past eight years were guided by a paranoid government. Fear motivates - has for centuries. Notice the mayhem? Death, wars, destruction? Pretty hard to miss, isn't it? Now it's also in the economic arena - worldwide. Had enough? You can stop it.

Lives dominated by a fear mirror that paranoid pattern. Constantly "putting out fires, fighting to survive." Attack and counter-attack. What fun in the sports arena. Not in life.

"Anxiety is a thin stream of fear trickling through the mind. If encouraged, it cuts a channel into which all other thoughts are drained." Arthur Somers Roche

Leaders take Big Risks, and the results are magnified in full public view.

Many leaders earning millions are driven by fear. Here's an interesting comment from a businessman. "How do you explain the success of Grove, the Intel CEO, who wrote, "Only the Paranoid Survive?" He was scared all the time. I am not very different."

Many see life through the eyes of "fear." Leaders are out in life in a Big Way. Trial and error is the path to success. But errors are amplified and affect many lives. As a leader's anxiety increases so do fear. Fear clouds thinking and make a bad situation worse. That's how fear "makes itself real", and paranoia is soon justified.

How "successful" is it to put out the fires you attract or ignite? Is this success? The fear is not a conscious choice. It's there in most everyone. Fear keeps many from even attempting leadership - or seeking fame and fortune.

Fear is a poor guide to success.

How successful has fear guided our nation? Companies? Economy? You? Fear is limiting you in the same ways.

Why not try something else? Pain, strife, stress, loss, war - aren't that much fun.

"Insanity: doing the same thing over and over again and expecting different results." Albert Einstein

Fear attracts itself (fear loss - and you lose; fear attack -- you attract it.) You find what you look for - and your "experience"

EMPATH

then validates the fear. Once caught up in that drama - it's difficult to see the alternative.

Know why? The alternative is overcoming fear: stopping it and refusing to get sucked into the limbic brain "fight or flight" response. It's a choice to stay mindful and find solutions instead. Next, you need a plan or vision of where you want to be - and you can train yourself to Focus on that instead.

Inspiration leading to solutions is a choice.

Everything you sense is vibration - and vibration exerts a "pull" like a magnet. Like energy attracts. Inspiration...with your Focus on your Vision or goal -- leads to solutions. That vision feels good - and so does pursue it. That's out of the range of the vibration of "fear." From the higher frequencies of "expecting" things to work out - they do. That's Law of Attraction in action.

The successful look for solutions and find them - sometimes with spectacular results. Fear is woven into the fabric of life. Many success stories reflect the constant struggle with fear...wins and losses...struggle and gain. That's the result of not overcoming fear, and instead of dancing with it.

Overcoming Fear.

Fear surfaces for everyone - you cannot get rid of fear (it's only a concept - a collection of thoughts. Like the number 3, you can't get rid of "3.") You can opt out, see fear as "the problem" and solve it. You can transform it by adding more to the old idea until it becomes a new idea - that's a habit too. Hard to believe? Only because you're in the "fear habit." Look beyond the familiar. You cannot solve your problems at the same level of fear that created them.

"I am an old man and have known a great many troubles, but most of them never happened." Mark Twain

Where does all the fear come from?

Your ancestors. Fear of failure and "bondage" are huge genetic patterns that interfere with creativity and success. Everyone's ancestors spent some time under the rule of a petty tyrant - either as a wife (50% of all genetic codes) or slave or servant or military. All ancestors failed many times - often with much pain and suffering. That fear is a part of your genetic blueprint. You can change it.

Not getting the success you want?

The only thing between where you are now and what you want -- is FEAR. Your genetic patterns limit you - nothing else - but an old habit. Some call that "fate". Now you know better.

What you have in your life is a reflection of your genetic blueprint - or your fate. That pattern in your subconscious built your experiences. Over many years you have modified and expanded it. You can change your fate. Is it time to change it again.

If you do not have the success you want - it is time for allowing more expansion - The fear of change and loss - can change too.

"Sure I am this day we are masters of our fate, that the task which has been set before us is not above our strength; that its pangs and toils are not beyond our endurance. As long as we have faith in our cause and an unconquerable will to win, victory will not be denied us."

Winston Churchill - Living with fear is living in chaos soup.

If you don't overcome fear - you continue to fight yourself, live in paranoia and stress - and eventually the fear wins out - and you get what you fear, along with whatever success you can hold onto. Ugh! Time to give that up. Life can be easy and fun - and successful. You need only choose it, act on the choice and live your Vision. If you're annoyed that it sounds too simple to be true - you're waking up.

Contraction and expansion is a natural creative process.

You have now outgrown your old habits of thought (and fears) and that is all that is limiting your expansion. How do you know? You want more. You feel limited, blocked and not much you try works well. Compared to where you want to be, you feel "contracted, boxed in and restricted."

When you feel you are not getting what you want and don't know how to get it: that feeling is what is keeping you stuck where you are. "Conflict" is the clash between vibrating or signalling what you want and your fear about it. Those double feelings are also called "stress".

Free yourself quickly. Simply see that you are only limiting yourself with unconscious fears. You are attracting the "fate" you fear when you allow fear to run rampant in your mind.

Get off of what is not working.

Give up hard work and action until you create a more expanded self-image - and feeling - you can't push through a genetic fear - and that's what is stopping your progress. You want what you want - and you fear (unconscious) what will happen to you if you get it. Overcome Fear Fast (at the end) can break you free of the bad habit.

"Every individual act and suffers by his peculiar teleology, which has all the inevitability of fate, so long as he does not understand it." Alfred Adler

How do you know if it is fear stopping you?

Is fear active in your life? Do you feel uneasy about being out in the world in a bigger way? Being more - expanding - new experiences - taking a chance -- new learning - giving up what you thought you wanted...looking for a new way to be and live?

Does changing your life routines, patterns, habits (friends, work, food, lifestyle) feel uneasy? It should - you have moved on and expanded - yet can't see how to get where you want to be.

Your fear is clouding your vision and inter-fear-ing with your Inspiration.

You overcome fear when you see fear as "the habit" that is attracting to you the very thing you fear. It might be the fear "I can't get what I want or what I want is outside my 'safe zone'.

That's a genetic fear - it's not about now, not true, and it's not for the reasons you think.

How do you know? Listen to your self-talk. Fear masks as "avoidance" too. Thoughts such as, "I don't care about money"; If the Universe wants me to have....; I prefer "behind the scenes;" I'm not seeking fame, or anything...just a little more cash..."

"Public opinion is a weak tyrant, compared with our private opinion - what a man thinks of himself, that is which determines, or rather indicates his fate" - Henry David Thoreau.

You are changing a habit, changing your fate.

The fear of "breaking free" was formed over centuries of many deaths and much pain and suffering. You can get over it by seeing it for what it is, and talking yourself into your "now" where you are safe, and those fears are no longer justified.

You can't get rid of anything - but you can transform it into something else. Bridge from the fear - to success "in a big way" - and it will be yours. When you stop the fear - you need a "bridge of thoughts" to walk yourself to your Vision (goal) of what you want. You must have a "destination" to shift the feelings and your point of attraction from fear to solutions.

How do you know it's working? You feel hopeful and begin to expect the new success you want. Your feelings (and point of attraction) shifted from doubt to expectation.

You always get what you expect. No exceptions. Use that fact to accurately gauge where you are - then you can get to feeling what you want.

Once you have removed or softened the barrier - your inspiration guides you to new opportunities. Test the new options compared to your Vision: If they match take action - if not, wait for the choices that feel good and match your Vision.

Make it easy and make it fun.

Spend time in nature - clear your mind, open your heart, mind and body and ask questions. Seek solutions and follow your Inspiration. You can do this.

Controlling Your Mind: How to Overcome Fear

Some fears are reasonable and helpful. Other fears are unreasonable and harmful. First, one must understand the difference and, second, one must learn how to banish those that are irrational. Here are seven guidelines.

How To Overcome Fear, Guideline One: It is reasonable and helpful to have a healthy fear of things like fire, tornadoes, falling out a window, sharp objects, thieves with weapons, and so on. When fears merely guide us to be careful, they serve a positive, protective function. Any fear that becomes debilitating, however, needs fixing. If one panics in the presence of a knife, open window, or flame on a kitchen stove, even those normal fears have become too extreme. How can you overcome these hurtful and limiting fears?

How To Overcome Fear, Guideline Two: Understand the source of irrational fears. They reside in the subconscious or Deep Mind. We aren't aware of its activities. It acts not by logic but by correlation - if A occurs before B then A probably caused B. Occasionally that is true. Often it isn't. The Deep Mind can't tell the difference; in fact, it is fully unconcerned about how logical a connection may be.

How To Overcome Fear, Guideline Three: When some hurtful or unpleasant occurrence takes place after a particular event or in the presence of some person, object, or place, the Deep Mind is likely to form a correlation. When that setting event occurs again the subconscious must send your conscious mind a message (called a directive) to become fearful. Perhaps a child gets startled or pummeled by a dog and understandably becomes upset. The Deep Mind may establish a correlation between dogs in general and the need to be afraid. When that happens (and sometimes for the rest of one's life) that child will feel great fear in the presence of dogs.

How To Overcome Fear, Guideline Four: The subconscious mind is so powerful that when it sends a directive, we have to act according to it. For instance, when the Deep Mind has created and held a fear directive, we will continue to experience fear in whatever context the correlation reflects. To get rid of a fear one needs to get rid of that specific fear directive. That may take specialized training from a professi onal, but there are some things you can try first.

How To Overcome Fear, Guideline Five: There is a process called Gradual Accommodation that often helps. You set up situations in which you begin experiencing the problem (fear producing) stimulus from a distance such that the event (or person, etc.) does not produce fear. For example, perhaps you watch dogs in a park while you are safely secured inside your car. The process involves gradually confronting the object of fear in tiny steps. You might take a second step as simple as watching those dogs with the car window opened, then the door opened, then standing alongside the car, then sitting on a nearby bench and so on. Don't move on to the next step until you feel no fear. Your eventual goal will, perhaps, be to be able to pet a dog. Gradually you accommodate to the fear-producing object. Be patient.

How To Overcome Fear, Guideline Six: Another approach could be called the Face Down. You just swallow hard and expose yourself to the feared object or person or situation. Find a dog known to be gentle, for example. Approach it, watch it, touch it, pet it, sit and hold it. The fear will initially well up inside you. In this process, the idea is to feel the fear left as you come to understand the situation no longer requires you to be fearful. (Not suggested for children.)

How To Overcome Fear, Guideline Seven: There are counselling methods that teach one how to overcome fear in short order and which have long-lasting effects. The typical talk therapies have a very poor track record when it comes to helping people quickly and permanently learn how to overcome fear. The so-called conditioning or desensitization therapies work best.

A Guide to Overcoming Stress, Anxiety and Depression

Scientific research is now validating that stress has a considerable influence on our body's physiology, contributing to many acute and chronic illnesses. A report by the World Bank stated that 1 in 5 people suffer from depression or anxiety. Typical stresses that may be encountered in daily life include physical, chemical, infectious and psychological stresses.

The stress cycle involves our thoughts, emotions, the chemical reactions in our brain, our body and the physical sensations we feel as a result of these. Once this process begins it snowballs, gains momentum and life may feel out of control. The first stage, our thoughts is the most powerful as it is not the event that causes us stress, but the way we react to it. Thoughts start in the cortex of the brain and move quickly to the limbic system or midbrain where our emotions lie. Negative thoughts trigger an immediate emotional response such as anger, fear, hatred, grief, regret, anxiety, sadness, embarrassment or jealousy. These thoughts stimulate our nervous and hormonal systems to release stress hormones, most notably adrenaline and cortisol from our adrenal glands (kidney bean shaped glands which sit above our kidneys). In response, chemicals are released throughout the body which reaches the pituitary gland in the brain and stimulates the release of more hormones and stress chemicals. The final stage of the stress cycle is activated as these chemicals alert every organ in the body to work faster. This results in symptoms such as sweating, tremor, anxiety, churning stomach, reduced salivation, dry mouth, increased muscular activity and hyperventilation, irregular heartbeat (palpitations), chest pain, visual disturbances and tingling and numbness, as well as muscle tremors, exhaustion, general weakness and sleep disturbances.

Once upon a time, it was very beneficial for the human body to undergo these physical changes, as the main emotion experienced by our ancestors was fear triggered by an attack from a wild animal. The stress chemicals released during the attack enabled the early humans to push their bodies to the necessary extremes and escape the attack. In the 21st century, however, more complex stress emotions are triggered far more often, and they don't necessarily require a physical reaction. As a result, this continual stress response starts to wear out the body - the overproduction of stress chemicals and hormones eventually take its toll on the body and may eventually lead to cell death. Cortisol one of the predominant hormones released by the adrenal glands in response to stress produces many of the adverse effects of long-term stress. This includes depletion of DHEA, a hormone which is important for the manufacture of sex hormones such as estrogen and testosterone; an antidepressant and our so-called anti-ageing hormone. A reduction in DHEA produces symptoms of fatigue, hormonal imbalance, depression and general unwellness. Consistently elevated cortisol levels may also lead to a reduction in serotonin neurotransmission. Serotonin is a neurotransmitter which is required for a healthy mood. Low serotonin transmission is a major defect in depression.

Stress Lowers Immunity

Immune system function is also adversely affected by excess cortisol leading to depression of antibacterial, antiviral defence and increasing our allergy response. This may result in symptoms such as frequent colds and flu, cold sores, hay fever, asthma, sinusitis, migraines, and food intolerances.

Stress Increases Toxins

Stress also has significant effects on toxicity. The intestinal barrier function is a major defence against an immense load of disease-causing microorganisms from ingested food, resident bacteria, invading viruses and other insults. Psychological stress has been demonstrated to disrupt intestinal permeability. Acute stressful events are closely associated with inflammation of the colon; cells of the mucous membranes of the colon have been shown to produce elevated levels of inflammatory substances such as prostaglandin 2 and cyclooxygenase 2. This situation not only increases bacterial adherence to the intestinal lining but also reduces the secretion of important immune system compounds such as immunoglobulin A. This may lead to a condition called leaky gut, whereby improperly digested food particles and other matter leaks into circulation leading to immune activation with subsequent enhanced stress response. Certain foods in particular seem to provoke this response, including wheat, dairy and yeasts. Symptoms of leaky gut include low appetite, bloating, flatulence, abdominal pain and cramping, irregular bowel movements, as well as sinus, headaches and skin rashes.

What Can You Do?

Fortunately, there is an abundance of treatment options for stress, anxiety and depression. If the symptoms are severe or have been persisting for a considerable length of time, it may be useful to combine several approaches as outlined below:

Herbal Medicine

Herbal medicines may be very beneficial for the treatment of stress, anxiety and depression. Many clinical trials have found herbs such as St Johns Wort to be as effective as pharmaceutical anti-depressants in treating mild to moderate depression. Other herbs which are useful for alleviating symptoms of stress, anxiety and depression, include Oats, Lemon Balm, Skullcap, Zizyphus, Passionflower, Verbena and Chamomile. Another class of herbs which assists our bodies to cope with stress are the adaptogens. These include the ginsengs, such as Panax or Korean Ginseng, Siberian Ginseng, American Ginseng and Indian Ginseng also known as Ashwagandha or Withania. Other important adaptogens include Rhodiola, Schisandra, Codonopsis and Gotu Kola. Since herbs are powerful medicines, it is best to consult a professional naturopath or herbalist who can prescribe an individual prescription containing a combination of herbs specific for your needs.

Supplements

Nutritional supplements may also be of benefit in times of increased stress since increased physical, emotional and mental demands increase our demand for certain vitamins and minerals, most notably:

• Magnesium required for muscle relaxation, energy production, hormone production and healthy heart function. Magnesium deficiency is a very common occurrence. Symptoms of deficiency include muscle cramps, headaches, neck and shoulder tension, premenstrual tension, period pain and low energy. Dietary sources of magnesium include: nuts and green leafy vegetables;

• B vitamins required for healthy nervous system function, hormone and neurotransmitter, production and energy production. As B vitamins are water soluble, they are easily removed from the diet. Consuming excessive amounts of diuretics such as tea, coffee and cola drinks as well as certain medications will promote their removal from the body. Good dietary sources include: whole grains, such as oats and brewer's yeast;

• Vitamin C is important for many functions in the body, including immune system function and adrenal gland function. It is also an important antioxidant and is required for collagen production;

• Essential fatty acids such as fish oil and evening primrose oil. These are essential for healthy brain function and are often deficient in the diet. Good sources include oily fish such as salmon, ocean trout, snapper, wild barramundi and deep sea cod. Evening Primrose Oil is best taken as a supplement. When buying oil supplements ensure you buy ones with added antioxidants such as vitamin E as all oil supplements are prone to oxidation. Also, since many fish are contaminated with mercury and pesticides, ensure you buy fish supplements which have been tested and purified.

Dietary Recommendations

In times of stress, we often go for an afternoon coffee or a cola drink with sugary snacks such as chocolate, cakes, biscuits, doughnuts, etc., which give us comfort and a short burst of energy. Unfortunately, these may be exacerbating our anxiety and in the long term promoting weight gain and reducing our energy and immunity. As a result, these foods should be kept to a minimum. During times of acute anxiety, it is best to avoid caffeine-containing substances altogether as coffee (especially instant), chocolate, cola and tea may precipitate anxiety and panic attacks. Instead eat a diet of whole grains including oats, grain bread, nuts, seeds and vegetables, particularly leafy greens such as broccoli, bok choy, spinach and rocket. Include more good oils in the diet, including deep sea fish, nuts (almonds, walnuts, cashews), seeds (sunflower, pumpkin) and good quality proteins such as eggs, lean pasture fed red meat and antibiotic free chicken.

Lifestyle Recommendations

There are many other therapies which are useful for reducing stress, including massage, hypnotherapy and acupuncture. Listening to relaxing CDs may also be beneficial. Practices such as yoga, meditation and tai chi are also beneficial as they not only calm our body by producing "feel good" chemicals called endorphins but also improve immune system function, bone density and promote the removal of wastes from our bodies.

As a Naturopath, I am passionate about educating people regarding drug-free alternatives to pharmaceutical medications to treat their anxiety and stress. One such alternative which I am particularly excited about is Brainwave Entrainment. Brain Wave Entrainment Technology has made it possible to alter your brainwaves by using audio technologies to tune your brainwaves to specifically designed brainwave states simply by listening to a CD or MP3 recording. The entrainment process has been scientifically proven to naturally synchronize your brainwaves to the embedded carrier frequencies on the CD. I have personally used these technologies for over a decade with great success for insomnia and anxiety issues as well as for memory enhancement. For detailed information on our brainwave CDs visit our website listed below.

You should also aim to get adequate exercise such as walking, swimming, cycling, aerobics or weight training at least four times per week for at least 20 minutes. This will not only improve your fitness levels and cardiovascular function but will also increase the body's production of endorphins-chemical substances that can relieve anxiety and depression. Scientific research shows that routine exercise can positively affect mood and help with depression. As little as three hours per week of aerobic exercise can profoundly reduce the level of depression. The most important thing is that you find something you like and do it regularly.

Below is a list of additional recommendations to help reduce stress:

• Develop a positive attitude about everything you do; associate with positive attitude people

• Make time to relax. If you don't know how now's the time to learn!

• Learn proper breathing exercises (yoga, taichi)

• Cultivate a good sense of humour & laugh more...

• Listen to relaxing music

• Pamper yourself or be nice to yourself, e.g. have a massage or facial visit with friends and do things that you enjoy

• Permit yourself to stretch from time to time

• Get out of the hum-drum and do something different (a vacation, bush-walk, picnic)

• Always get proper rest

• Learn about your inner spirit, pray or meditate according to your conscience and beliefs

• If you're not enjoying yourself, ask why & do something about it - Life's too short

• Keep a diary of your feelings to monitor your progress

• Find something to appreciate about life every single day!

Face-To-Face With Your Fear and Anxiety

In many ways we may try to get rid of our fears and phobias by taking medication (or alcohol and drugs), going to psychotherapy, reciting affirmations, listening to hypnosis tapes, or by simply avoiding environments where we feel too much anxiety and worry.

But the truth is that experiencing some fear and anxiety is unavoidable, and it's a good sign of a healthy mind. Often, by acknowledging our fears (not avoiding them or suppressing them) we gain insight into areas in our life that we may need to improve upon.

Fear as a compass.

When your hand touches a hot stove, it feels pain, and that pain motivates you to move your hand away. In the same way, fear is an important signal and motivator that can help guide our behaviour.

Sean Cooper, author of "The Shyness and Social Anxiety System," describes fear as a kind of compass:

"Fear is like a compass that points you towards the life you want. All of your deepest desires are fear-ridden, from approaching someone you're attracted to, to starting a new business, to conquering your social anxieties. Whenever you feel fear, you know that you are going after what you truly want and growing as a person."

The truth is that whenever you try to make a significant change in your life, that change will usually be met with some kind of resistance or fear. This is because making changes requires that you start engaging in new and unfamiliar behaviours. And when engaging in these new behaviours, there will always be a degree of uncertainty - you've never acted in this way before, so you aren't sure exactly what the rewards or consequences will be. This uncertainty can be a huge contributor to our fear, anxiety, and worry. But we have to learn how to embrace it anyway.

Confronting your fears face-to-face is the only way to truly overcome them. Avoiding fearful situations only exacerbates the problem. But when you begin to see fear as a sign of growth and boundary-pushing - when you are willing to step outside of your "comfort zone" - then you give yourself an opportunity to learn more about yourself and improve your life in the face of those fears.

You can't get rid of these fears completely - you just have to find ways to embrace them in positive ways.

DIWA: Do It While Afraid

Fear doesn't go away by learning about it. You need to actively seek new experiences and gain confidence in facing these physical and psychological obstacles. Only by exposing yourself to these new experiences do you begin to rewire your brain and habituate to these new environments and situations.

Sean Cooper has a mantra that helps him overcome fear: "acknowledge feelings and take appropriate action."

There is no sense in suppressing or ignoring these feelings when they exist. Often the more we ignore or suppress our feelings, the bigger the feeling builds up inside of us. I like to sometimes think of our emotions as a baby throwing a temper tantrum. If you try to ignore the baby, it will only get louder and louder until it gets your attention. Our emotions work the same way - they are calling to us to get our attention.

Therefore, it's crucial to acknowledge and accept our feelings. And while doing this, we can often become more aware of what causes our emotions, what they are trying to tell us, and how we should act in response to these feelings.

7 Tips in Having the Right Mindset to Overcome Fear

Fear can hold us back from realizing our biggest dreams. You have to understand that fear and success can and will never go together, you have to let go of one, and if we don't overcome it, it would be impossible for us to achieve and succeed in reaching our dreams.

But as a person, you were born strong; you were born unafraid, you were born confident, you were born capable of achieving anything you could think of. It is important for us to understand the root of our fears so that we can eliminate it. It is usually from what we see, what we hear and failing to look beyond our fears that hold us back, to let us feel that we should be better of giving up than going for it. I for one was able to overcome my fear, and it took some time, it took a lot of obstacles that I had to overcome, but eventually, every bit of it was worth it. I was able to start my very own multi-million property business, and I want you to realize that your dreams can be achieved, it is possible, and you are a possibility.

Overcoming our fears is liberating and is setting our selves free from serving a lifetime of regrets and "what if's".

Here are my tips to help you overcome your fear and help you have the right mindset in reaching your dreams.

1. IDENTIFY THE THINGS THAT ARE HOLDING YOU BACK - You have to identify what it is that you're afraid of, are you afraid of failing? Are you afraid of letting go and being away from your loved ones? Whatever it is that you are afraid of, identify the root cause of it and from there on you have to confront them that they're not going to stop you from what you want and what you deserve. You have to look beyond your fear and see that an endless amount of possibility is out there only if you let go of your fears.

2. SELF-MOTIVATION - Self-motivation is very powerful in changing one's ability to handle and confront fears. If you are having doubts, each day writes something positive that you can repeat to yourself every morning. Write down the things you want to happen and the things you want to accomplish each day. Make everything you write down as positive and as motivating as it can be. It will help you get through.

3. DO IT ANYWAY - Fear may stop us, either temporarily or permanently but we have to face the truth that if we do not get it over it, fear will eventually find its way back to us in other ways. The best way to overcome it is to decide that fear will not stop you. Your dreams are too important to just write them off due to fear.

4. REALIZE THAT YOU ARE A POSSIBILITY - From the moment you were born, you were already a success. You have the God-given capabilities, skills and life to do all that you can accomplish. Don't waste life by taking a step back and live it by wishing you could have done better, act now because now is the time to do better. What you dream of is POSSIBLE if you decide to make it happen.

116

5. BE POSITIVE AND BE WITH POSITIVE AND MOTIVATIONAL PEOPLE - One way to overcome your fear is by living day to day positively and surrounding yourself with positive thinking people who can give you the confidence, who can support and motivate you into becoming the best that you can be. Negative people will only see your weakness and bring you down. Stay away from them and be with the right group who can keep you positive.

6. DO YOUR RESEARCH - If ever you are afraid of failing, study it. Learn what you need to learn from the experts to minimize the risk of failing, to know what to do and to avoid what not to do. Learn as much as you can, keep it in heart and mind and gain as much experience, values and lessons as you can. You can even get yourself a mentor to guide you and get you through the process of living your passion.

7. PRAY AND STRENGTHEN YOUR FAITH - Fear is usually the result of weakness inside, and we can ask help by Praying to God, He will always be our stronghold, and He will always plan what is best for us. When you have God with you, nothing and nobody, not even fear can hold you back from what you are destined for.

How to Overcome Fear - 7 Tips to Help You Overcome Fear

- Public speaking

- Dogs

- Spiders

- Going somewhere new

- Ageing

- Socialising

- Losing a partner

- Starting a new job

- Trying a new activity - particularly on our own

- Moving from the area in which you live

- Flying

Do any of these things fill you with dread? Well, you're not alone!

We all feel some or all of these fears and many others to boot! Whatever our excuse for not achieving something, fear is usually involved in it somewhere.

It's not just our doubts that stop us from moving forward, very often it can be our friends and family that are very happy to give us their opinions that just pile on top of the self-doubt that we already have.

Can we live fearless lives? Actually no, but we can become far better at being able to overcome fear and thus substantially reduce it's negative effect on our lives. Some fears we need to have to alert us of danger, but it is the ones that stop us from progressing positively in life that we need to learn to put in perspective.

It's a well-known fact that most of us only achieve a small percentage of our full potential in life; wouldn't it be great to increase that potential?

From the Cradle to the Grave

One of the main problems is that we are all told from the cradle to the grave, be careful with this, don't do that it's dangerous, I wouldn't recommend that it's too risky, I don't think you'll be able to do that.

We have so much reinforced negative conditioning. We are taught to fear but rarely taught how to overcome fear. Of course I realise that when your parents advise you to pay attention when crossing the road, this is obviously sensible and is the correct advice, but when making a decision where your life is clearly not at risk, we must assess for ourselves the real risks involved.

That said, some people do have to make decisions which may result in a situation or activity where their lives could be at risk, but they still go for it anyway. If this was not the case there would be a lot of sport not played, planes not flown, wars not fought, countries not governed and challenges not taken.

Here are seven tips to help you overcome fear and grab the life you deserve:

1. The "No Lose Scenario"

When you've made changes in your life previously, what were the outcomes? In most cases, the outcomes were probably good or fairly neutral. Occasionally you may have made a decision that you now feel was wrong. But, in making what you see as a wrong decision, you learned something, so in a way, none of the decisions was wrong. Given those results, can we say there is no "wrong" decision, I think so? Also, don't forget that sometimes what you previously thought was a bad decision, may lead you to the right place in the end. Things often happen for a reason and happen when we are ready for them.

2. You Need To Make Mistakes

We are all going to make mistakes, so get used to it! We all make mistakes - all the time. If we didn't, how would we learn? Have you ever heard the saying: "There's no such thing as failure, only feedback."?

Not everything in life is explained in a textbook, and even if it were, you wouldn't remember it all anyway. We remember better when we have experienced something because we have more senses attached to that memory. If we burn ourselves on a hot pan, we will certainly remember to be more careful in future as we know what it FEELS like if we touch a pan that is very hot. Get used to mistakes, expect them and most of all learn from them!

3. The Things You Want To Do ARE Achievable

Nearly all the things that we could possibly think of doing have been done before which means they are achievable. Therefore, if it's already been done, there's a good chance that you can do it too, you just need to learn how and then do the work necessary to get you there.

4. You Will Handle It

One of things that Susan Jeffers says in her book; "Feel The Fear And Do It Anyway" is to think to yourself that whatever comes your way, you'll handle it. Think about your life, isn't that true? You have handled everything that has come your way so far, one way or another and you're surviving to tell the tale!

5. Reduce Worry And Stress

If you learn to overcome fear more effectively, you will reduce the amount that you worry. If you reduce the amount that you worry, you will reduce your levels of stress. If you reduce your levels of stress, your health will undoubtedly benefit.

6. Be Happier

Think for a moment, if you were able to substantially reduce your fear, what things would you like to do? And if you did those things, how do you think you would feel? Wouldn't your life be so much more exhilarating? So many new opportunities would be available to you. Your life would carry so many more great experiences and achievements which could only make you happier.

7. You've Already Done It

You will have made many decisions throughout your life and your life has probably changed many times, so it's a good thing to look back and say, I was scared but I went ahead anyway. Remember the sense of achievement that you felt when things went to plan or the enjoyment you felt when you tried an activity that you were scared of beforehand.

And Finally - Why Is It So Essential That You Learn To Overcome Fear?

The thing that we should fear the most is the prospect that our lives will never change, that we will never grow or learn anything else for the rest of our lives because of fear. Surely that would be the worst thing and such a waste of a life where so much is possible for us.

Learning how to overcome fear is essential for us to make our lives worth living.

Overcoming Fears with Psychic Abilities

Did You know that You have the power to overcome fear by using your psychic skills? Well, You do. By tapping into the unseen powers around and within, You can leave yourself feeling relaxed, empowered and ready to face what comes.

First of all, the root of many fears stems from worry about the future. We lose our center thinking about situations out of our control. For example, being afraid the plane will crash, a tornado will strike, or our loved ones won't arrive safely. We take ourselves out of alignment with our Higher Selves when we fear things won't work out the way we want them to. We start focusing on the worst case scenario and drain our energy. All the what ifs start to hold us in a state of fear.

Remember that when faced with actual bodily harm You can trust yourself to know what to do in a scary situation when it's right in front of You. What I'm talking about here is how to feel better in the now. You have the psychic power to release the fears holding you back and leave yourself feeling calm, centered, peaceful and confident in the now.

Here are some ideas that can help You with overcoming fears.

Trust All is Well and everything is in Divine Order. Allow yourself to know in your heart and mind that whatever comes your way, You are OK.

See and feel yourself succeeding. You can project your consciousness into the future and notice what it's like to have lived past the event that had You feeling scared. Allowing yourself to feel in the now that You made it through the hard time and you've thrived.

Take time to mediate and allow yourself to be grounded with the earth energy and connected with the cosmic energy. This will keep You in the now. In the now is where your personal power rests.

Ask your guides or angels for help. Archangel Michael's expertise is in removing fears.

Remember the law of attraction says whatever You give your attention to grows stronger. Figure out what it is You want to happen and focus on that. Or just pay attention to things in your now that you appreciate, things that make You feel good.

What if You try a bunch of techniques and You still feel afraid? Try playing the even if... game. This tool has You project yourself into your fear and You see and know you'll be OK no matter what. Even if (fill in the blank) happens, I know I'll be ok.

I've found the even if tool helpful for overcoming my fears — for example, the fear of dying while my children are young. Even if I die while they are young, I know they will be ok. Another example, worry about getting in a car accident. Even if I get into a car accident, I know I'll be ok.

Just by using the even if tool I was able to stop focusing about what I didn't want because I was able to feel in my body, heart and mind that I am OK and would be OK no matter what.

Underlying a lot of fears is the fear of dying. If You are attracted to this site, You most likely have awareness of yourself as an eternal and spiritual being. If You see death as a transition to a different realm, then there isn't really much to fear

CHAPTER 5

SURVIVAL GUIDE FOR EMPHATIC AND HIGHLY SENSITIVE PEOPLE

Emotional Intelligence and the Empathic Spirit

The mood was festive and joyful. The ambience of the large and magnificent arena concurred with the joyful energy that permeated the room. The Master of Ceremonies had prepared a first Class meeting as usual. I had noticed that the MC has a habit of doing a first class job at everything he does, this habit must have something to do with his childhood, I was thinking.

The kind Gentleman walked up to the podium and my chagrin, he told a story about a child, we were all ears. Now, I will share the story with you, as best as I can remember it.

There was a young lad in a past age, Let's call him Hans, in a country where they set buckets of water on the floor to use as fire extinguishers. Hans had been taught well by his parents; he was well versed with truth and the propriety of his society. Hans was the boy that everyone knew was going to do right all of his life. This was the boy that always had his homework done and done right. Everyone who knew him expected him to do what was right, and do it on time.

It was the beginning of a new school year, complete with all the joy, jokes, the hope of a new beginning and the nervous anticipation that goes along with such events. Everyone who had anything to do with the school was attending. Hans was sitting on the front row.

Children can get very nervous on the first day of school and this day was no different. Hans noticed the young girl on his left side. She appeared to be more than nervous and sorrowing with anxiety, shame and very troubled.

Hans walked over the hallway, picked up one of the buckets of water, walked back with everybody now watching him and poured the entire bucket on the young girl. Pandemonium erupted in the auditorium. Teachers moved to her defence and Hans was in a lot of trouble.

Hans was taken to the principal's office and was questioned there. Hans never spoke a word but rather took his punishment like a man. Nobody could get a single word of explanation from Hans, about the incident that entire year.

He held his peace. As time went on the incident began to dim in mind and memories of the students and faculty. It was now the last day of School, and his schoolmaster stopped him on his way out and asked him why he poured the bucked on the young girl.

Hans replied; "Sir, she had wet her dress. I could see that she could not take the shame. I poured water to spare her the humiliation. "But Hans, you got into a lot of trouble over that," said the schoolmaster.

127

Then Hans said: "I know, and I could take the punishment" "But she was not strong enough to take the humiliation".

Listening with great care as the first class speaker delivered this story, it hit me. That is the truth being taught hit me; I got it. The truth received that day was as magnificent as the expansive auditorium and as awe-striking as the joy and energy of the crowd.

The truth received, will not openly be written here because you can figure it out on your own. However, I will leave you with this statement; this is the kind of thing that God does for us.

Resources for Empaths and Emotionally Sensitive People

Empaths have a natural ability to sense not only their own but also the emotions of others. This innate skill can be observed in babies. This ability usually subsides in childhood as we learn to focus more on verbal cues than emotional ones.

But for some people, the flow of emotional information just keeps coming. This can lead to powerful internal conflicts as they pick up incoherent verbal and emotional messages from people (such as when someone lies or suppresses anger). It can also quickly become overwhelming in social settings where the sheer quantity of emotional information can be too much to handle.

Emotional Intelligence is defined as "the ability, capacity, or skill to perceive, assess, and manage the emotions of one's self, of others, and groups" (Salovey and Mayer, 1990). Developing your Emotional Intelligence means that you have tools and processes to manage these emotional data.

If you are interested in Emotional Intelligence i've wrote a good introduction book of Emotional Intelligence, the title name is "Introducing Emotional Intelligence" by the way of course by Daniel Anderson.

Are you an Empath?

• Do you feel anxious or nervous in a crowd (4+ people)?

• Does your mood vary seemingly at random (getting angry or sad for no apparent reason)

• Do you feel a change in your physical energy level when you're in a crowd (tired, wired)

• Do you have a hard time falling asleep before midnight or do you procrastinate going to bed?

• Do you have physical symptoms that related to hearing (ringing, popping, itching in the ear)?

• Do you feel emotionally uncomfortable when someone touches or is close to you?

Disclaimer: This checklist is not a diagnostic or treatment tool. Some of the characteristics of Empaths can be diagnosed as ADD, agoraphobia or clinical depression. Contact your health care professional if you have any questions, need diagnostic or treatment for a mental health issue.

Empath Resources

Fortunately, there are more and more online resources available for Empaths. Unfortunately, most of these resources suggest a process that is likely to make things worse for you! Any kind of "protective mental shield" is based on the assumption that emotional information is threatening. If you go down that path, you will have to "defend" yourself for the rest of your life. How exhausting does that sound?

My work is result-based: if it works, keep doing it! As an Empath, these are the three tools I find most effective to manage the flow of emotional information I receive constantly. Try them out and see for yourself which one works best for you.

Being Transparent:

When we feel threatened by our surroundings, we become physically tense, and our energy field (the magnetic field that wraps around our body) becomes dense and constricted.

When you notice this tension, imagine that your energy field is expanding, like a gas. The particles are getting more and more spaced out, making your energy field thinner and much bigger. As your energy field becomes looser, emotions go right through you, like a rock falling through water. Instead of being caught in your dense energy field, the emotions of others will simply flow through you.

Adjust the Volume:

Sometimes the noise from other people's emotions gets so loud that we can't hear ourselves think! We get confused, hesitant, frustrated. Close your eyes and imagine two volume dials in front of you that go from 0 to 10. One says "Me", and the other says "Everything else". Turn the "Me" dial to 10, and the "Everything else" dial to 0. Instantly, your mind will respond to this request, and the chatter will calm down.

Progressive Affirmations:

Progressive affirmations can help you build up to where you want to be. Keep in mind that affirmations must ALWAYS feel good to be effective. So start at the "easiest" affirmation and say it for a few days. When you feel ready, move on to the next level for a few days until you can say the "top" affirmation while feeling good.

"I am willing to master my Empath abilities."

"I am ready to master my Empath abilities"

"I am choosing to master my Empath abilities."

Keep in mind that practice makes perfect. Try doing it in your head before you throw yourself in a tough situation (such as the mall or a party).

Once you are comfortable managing your Empath skills, you are ready to move on and develop your Emotional Intelligence by productively using emotional data in your daily life.

4 Steps to Turn Your Sensitivity into Your Superpower

Have you ever been told you're too sensitive? Or, to grow a thicker skin? Do you have a habit of taking on other people's pain? Do you consistently put others' needs before your own? Do you struggle with your sensitivity, at any time, in any way?

If you're like me, you might be an empath, a highly-sensitive person, or maybe someone with an extra dose of sensitivity. There's a spectrum, and if you find that you have heightened sensitivity, you likely fall somewhere within the spectrum of empaths.

Although, as sensitive souls, we know how painful it can be, it's important to know that sensitivity is a source of inner power. What's tricky, is knowing how to manage sensitivity -- so that rather than disempowering us, it empowers us instead.

There's no question in my mind that sensitive people must be vigilant about self-care. Daily self-care is not an option if you want to thrive as a sensitive person. And, fortunately, with the right methods and tools, it's possible to turn your sensitivity into your superpower!

What do I mean by turning your sensitivity into your superpower? I mean nurturing your inner gifts, such as intuition, inner vision, deep knowing, psychic ability, love, compassion, healing energy, creativity, artistic vision, and so many more -- and letting them shine.

Our creative abilities come from our senses, and we help them flourish by creating a nurturing inner environment.

Here are 4 Steps to Turn Your Sensitivity into Your Superpower:

STEP 1: EMBRACE

This is where you start. Tune your awareness to what lies within you. How does sensitivity show up for you? How does it assist you? How does it hinder you? Embrace everything that shows up with love, and acceptance. Let go of judgement.

Write a list of all the things you love about your sensitivity. Write a list of all that is painful. Practice embracing yourself with love, when you notice either the pleasurable or painful aspects of your sensitivity.

For one of my clients, when she learned how to embrace her sensitivity, without making it wrong, she was able to harness it in her work as an artist. Now she infuses her sensitive gifts into her creative projects, and her work has blossomed.

STEP 2: CLEAR

This step creates space for the magical part of your sensitivity to assist you in ways you could never imagine. Freeing ourselves from judgement, other people's opinions, other people's feelings, and all the old emotions we've stuffed down is the key to allowing our sensitivity to shine.

Sensitive people are prone to experiencing intense bouts of self -doubt, anxiety, fear, sadness, and overwhelm. Also, because we are sensitive, we're sometimes more likely to accept beliefs that aren't even ours. When these emotions and beliefs get stuck in our system, they contribute to persistent limiting patterns.

Clearing out old stuck emotions, and releasing limiting beliefs and patterns is crucial for our sensitivity to thrive truly. Clearing techniques include meditation, deep breathing, yoga, EFT tapping, matrix reimprinting, heart breath, and various talk and touch therapies.

Experiment with what works for you. Many times, if not most, it's helpful to enlist professional help when dealing with old persistent patterns and stuck emotions.

And, remember, self-love is the healing elixir for clearing any, and all, old negativity.

STEP 3: RECHARGE

Cell phones, with all of their amazing apps, only work when they're charged. Think of your superpower, or your inner power, like a battery that needs recharging regularly. When we don't recharge, we lose power. Recharging is essential.

Recharging for sensitive people often means a daily self-care ritual, perhaps combined with services such as massage, sauna, salt therapy, and energy therapies.

It also means creating healthy routines to allow for alone-time, creative expression, sleep, and time in nature.

And perhaps the most important aspect of recharging is the presence of healthy boundaries. Without them, overload and burn-out are almost guaranteed. Boundaries can be firm, hard, loose, stretchy, soft, or any way you want them. However, you decide to create them, remember that boundaries are essential to protect yourself from unwanted energy, people, ideas, and anything else that's not a match for your system.

STEP 4: ACTIVATE

Once you've become clear on the different aspects of your sensitivity, you've begun to clear out old, stuck energy, and you're regularly recharging your inner power, you're ready to active your gifts. As with anything, this is a process. The more you repeat the steps in the process, the easier, and more powerful it will become.

Decide now, which of your sensitive inner gifts will you expand? Which of your natural sensitivities will help you enrich your work life? Your relationships? Your Health? Your Spiritual Life? Your creative life? How will you shine your gifts, and with whom?

When you begin to see the picture of how sensitivity can flow through your life, activate one aspect of your sensitivity. For example, if you have a lot of compassion, you might choose to volunteer as a way to share your compassion. Or, if you have a gift for sensing subtle energy, you could expand your knowledge of energy therapies. The possibilities are endless. The goal here is to expand what you already possess, in the way that enriches your life. This is what turns your sensitivity into your superpower.

Throughout the process of activating your inner gifts, it's important to recycle through the first three steps: embrace, Clear, Recharge. A continual act of self-love will help you continually activate your brilliance.

You deserve your magnificence!

Here's to Bold Sensitivity!

9 Tips for the Spiritually Sensitive and Empaths

An empath is a highly sensitive person who can feel the emotional and physical states of the people around them. This, of course, can be problematic for the individual while walking through crowds or being around people who are in a negative state of mind.

They also have the ability, if they set aside any bias or emotional attachment, to sense truth and the motives of others.

Unfortunately, there are many people who are highly empathic and don't realize it. They struggle daily with not only their emotions but those of everyone around them. Some attempt self-medication with alcohol or drugs, or are prescribed drugs, that compound the issue, by doctors who don't understand the problem.

Thankfully, if you're an empath, there are other ways to deal with it. Below are things we've learned, as empaths, that we must do if we want to feel good daily.

1) Diet is key. You must be careful about how you fuel your body. Sugar and junk food will affect how you feel more so than other people, so it's best to avoid it as much as possible. Also, go easy on fruit sugar and make sure you are getting enough quality protein (not non- fermented, processed soy).

2) Regular exercise makes everyone feel better, and it's especially important for empaths. You don't need to go to a gym to exercise, of course, and a crowded gym might not be

the best place for you.

3) Make sure to schedule alone time to recharge; reading or walks in nature are two good ways. Regular solitude is a healing balm to the spiritually sensitive.

4) Be careful of who you allow in your inner circle. Don't try to save toxic people.

5) Meditate daily to clear your mind and calm your energy. There are many ways to meditate. For beginners, we recommend just sitting quietly with your eyes closed, and focusing exclusively on your breathing, a mantra, or counting from one to 500.

6) Burn white sage or use other energy clearing and protection methods to keep your space energetically clean.

7) Know that you always have access to spiritual help and protection from the other side. We call upon Arch Angel Michael for clearing and protection often, and there's no such thing as asking for too much help of him, or other helpful guides and beings of the Light, or God.

8) When you are feeling down, anxious, or otherwise negative, stop, breath, and ask yourself, "Are these feelings from me or someone else?" even if you are alone, you may be picking up other people's thoughts or energy from many miles away. You have the option to reject outside, negative energy and the right to feel good. Stand your ground and refuse to take on the energy of others. Sometimes you just have not to care.

9) Finally, you need to be aware of the information we've shared previously about spirit attachment and possession,

which can be more of a problem for empaths. A weakened energy state, due to various reasons such as excess drinking, drugs, or stress, can inadvertently invite toxic energy in the form of stray souls, entities, or even demonic energy, which can greatly interfere with all areas of your life.

It isn't easy maintaining a balanced state of mind as an empath but following these tips will help you feel better. You'll also have more energy to use your empathic ability in positive ways, such as being able to understand others' perspectives acutely well, and offering guidance when appropriate.

A Survival Guide for Empaths and Highly Sensitive Persons

Empaths are very special people and face multiple daily challenges. You connect with the energy of others sharing your space, and also your environment (through energy imprints). This can be overwhelming at times, and to gain control and manage your energy, a few tools can be essential. Here are some tips and techniques that have proven to be valuable assets for the empath's toolbox.

Learn how to disengage from the energy of others. How do you accomplish this? You must first know your energy. The awareness of what is yours versus other people is key to this step. I suggest reading Yvonne Perry's book, Whose Stuff Is This? This is an excellent reference book to begin learning about energy management. Distress and relaxation space is another necessity. It can be your man cave, your reading nook, or porch swing. It just needs to be a space where you can go to have time out and be away from the energy of others so that you might centre and recharge yourself.

Positive affirmations are also very helpful. A positive affirmation is a short sentence or two that supports positive thought patterns and can re-train your brain (The Audiobooks of Anthony Proctor are a really good choice) . An example, let me receive what is in my best and highest good at this time, is both raising your energetic signature and open-ended. Why is open-ended a good thing? It doesn't define, which can sometimes place limits or expectations providing an unintended consequence. What is what is the best and highest good is better than you have imagined? If you leave it open ended, it can flow right to you. I enjoyed, Outrageous Openness by Tosha Silver, which did a wonderful job of breaking this down and giving more insight into how this works.

Shielding is another tool you can use when you are just getting started. This involves calling in a high vibrational energetic field to protect you. You can call in Angels and see them standing by you in your mind's eye, or imagining a white light encasing you. Another method is to see yourself in armour made of mirrors which send energy right back to its source. A developed empath will be able to allow energy to flow through without absorbing any. This takes confidence and skill. You can develop this with practice. It is the knowledge that any energy that flows towards you is temporary, like a breeze. It can flow right through you. You can feel it, know it does not belong to you and allow it to pass through without absorbing any of it.

Good energetic hygiene is a must for any empath. It starts with a basic understanding of chakras, and then a simple visualization of cleansing them. Some people see the chakra wheels of colour and imagine them spinning with bright, healthy colour and any dark spots of negativity are removed. Doing this in the shower can be quite effective as any negativity goes right down the drain with the dirty bath water! You can also imagine white light coming in through your crown chakra, nourishing and replenishing the chakras.

Meditation and centring are also valuable assets for your empathic toolbox. Meditation for 10-20 daily will bring profound change. Centring involves coming back to self.

Empaths connect with others, and it's like an energetic handshake. Your energy goes out to meet and greet others, and centring brings you back into your body fully. This allows you to align with spirit/source energy and step out of ego. Mindfulness is great for centring. Try to live in the moment, and whatever emotion comes up to acknowledge, express and then release it.

Stones and essential oils can also be helpful. Depending on how you are wired you might prefer one more than the other. Remember you are an individual, your expression of empathic ability and empathic experience may be similar to another person's. However, the truth is you are a unique divine expression. That means you will vibe strongly and have an affinity with some things and not others. That's your beauty a nd why the world needs you!

Forgiving others and forgiving self is one of the most powerful tools you have. It will clear your energy and raise your vibrational rate. Remember forgiveness is for your well-being; the other person doesn't need "to forgive you" for the benefit. It can be a challenge to do this. However, it is necessary for your growth and evolution. No one has walked this earth and not harmed, intentionally or unintentionally, another being. It is part of the human experience. So like the prayer says... forgive others and forgive yourself.

The root chakra connects us to the earth. Be aware of this and using visualization ground into the earth. See (using your mind's eye) a cord connecting you to the earth. You can then use it to send negative energy into the earth where it is absorbed and to draw up nourishing energy from the centre of the earth. Doing this will increase your energy flow.

Others helpful techniques include listening to music or nature sounds. Spending time in nature and with your pets is a great way to relax, clear your energy and centre yourself. Exercise programs will support a good energetic flow. Yoga is really good because it combines breathing with poses that encourage alignment and flow of energy.

Keep your environment clear of negativity. Raise those vibes! The Native Americans' have been smudging with great results for years. Burning sage while stating an intention is a great method for clearing energy. In your office area, you can use a spritzer bottle with water and salt, or make an aromatherapy spritzer. If you use essential oils remember that oil and water don't mix so, you'll want to add some witch hazel or alcohol to the water and oils. A cup of water, ¼ cup of witch hazel and 7-10 drops of oil. Journal the gratitude! Ending the day by writing a list of things you are grateful for in a journal and then stating an intention or affirmation keeps the positive energy flowing.

NARCISSIST

*Discover the true meaning
of narcissism and how to avoid their
mind games, guilt, and manipulation*

By

DANIEL ANDERSON

this book has been derived from various sources. Please consult a licensed professional before attempting any techniques outlined in this book.

By reading this document, the reader agrees that under no circumstances is the author responsible for any losses, direct or indirect, which are incurred as a result of the use of information contained within this document, including, but not limited to, — errors, omissions, or inaccuracies.

TABLE OF CONTENT

CHAPTER 1
BASIC KNOWLEDGE ON
NARCISSISM

Narcissism and Its Traits

Narcissus was a mythological Greek male who looked adoringly at himself in the reflection of a stream and became forever in love with his image. From that mythology, a definition of a type of personality was born...Narcissism. In its extreme, it is known as Narcissistic Personality Disorder (NPD). This type of disorder is characterized by an all-consuming focus on oneself to the exclusion of anyone else.

This person has no regard for anyone's feelings, is without empathy, usually takes advantage of others for personal gain, seeks admiration from all he comes in contact with and is likely to be caught up with the fantasy of his self-importance. Narcissism is more often found in men than women (3 times more men than a woman).

NPD is at the end of the spectrum, and there are many more people with narcissistic traits than those with NPD. However, I will be focusing on NPD in this book.

There are many attributes that can be used to help one to identify a narcissist. Since becoming involved with someone who has this disorder will likely turn out to be a very negative experience it is a good idea to know what to watch for.

He needs to be right all the time. This is part of the inflated ego of the narcissist, never admitting wrongdoing or misjudgment. He will try to manipulate the data and the conversation in such a way as to find fault with everyone but himself.

He exaggerates or lies about accomplishments. This trait is part of the need to feel superior by using grandiose statements to boost his feelings of self-importance.

He expects special treatment wherever he is and whatever the circumstance. This could see as obnoxious or overly pushy behaviour in a restaurant or theatre, as though he deserved a certain "celebrity" status.

He craves admiration or adoration from everyone. If he can't get that need met he may become angry or hostile like some petulant child who can't get his way.

He has no concern for others. He lacks sympathy or empathy and acts as if other people's feelings are not important.

He will often try to dominate a conversation, as though his input were far more valuable than anyone else's.

He tries to manipulate or even brainwash others into believing what he wants them to believe.

He is often envious of others who he sees as celebrated or rich. He also believes others are envious of him, supporting his fantasy that he is more powerful, smarter or even richer than he is.

Self-Love is Not Narcissism!

Not only is self-love not narcissism; unfortunately, narcissists do not know how to begin to love themselves! Keep reading to discover the difference and to learn why self-love is vitally important today.

I have heard people describe narcissists as persons who love themselves - or love themselves too much! Because I was blessed to be taught self-love, I bristle every time I hear that description.

At MayoClinic.com, I found the following definition of narcissistic personality disorder: "Narcissistic personality disorder is a mental disorder in which people have an inflated sense of their importance and a deep need for admiration. They believe that they are superior to others and have little regard for other people's feelings. But behind this mask of ultra -confidence lies a fragile self-esteem, vulnerable to the slightest criticism."

A true narcissist considers himself to be of greater value than others, believing he is entitled to the best of everything. Narcissistic personality disorder should not be confused with healthy self-esteem. Although truly confident people are in touch with their gifts and talents, they do not consider themselves superior.

If self-love is not narcissism, what is it? Self-love is the ability to extend kindness and compassion to yourself. It is the ability to extend kindness and compassion that is sometimes nurturing and other times confrontational. You can be honest with you about motives, intentions, choices, behaviour, and words. Further, it is your ability, to be honest without hurting you over it! I like the way Joseph sums it up; self-love is the willingness to embrace all that we are. The way I sum it up is that self-love is when you give yourself the kind of love, affirmation, and boundaries that you wish your parents had been able to give you.

Many of us were taught as children to forget ourselves in deference to those around us. Some were encouraged to be selfless as a morally right way to be. Others were encouraged to put themselves last because the adults around them were emotionally needy. Surrounded by genuine need, some learned to set their own needs and desires aside.

Of course, selflessness is a good trait. There are problems in the world that would go unsolved without it. The problem for individuals arises when after an extended time of giving selflessly to others; our inner wells of love begin to run dry. When selflessness is part of a dysfunctional relationship, the insecurity driving it undermines other aspects of our outpouring love, causing self-hate to fill that inner well of love.

When we attempt to pour out love and to care without having nurtured love for ourselves, resentment invariably comes to the surface, sabotaging our efforts to love others. Those who have come to depend on our ability to fill them up with love, become frightened and needy when our selflessness begins to dry up. We create a cycle where manipulation and resentment take the place of love and generosity even as we attempt to extend love and generosity.

The answer to this conundrum is simple but challenging! Practising the discipline of self-love will turn it all around, slowly but surely. Not only will you get your love and generosity back. Practising the discipline of self-love will teach you to set boundaries with those who pull on you inappropriately, which is a greater act of love toward others.

The practice of self-love brings us back to facing that old nemesis, Narcissus! Do you remember how Narcissus gazed at his reflection in still water? Well, a good place to begin the practice of self-love is by looking at your own reflection in a mirror and saying to yourself, "I love you," over and over. Repeating it the way you might soothe a child with the words.

The difference between this practice and the myth of Narcissus is when we say, "I love you" to our own reflection in the mirror, we put ourselves in a humble place where we will confront everything we do not like about ourselves. From a wrinkle or hair out of place, to the way we spoke to our spouse last night, to the way we dismissed that irritating person at work, to the motives behind the excess food we ate, etc.; when we make the commitment to say, "I love you," to ourselves, we invariably confront everything we dislike or hate about ourselves.

This is a good thing. It means we get to tame the dragon inside who are trying to consume us before we do more damage to others or ourselves.

Rilke said, "Perhaps all the dragons in our lives are but princesses that are waiting to see us act just once with beauty and courage. Perhaps everything terrible is, in its deepest essence, something helpless that needs our love."

You need your love. You deserve your love. Take a risk today. Risk your inner voice calling you a narcissist and tell you that you love you, unconditionally and unequivocally! Your heart, your inner child, you will be glad you did.

Narcissism: Ancient and Modern

Modern psychology presents the importance of narcissism, self-absorption, in the construction of mental illness. Evidence of narcissism indicates mental instability. Ambitious individuals have, from this perspective, damaged psyches. Freud saw Narcissism as a default mechanism, energy that should have been going outward being turned inward with destructive effects. It can be observed, if one chooses to do so, in some psychotic and sociopathic conditions. This part will consider the one-dimensional nature of such an approach, and how the Narcissus and Echo myths, utilized by Freud, demonstrate wider cultural truths and that the insights of ancient people were deeper more compelling than those of recent modern thinkers. It suggests that the modern belief in healthy relationships as evidence of psychic health and unimpeded emotional growth is absurd.

The book will look at the Narcissus and Echo myths, considering their relevance to the Ancient Athenians, the Roman poet Ovid, as well as to psychoanalysis, critiquing the views of Melanie Klein, Alice Miller (who rejected psychoanalysis) and the Object Relations' School and examine what can be learned of differing cultural perspectives on human behaviour, and what light this throws upon psychoanalysis, exploring the contradictions and similarities of the different approaches, placing the psychoanalytical understanding of the myth in its cultural context. Psychoanalysis is in this view, only another cultural interpretation.

Both psychiatry and psychoanalysis insist on the differentiation of human beings according to largely subjective categories, so ambition, success, exemplary achievement is re-classified within various terms denoting pathological behaviour. This book rejects such ideas.

The Ancient Athenian Concept of Human Nature,

With the evolution of the Greek polis or city-state, there existed a tension between ideas of civilisation, civilised nature and the natural world. Athenian men, as citizens of the polis, distinct from women, symbolised the concepts of reason and rationality. The perfect expression of humankind was a man who lived within a city and was part of a city community. The notion of an individual set apart from a city was not understood, viewed as an aberration or as a primitive form of consciousness.

Homosexual relationships were normal in most ancient Greek societies during adolescence, usually between a younger and an older man. Male romantic passion was reserved for their sex rather than towards members of the opposite sex. The friendship between men was prized above all. Lastly, in Athens, there was a sharp division between public life, a male domain, and private life, a female domain.

The Attia of Flower Myths.
(Metamorphosis)

'And in its stead, they found a flower-behold/White petals clustered round a cup of gold.'

There were different versions of the myth in ancient Greece, used and developed mainly by Hellenistic poets, serving a didactic purpose. The myth may originally have concerned the worship of Eros. Ancient Greek myths which detailed metamorphosis into flowers usually had an erotic connotation, linking youth and beauty, often telling of boys dying young with their virginity intact and their metamorphosis into beautiful, useful plants. The metamorphosis stories, while erotic, do not end in sexual fulfilment and fertility. According to Forbes Irving, the metamorphosis of humans or deities reflects human development, or in the case of transformation into plants, evidence of early cults. It involves the primitive side of human nature before socialization and urban life.

Narcissus is warned that he will die young unless he learns to know himself. Such knowledge comes from sharing in a relationship. Narcissus sees his reflection in a pool, falls in love with it, and slowly dies, transforming into a flower. He did not understand that his image was his. He did not, therefore, know himself. The flower is a narcotic, suggesting the transformational effects of such plants and the subsequent self-absorption. The point is, by expressing fertility a youth becomes a man, that is a citizen of a polis. Ovid's myth concerns the essential value of human development, growing sexually and emotionally.

To the Greeks, the myth also expresses the problem of excess. Too much beauty meant that Narcissus was competing with the gods and had therefore to die. Also, the natural world was unable to tolerate too much wealth, luck or beauty and destroys it. The same responses can be found in our world with the sometimes hidden anger towards celebrities and the more fortunate. For Klein excess encourages the envy of others. Narcissus suffered not only from an excess of beauty but also from his virginity, in the latter offending Eros, according to Bremmer.

Echo. 'Her love endures and grows on grief.'

It is likely the first connection between Narcissus and Echo was made by Hellenistic poets, not Ovid.

Narcissus was unable to love Echo, a nymph of trees and springs. He rejected her, and she faded away until only her voice remained. I suggest that Echo personifies bestial sex through her relationship with Pan, with whom she had a son, and through being a woman. In ancient Athens women symbolized irrationality. They were associated with nature, the uncivilized part of humankind and unbridled lust.

The destructive relationship between Narcissus and Echo may, therefore, have reflected the tensions between civilized man and nature. Narcissus declares in Ovid: 'Keep your arms from me/Be off! I'll die before I yield to you.' This may not simply be youthful arrogance. It certainly looks like that stage when a youth becomes a functioning sexual being or symbolic of exclusive homosexuality. Echo's decline into a voice repeating the last word of other's sentences may symbolize the suppression of Athenian women and their lack of involvement in the polis.

The Athenian males' suppression of women may have had its roots in their upbringing. Exclusively cared for by their mothers until adolescence they were then brought up by their fathers and taught to despise and fear women. This presents an alternative to Klein's view that the primitive emotions of 'envy and gratitude' stemmed from reactions to the primary object. The mother. Athenian's present such emotions as subject to ritualised behaviour, motivated by community drives. The primitive emotions envisaged by Klein would have been modified for use by the community, aiding the polis, as a community run by men with an emphasis on militarism, debate and public work, with all the intellectual contracts of rationality and reason that ensued.

The myth may reflect the tensions of the time within society between gender and the nature of erotic love. It is thus inappropriate to attach individual psychological positions to Narcissus and Echo. The two stories concern reciprocity, which obsessed with ancient Greeks. The relationships ancient Athenians enjoyed with their wives carried less emotional value than in the present day. The sex act between men and women was practical, assuring women lacked influence in society. In ancient Athens, a man's individuality was expressed as a component of the community, not as modern-day individuality. Narcissus' metamorphosis returns him to the natural world, where, because of the medicinal powers of the plant he becomes more useful to society. The narcotic qualities of the flower express, I believe, fertility rather than obsession or addiction.

The Myth According io Ovid:

Perry: 'True perceptions cannot be distinguished from false ones, for every perception that is true, there is one resembling it that is false.'

Ovid composed in the Classical Tradition, meaning he imitated and referenced Greek and Roman writers before him. His poetry is didactic in the manner of Callimachus, the Hellenistic poet, and Metamorphoses debates the nature of literary form, reality and the materialistic philosophy of Lucretius. Ovid changes the myth from a homosexual to heterosexual account.

I will look at Ovid's rendering of the myth of Narcissus to find if he agrees with or throws light onto the Freudian interpretation with his focus upon individual character as understood through sexual nature. I will examine Ovid's understanding of love, reality, experience, gender, paradox and fate. Certainly, Narcissus' predicament reflects for Ovid Plato's views of knowledge and reality.

Ovid questions the validity of perception through love and permanence of gender. Tiresias, who foretold the future, was for a brief period transformed into a woman, experiencing sex as both a man and a woman. By so doing, the unfixed nature of sexuality was emphasised. Freud sees sex as fundamental in the development of human character, interpreting the objective world through sexual drives, childhood trauma, memory and ego. For Ovid sexuality concerns the ontological nature of reality. He perceives human sexuality as more fluid and less liable to categorisation than Freud.

Narcissus' love for his reflection concerns for Ovid the deceptiveness of love and shows how falling in love can distort reality, confusing boundaries between subject and object. This perhaps more reflects Klein's views on 'the defences of the early ego', whereby reality is structured by the early development of the self through its relation to an object. Subject and object become confused.

Narcissus' nature in Ovid, transfixed like a stone by his reflection, suggests his character before metamorphoses according to Forbes Irving. This is not about the 'tragedy of the loss of self', as Miller believes, denied by the effects of grandiosity from adapting to the needs and desires of others, but about his ability to deceive. He is deceived by the fluctuating nature of reality ('You see a phantom of a mirrored shape') and the demands of his fate.

For Ovid, Echo serves as a further example of the insubstantiality of reality, rather than the individual, as understood in modern psychological theories, caught within a dependency relationship upon another. Echo reflects vocally in the same fashion as water reflects Narcissus' image. Also, it may concern how language forms an identity, prefiguring Freud's grabbing with the matter. As with the Greeks from whom Ovid took many of his ideas and literary forms, the paradoxes' of reality contained within the myth are transformed into something of greater general use.

Narcissus and Psychoanalysis:

Freud believed that narcissism is the 'libidinal complement to the egoism of the instinct of self-preservation.'

In this section, I aim to show that psychoanalysis represents a shift in perspective about our understanding of objective reality from an emphasis on the external world and humankind' relationship to it to an emphasis on an internal world, with a corresponding shift in the understanding of reality and experience. Subjective reality became thereby a consequence of individual experience, and splitting of reality becomes apparent. Individuals relate to only part of the world rather than the world as a whole. The later concepts of Freud (Civilization and Its Discontents) merely acknowledge the importance of external reality, which is a commonsense strategy, but not its part in constructing objective reality. He perceives the external world as providing stimuli for the structuring of reality through individual impulses.

This encourages the view that individual sexual drives or ego create events.

Such a perspective can be observed in Klein's views on the child's internalization of external objects and the introjections of the 'good internalized breast and the bad devouring breast' which underlines her understanding of Narcissism. The myth shows Narcissus metamorphosed into an element of the greater world, becoming a flower of beauty and medicinal qualities. In psychoanalysis, individuals become defined through their relationships with others, not through relationships with ideas, God, or the greater world. In object relations (Winnicott and Kohut) this is often reduced to a relationship with the primary object, the mother. It is a lesser world.

The Narcissistic Personality: 'so long as he suffers, he ceases to love.'

Freud perceives the self-absorption of Narcissus as primary narcissism, the 'libidinal cathexis of the ego', and preceding cathexis of the primary object, the individual's first nurse, and an inability to properly relate to others if continued into adulthood. They could not relate to or love others. Freud perceived these characteristics within psychotic personalities, who appeared unable to exhibit interest in the external world but showed interest only in themselves. He also saw it in paranoiacs and homosexuals who may have identified with the mother when children. Narcissus' rejection of intimacy in Ovid's telling of the myth is not, according to Freud, about the mutable quality of reality but the individual's creation of an ego-ideal that results in 'overvaluation' of their qualities and capacities.

Freud's observations seem to have been exclusively connected with the apparent self-absorption of psychically damaged individuals within his practice, or those suffering addiction. This one-dimensional characteristic may have been exaggerated by Freud due to his limited exposure to the ordinary activities of his parents. His relationship with his patients was limited to their relationship with themselves, with others through their interpretation, failing to invest them with a valid intellectual life or allowing any influences to bear beyond the narrow focus of their sexual and emotional lives and those of others acquainted with them. The Narcissist of Freud appears attached to a smaller, sterile world, bound by individual egoism or libidinal drives compared to Ovid's Narcissus. Freud's early association of Narcissism and homosexuality may have had its roots in the specific delineation of gender attributes of his period.

Klein: 'the mean and grudging breast.'

Beautiful Narcissus, for the ancient Athenians, was the envy of others. That decided his fate. Klein sees such narcissism as evidence of the sufferer's envy. The world is perceived from the inside out, the individual born with an un-cohesive ego and temperamental predisposition restructuring the world according to early experiences with a primary object. This can be altered through the later Oedipus period and the depressive position. For Klein, the destructive envy of Narcissism begins early, and, the prime object of envy, as a consequence of dependency and subsequent fear of annihilation, is the mother's breast. The mother becomes the bad object; a function of the baby in the paranoid-schizoid position before the baby has a perception of the mother's being a separate object. Fairbairn appears to view the mother as determining the development of psychic problems. The death of Narcissus' putative lover, himself, and Echo's fate, from this perspective, is part of the envious destructive quality of narcissism. The 'scooping out, sucking dry, and devouring' of 'the breast'. The destruction of the creativity the Narcissist envies in others. This envy prevents the proper development of object-cathexis, focusing upon a mature love object. The baby's ego is early split between itself and the primary object, which is usually the mother.

For the Athenians, Narcissus and Echo represented the tensions specific to the polis, their relationship to the erotic, homosexual inclinations they owned, and to the journey of early life that culminated in an assumption of communal responsibilities. Childhood was part of that journey, regarded as a preparation for the real business of life, serving the community. This youth did at nineteen when they were expected to fight for the city-state. The years with their mothers were to ensure preservation. Learning began under the auspices of fathers. The traumas itemised by Freud and Klein would, assuming they exist, have been subsumed into the drives of the whole community. The early years of manhood were considered of far greater importance than childhood, an unproductive period of dependency. Children were not useful. Narcissus occupied the point between unproductively and usefulness.

Ovid dealt with the complexities of reality, the fashion that love, erotic intimacy, reflects that complexity. He understood the world intellectually and would probably have dismissed Miller's refutation of intellectuality as a source of self-knowledge on the basis that reality is not determined by feelings or individual histories. Freud, Klein, Miller and the Object Relation's School appear to have believed this disturbing notion. People's relationships are perhaps a reflection of different notions of reality and do not construct it. Both the ancient Athenians and Ovid emphasized the drives of communities and ideas beyond themselves. Psychoanalysis and Psychiatry view drove, high accomplishing individuals as exhibiting evidence of Narcissistic personality disorders when their drives are more complex than self-absorption and often informed by intellectuality which neither of the above considers a formative force.

Object Relations' School

This mainly British version of psychology views relationships as the goal of human existence, and all other endeavours as distractions from this goal. These other endeavours, creating a business empire, writing books, other less agreeable activities, were put down to self-grandiosity (see Miller, 2001). Neither the ancient Athenians nor Ovid would have understood this notion. The Athenians would have considered it shocking. While they would have appreciated the association with hubris, the alternative focus on relationships would have horrified them. Ovid would probably have viewed it as an absurd trivialization of existence.

In societies where the individual was an expression of greater ideals, the polis or Imperial Rome and its mission, perceiving life as being about the pursuit of healthy relationships would have been treasonable or childish. Historical drives, for at least the elite, took the place of individual drives. Sexuality was not necessarily connected to individual happiness, conceived of as either a deeply serious matter (Athens) or connected to power and the state (Rome), it was far too important for that. Object Relations foisting of later individual development on the mother alone appears like an assertion of masculinity as a reaction to Britain's loss of Imperial and political power.

You are viewing individual drive, intellectuality and choice as simply evidence of a damaged psyche, controls and limits self-expression, individuality and creativity. It was, and remains, a dangerous step forward — the accompanying celebration of relationships sanctions conformity and mediocrity.

Narcissism and Today's Society

The subject of 'Narcissism' has intrigued us for many decades, but social scientists now claim that it has become a "modern epidemic". The term 'Narcissism' originated more than 2000 years ago when Ovid wrote the 'Legend of Narcissus', which tells the story of a beautiful Greek hunter, Narcissus, who, one day, sees his reflection in a pool of water and falls in love with it. He becomes obsessed with his beauty and is unable to leave his reflected image until he dies. The concept of Narcissism was first introduced by the famous psychoanalyst, Dr Sigmund Freud's essay 'On Narcissism'. He popularized this new concept through his work on the 'ego' and its relation to the outside world. Narcissism can be defined as the pursuit of gratification from vanity or egotistic admiration of one's attributes. The 'American Psychiatry Associ ation' has classified this as 'Narcissistic Personality Disorder' (NPD).

Narcissism lies on a continuum from healthy to pathological. Healthy narcissism is part of normal human functioning. It represents the required self - love and confidence based on real achievements and the ability to overcome setbacks. But, narcissism becomes a problem when one becomes excessively preoccupied with the self and seeks complete admiration and attention, with complete disregard for others' feelings. Lack of satisfaction of this need leads to substance abuse and major depressive disorders. In adolescents, this causes 'Substance Dependency Disorder' (SDD) - they display overt narcissistic and prosaically behaviours, which show a connection between self - centeredness and addiction. These substances include sedatives like alcohol, psychedelics and hallucinogens like marijuana and LSD, stimulants like cocaine, narcotics like opium, heroin, and morphine, and anti-anxiety drugs like Xanax.

"Narcissists unconsciously deny an unstated and intolerably poor self - image through inflation. They turn themselves into glittering figures of immense grandeur, surrounded by psychologically impenetrable walls. The goal of this self - deception is to be impervious to greatly feared external criticism, and to their rolling sea of doubts." This is how Elan Golomb describes NPD, in her book 'Trapped in the Mirror'. The narcissists fail to achieve intimacy with anyone as they view other people like items in a vending machine, and uses them to serve their own needs, never being able to acknowledge that others might have their feelings too.

Narcissism is filled with irony and paradox, whether as a character trait or as a clinical disease. Emily Levine says, "I thought Narcissism was about self - love till someone told me there is a flip - side to it... it is unrequited self - love." It must be remembered that Narcissus weeps to find out that his image does not return his love. This indicates that a loving engagement with the self does not, and cannot, come from putting on lofty airs, acting with self - satisfied arrogance or being obsessed with assorted fantasies of ideal brilliance or beauty. Healthy, non - egotistical self - love arises from an unconditional acceptance of the self, without having to declare superiority over others. Deep down, the narcissists know, albeit unconsciously, that they are not really what they project. One of their central defences is to endlessly project onto others the very flaws and fears that they are unable or unwilling, to allow into awareness. They are critical of others' shortcomings but completely blind to their own - their self - love must be seen as an illusion, a spectacular triumph of self - deception. They can only love their false, idealized self - a mirage that cannot possibly return the fantasy-laden love. Their flawed self, hidden beneath their outward bravado, remains locked up and placed in permanent exile. And, to continuously safeguard themselves from a reality that so freq uently contradicts their grandiose assumptions and pretensions, they are forced to employ a massive defence stratagem, with extraordinary rigidity.

Although very few of us are diagnosed with NPD, almost all of us are guilty of sharing certain narcissistic tendencies. So, Todd Solondz says, "Narcissism and self - deception are survival mechanisms without which many of us might just jump off the bridge." For true narcissists, the defences are necessary to compensate for their ego deficits and reduce feelings of shame. Without them, they might result in a state of suicidal depression; for, narcissists do not like themselves - the more they boast and demean others, they are more likely to cover up for their deeper, largely hidden feelings of inferiority and lack of love. Blinded by their idealized self - image, they try to project themselves as gifted, exceptional and unique - that in turn makes them egotistical and arrogant. According to TS Eliot, "... half the harm that is done in this world is due to people who want to feel important. They don't mean to harm but the harm [that they cause] does not interest them. Or they do not see it, or they justify it because they are absorbed in the endless struggle to think well of themselves." This shows a distinction between narcissists who are malevolent and those who simply lack concern of how their behaviour might adversely affect others. It is yet another way of gaining attention to their supreme self - absorption, which makes it impossible for them to identify with others' feelings.

Kurt Cobain says, "I don't care what you think unless it is about me." This shows the narcissist's indifference to the outer world unless it specifically relates to them. They are completely incapable of a genuine interest in others' matters unless they are needed for the former's assertion of superiority. Narcissists are also great con - artists; after all, they always succeed in deceiving themselves. It becomes particularly painful when they suffer from memory loss, when, they lose out parts of the person they love the most. In general, a narcissist "devours people, consumes their output, and casts the empty, wreathing shells aside", says Sam Vaknin. Hate is a complement of fear, and the narcissists like being feared - it provides them with an intoxicating sensation of omnipotence. The difference between Narcissism and self - love is a matter of depth. Narcissus falls in love not with the self, but with an image or reflection of the self, with the persona, the mask. Narcissists see themselves through the eyes of others, changes their lifestyle and behaviour and expression of feelings, according to others' admiration. Narcissism is voluntary blindness, an agreement not to look beneath the surface. Oscar Wilde says, "To love oneself is the beginning of a life - long romance" - this notion of self - love leans towards the pathological and the autoerotic as well.

Prof. Jean Twenge differentiates narcissism from the idea of self - esteem. One high in self - esteem, values individual achievements, but they also value their relationships and caring for others. Contrarily, narcissists miss out on valuing and caring their relationships, as they lack empathy. Prof. Twenge and Keith Campbell, a specialist on Narcissism, joined hands to investigate whether people born in more recent generations score higher against Narcissism measures than in previous generations. The tool they used to assess their subjects is the 'Narcissistic Personality Inventory' (NPI), created in 1988. It is the most widely used measure of Narcissism in social - psychological research, where a 40 item forced - choice version is the one most commonly employed. Following Freud's and Kohut's theories, individuals would be diagnosed clinically as patients of NPD, if they fulfil the following criteria:

A. Grandiose sense of self - importance or uniqueness

B. Preoccupation with fantasies of unlimited success, power, brilliance, beauty, or ideal love

C. Exhibitionism

D. Cold indifference of marked feelings of rage, inferiority, shame, humiliation or emptiness in response to criticism, the indifference of others or defeat

E. At least, two of the following characteristic disturbances in interpersonal relationships:

I. Entitlement - the expectation of special favour without assuming reciprocal responsibilities

II. Interpersonal exploits

III. Relationships that characteristically alternate between the two extremes of over idealisation and devaluation

IV. Lack of empathy

F. Vulnerability to shame, rather than guilt

G. Denial of remorse or gratitude

In this regard, reference can be made to Hotchkiss's 'Seven Deadly Sins of Narcissism', which include shamelessness, magical thinking, arrogance, envy, entitlement, exploitation, bad boundaries.

The 'narcissistic dilemma' is seen when, being criticized, the narcissists show themselves pitifully incapable of retaining any emotional poise or receptivity. But, these disturbed individuals also display an abnormally developed capacity to criticize others. Their dilemma is that the rigidity of their defences, their inability ever to let their guard down, even among their closest people, guarantees that they will never get what they most need, which, unfortunately, they are themselves oblivious to. People are never born narcissist; it is powerful environmental influences that make them so. Being neglected and ignored, or constantly disparaged or berated by parents in childhood, they form unrealistically high standards of behaviour. Unable to meet up to their parents' unreasonable, perfectionist expectations, they create an imaginary "ideal self" that could receive parental acceptance, even adulation, which they yearn for. The main elements of narcissism are narcissistic supply, narcissistic rage and narcissistic injury, and narcissistic abuse. Narcissism can be of various types, and its causes are not yet well - known. Inherited genetic defects are thought to be responsible in some cases, along with envir onmental factors:

1. Childhood abuse or neglect

2. Excessive parental pampering

3. The unrealistic expectation of parents

4. Sexual promiscuity

5. Cultural influences

A study shows the changes in levels of Narcissism over the past few decades, among the college-going students, i.e. the youth; it is seen rampant in the society of the USA today, because these youths are the future leaders, and Narcissism is very harmful to the society as a whole and can cause failure in academic and other endeavours. Twenge and Campbell surveyed American institutions from 1979 - 2006 and found an upward shift in scores on the NPI, meaning that, now the average college student embraces narcissistic tendencies more than their counterparts, two decades ago. The rise in Narcissism in the American population might be because now, from a young age, Americans are taught that they are very special and unique, that in turn increases their self - esteem. Extroversion and assertion are the key factors of Narcissism. It is also due to the large emphasis on materialism and wealth, with a focus on an individual's pleasure and success, in the current American society.

Today, Narcissism has gripped the entire world, as indicated by the rapid change in society that occurred during the industrial and post-industrial times. The past few decades have witnessed a societal shift from a commitment to the collective to a focus on the individual or self. Here comes in the 'self - esteem movement' which became the key to success in life. The parents tried to "confer" self - esteem upon their children rather than allowing them to achieve it through hard work. The rise of individualism and the decline in social norms that accompanied the modernization of society led to a shift from the concept of what is best for the others and family to what is best for "me". The commercial world with a total focus on wealth and fame created an "empty self, shorn of social meaning". Today, the generation of young adults - the 'Generation Y' - also known as the 'Millenials' and 'Generation Me', comprising of individuals born between 1975 - 1995, are condemned for being narcissistic, selfish, self - entitled, and having unrealistic expectations from life.

The rise in technology and the advancement of immensely popular social networking sites like Facebook, Twitter, Instagram, MySpace, YouTube have changed the way we now spend our leisure time and communicate with others. Internet addiction is a new area of study in mental health, and many researchers show that addiction to Facebook, Twitter is strongly linked to narcissistic behaviour and low self - esteem. The notion that the current generation is increasingly becoming narcissistic, as a product of the "like effect" (a theory where the number of 'likes' on social media produces greater self - esteem) has been widely debated. This effect creates negative self - esteem contrary to egotism due to modern youths constantly comparing the quantity of 'likes' or the quality of a picture to that of another. The ego can never be satisfied with an increasing number of 'likes'. Also, the total control over one's perception of social media allows modern youth to see an unrealistic, distorted image that they will compare themselves to. Thus, regular posting of 'selfies' on social media promotes Narcissism, that is a cry of ego - satisfaction. Social networking sites are believed to be outlets for narcissistic expression, and Gen Y, aged between 17 - 21 years, are particularly vulnerable to its negative effects. Lucy Clyde says, "If you are a narcissist, you are looking for a positive reflection of yourself, the world is your mirror, and you are constantly looking for affirmation. For this reason, you're probably curating your own life very heavily on social media."

Named 'Word of the Year' in 2013 by the Oxford English Dictionary, the term "selfie" has become very common among all teens and young adults, in today's technological era. A "selfie" is defined as "a photograph that one has taken of oneself, typically one taken by a smartphone or a webcam, and shared via social media". For Gen Y, taking selfies and posting them on social media has become inevitable parts of daily living, promoting Narcissism. Millennials, aged 18 - 33 years, are hyper-connected with little awareness or concern for the others.

"Generation Me", today, is a victim of the 'Selfie Syndrome' - they post, tag and comment on self - portraits, believing that others are interested in their daily activities, and they want to tell others what they are doing. Selfies symbolize that shamelessly flaunting your Narcissism is trendy; if you put an inspirational quote under your selfie, no one can see your Narcissism. A selfie a day keeps insecurities away - "constantly taking selfies will not make you prettier; may you someday find someone to love you as much as your selfies indicate you love yourself." Today, the confidence level is measured by "a selfie with no filter". Never before has a generation so diligently recorded themselves, accomplishing so little - "if you could take selfies of your souls, would you find it attractive enough to post?"

It seems those people who constantly post selfies must not own mirrors like the rest of us; but again, mirrors should not be taken too seriously, as one's true reflection is in his heart. Increase in Narcissism pose a threat to the emotional and psychological health of the youth - it results in self - enhancement and self - promotion, preventing them from establishing lasting intimate relationships. Also, they tend to be prone to respond to violent and aggressive behaviour after being criticized. Online relationships may appeal more to narcissists, who are otherwise unable to, or unwilling, to form meaningful relations that demand any time or emotional attachment. The increase of smartphones and many new sophisticated gadgets allow people to access social media very easily, contributing to widespread Narcissism. Managing and revising one's online profile content is a vital aspect of the youth's online identity and "e - personality". Social networking sites give narcissistic individuals the chance to keep the focus of their profile's content solely on themselves. By this, they post status updates, comments and photos that depict only themselves, and not others, perpetuating their selfish nature. The online profiles allow them to achieve a type of social identity that they wish to portray, through exaggeration of certain character traits and present a persona that they believe is appealing to the world, at large.

Lack of empathy for others causes a preoccupation with the Gen Y's frustrated selves and emotional distresses, while growing up - they go out of their houses, but focused on themselves only, taking selfies - and thus, can never completely come out of their selves. They lose out on moral values and find it difficult to come out of their fears. The increasing demand for plastic surgeries, worldwide, to look b etter in the eyes of others, is also an unfortunate consequence of the rise of Narcissism. They always remain emotionally and spiritually unfulfilled, hungry for a nebulous something they cannot even conceive, and project a constant detachment in all relationships, even in the most intimate ones.

Treatment of 'Narcissistic Personality Disorder' (NPD) is possible through psychotherapy, or talk - therapy. But Narcissism has certain beneficial effects too. It has a fundamental connection with leadership, as both notions have the common factors - dominance, extroversion, confidence and power. Because of these, narcissists become good and successful leaders, provoked by their desire for self - assertion, glory and power. But today, individualism is co-related to materialism and Narcissism. So, together, the world's Narcissism is huge - the collective Narcissism results in the destruction of the planet. Together, we are wiping out one species after another from this world, fuelled by consumerism and our growing self - importance. Our Narcissism may eventually turn out to be our Nemesis, in the end.

CHAPTER 2
THE SIGNS AND RED FLAGS OF NARCISSISM IN RELATIONSHIPS

Can You Tell if Someone Has a Narcissistic Personality Disorder?

It is not easy to tell whether or not someone has a Narcissistic Personality Disorder.

However, you may find many telling signs of a Narcissistic Personality Disorder when reading about its symptoms and behaviours. One of the first indicators of a person with Narcissistic Personality Disorder is that they have a larger-than-life personality or a grandiose sense of themselves. They often are braggarts who are always holding onto the belief of others being jealous of them. But in reality, it is quite the opposite. They are the ones who, because they have such low self-esteem, are jealous of others. A common trait in someone who has Narcissism is excessive negativity to constructive criticism. Their ego identities are so fragile criticism is often unbearable for them. In response, they often put others down to build themselves up. The first sign of someone who feels intensely insecure is acting as though others are inferior to them. It is common to label this type of person as having a superiority complex. But again it is the feelings and emotions of not being good enough that fuels their self-serving behaviours.

People with Narcissistic Personality Disorder expect others to work with them to achieve their hopes, goals and dreams regardless of how unrealistic or unattainable those goals are. People with Narcissistic Personality Disorder are insecure and have low self-esteem even if they do not appear that way. Outwardly they are usually perceived as being insensitive and unemotional. As a result, they alienate people and will often have negative relationships with people in both their professional and personal lives.

There is treatment for people who have Narcissistic Personality Disorder, once these symptoms have been detected. To get a Narcissist to admit that he has a problem is very difficult. You would have to work very hard at attaining their acceptance and trust to be able to bring them to this point of their journey. That is why it is more helpful and effective to study about Narcissistic Personality Disorder and educate yourself about how you can change your role, which may well be as a Codependent, in your relationship with a Narcissist. Relationship experts on NPD will help you learn the skills and behaviours you need to adapt to change the dynamics of your relationship with a Narcissist.

Signs of Narcissism

At certain times, we all have narcissistic tendencies. We want our way, we like to be admired for our looks, body or brain and we react negatively to criticism. In a nutshell, within limits, those very traits can be relatively normal. It's important to note, however, that there are extremely unhealthy levels of the narcissistic personality. These high levels of narcissism will take out the innocent and the weak of heart before they can even realize what hit them.

Since someone with Narcissistic Personality Disorder (NPD) doesn't normally wear a sign around their neck, how do you spot them?

•   According to the Mayo Clinic, narcissistic symptoms may include:

• The belief that you're superior to others

•   An exaggerated fantasy of power, success, status and attractiveness

- Exaggerating your achievements

- Lack of empathy

- Using others to get your way in business, relationships or other aspects of day-to-day life

- Setting unrealistic goals

- Appearing tough-minded/unemotional

- Difficulty keeping healthy and lasting relationships

- The appearance of over-confidence and or arrogance

- Monopolization of conversations (constantly interrupting)

- An attitude of entitlement

- A 'look at me, look at me' attitude

There are several very big clues as to if someone you're in a relationship with is a narcissist. Since in the narcissist's mind they are ultimately more important than others, you can detect narcissistic personality traits by their extreme self-centeredness, manipulation tactics and lack of empathy toward others. Narcissists rarely feel guilt or shame for their behaviours and often place the blame for what they've said or done on someone else (projection); i.e. 'It's your fault I did that. If you hadn't done that, I wouldn't have responded that way.'

A word of caution: People with NPD can be very charming, but are also very hazardous to your emotional well-being. They and are constantly looking for their next "victim" or "narcissistic supply source". The narcissistic supply source is someone who will feed their ego and tell them how wonderful they are, how intelligent they are, that they're a GREAT employee, lover or spouse, etc. The narcissist tells you how hot they look, how in shape they are or how much they're going to make on their next big deal (usually one of many fantasies they wish were real). In essence, everything is about them. Once the narcissist has obtained what they need from you, they'll dispose of your relationship to them (whether they're married to you or not) and leave you wondering what you ever did to make them love you one moment and discard you the next.

Additionally, most people with NPD also have a problem with at least one addiction. For some its drugs, for some it's alcohol, and for other's, it's some sort sexual addiction. Regardless of which one it is, all are extremely dangerous to not only the narcissist but those in closest relationship to them as well.

Recognizing the Signs of Narcissistic Personality Disorder

Narcissistic Personality Disorder is distinguished by a long duration pattern of grandiosity (either in delusion or real-world conduct), an overwhelming wish for admiration, and generally an absolute lack of concern toward others.

People with this sickness typically think that they are of paramount relevance in everyone's life or to anyone they connect with.

A particular person with this particular problem could very well whine about a clumsy waitresses "rudeness" or "ignorance" or end a medical-related evaluation giving a condescending evaluation of the medical profession.

In layman terms, a person with this disorder may be described just as a "narcissist" or as somebody with "narcissism." Both of these terms largely refer to anybody with a narcissistic personality disorder.

Signs of Narcissistic Personality Disorder

For anyone to be identified as having a narcissistic personality they need to match 5 or more of the following symptoms:

Is obsessed with fantasies of inexhaustible achievement, authority, splendour, attractiveness, or perfect love.

Boasts a grandiose feeling of self-importance (e.g., exaggerates accomplishments and skills, wants to be recognized as exceptional without having commensurate achievements)

Thinks that he or she is "extraordinary" and unique and can only be understood by, or should associate with, other unique or high-status men and women (or establishments)

Will require an excessive amount of appreciation.

Is exploitative of other people, e.g., will take advantage of other folks to gain his or her ends.

Has an incredibly strong feeling of entitlement, e.g., unreasonable expectations of specifically favourable treatment or instant concurrence with his or her expectations.

Is short of empathy, e.g., is reluctant to recognize or identify using the emotions and needs of others.

Frequently will show egotistic, haughty behaviours or conduct.

Is usually envious of other people or thinks that others are envious of him or her.

A narcissistic personality disorder is a lot more prevalent in males as compared to women and is particularly believed to develop in much less than 1 per cent of the normal population.

Similar to most personality disorders, narcissistic personality disorder nearly always probably will reduce in seriousness with age, with a lot of people struggling with a couple of the most significant indicators and symptoms once they're inside the Forties or 50s.

Exactly how is Narcissism Diagnosed?

Personality problems like narcissistic personality disorder are typically clinically determined by a q ualified psychological wellness expert, for example, a psychologist or psychiatrist.

Household physicians and common practitioners are often not properly trained or well-equipped to create this type of mental health diagnosis

A diagnosis for narcissistic personality disorder is normally made by a mental health specialist evaluating your signs or symptoms and life history with all those listed here.

They're going to decide whether your signs or symptoms met the criteria required for a personality disorder diagnosis.

Treatment of Narcissism.

Proper treatment of narcissistic personality issues almost always will involve long-term psychotherapy with a therapist that has expertise in treating this kind of personality disorder.

Narcissistic Pointers in Relationships - 8 Signs of Narcissism in Your Partner

Relationships have their challenges for everyone. With effort and commitment, two reasonably balanced and emotionally healthy individuals can forge a relationship that is mutually supportive and fulfilling. However, there is a segment of the population that is hard wired with personality disorders. Narcissism is a disorder that often drives the affected individual to act in ways that are very destructive to intimate relationships. The non-disordered partner is often left feeling bewildered and hurt by his or her narcissistic partner's behaviour.

Affairs are extremely painful and shocking for many partners who find out that their partner has not been faithful. While a relationship can survive an affair if both partners recommit and establish excellent communication and accountability, there are instances where affairs can be a sign of more than just an issue in the relationship of origin. A segment of our population is afflicted with a personality disorder, and a common disorder of this type is narcissism. Sometimes, affairs can be an indicator, along with other criteria, of the presence of narcissism in an individual. While only a licensed mental health professional can diagnose narcissism, it can be helpful to know what you are looking for.

Here are eight signs that your partner's affairs could be a deeper sign of narcissism:

1. Poor behavioural control and a tendency toward impulsive behaviour. This can lead to addictions or compulsive sexual behaviours.

2. Lacking in empathy. The narcissist cannot put him or herself in another person's shoes. This leads to acts that appear callous and selfish.

3. An inflated and exaggerated sense of self-worth. Your partner may brag about accomplishments and build them up past their real merit.

4. The sense of entitlement. Your partner might act as if he or she deserves special treatment, and ought to know and associate with others who are special. Often, there is a haughtiness in attitude and a sense of superiority present.

5. A willingness to exploit others for his or her benefit.

6. Jealousy toward others. Your partner might even become enraged at the successes of others, upset that attention is being paid toward anyone else.

7. Needs extreme amounts of admiration from others. This source of admiration is termed "narcissistic supply," and is much like a drug that the narcissist craves.

8. Thinks in ideal terms, such as "perfect" love, beauty, and power. You may be perceived as ideal for some time, then discarded and considered worthless with nothing in between.

"Brattiness" May Be Narcissism

Would you know a Narcissist if you met one? You will find them around your town, on the sports field, and even in your own home. You probably know many kids who you consider to be 'bratty.' Don't expect their parents to do anything about their bad behaviour because the brats I am talking about are now adults — big adult brats, but not necessarily grown-ups.

What causes narcissism? Narcissistic Personality Disorder, that's what. Do you remember that girl at school who stole things, or started rumours (about those least able to defend themselves) but always got away with it because she always charmed or connived her way out of any situation? We all remember kids like that, don't we? One of the hallmarks of a narcissist is blaming others.

If you ever wonder what happens to brats who turn into adults before ever learning good social skills, well ...With a good education they may end up in charge of other people's resources, and possibly run an otherwise healthy company into the ground, or cause a nation's financial ruin. The less educated narcissist men; the ones who use their charm and manipulation to work the system are more likely to end up in jail. Narcissistic women, once they are too old to seduce and exploit men any longer, typically end up dying alone; rejected and despised by all.

Brats bring their narcissism and awful social skills right along into adulthood. They are brash and blame the very people they abuse for causing their actions. "I couldn't tell you I took the money out of your purse. You would have gotten hysterical. I can't even talk to you." Or (after they have yet again exploited you in any number of ways), "I can never talk to you. You never listen to what I want."

10 Signs That You're in a Relationship with a Narcissist

Narcissism is often interpreted in popular culture as a person who's in love with him or herself. It is more accurate to characterize the pathological narcissist as someone who's in love with an idealized self-image, which they project to avoid feeling (and being seen as) the real, disenfranchised, wounded self. Deep down, most pathological narcissists feel like the "ugly duckling," even if they painfully don't want to admit it.

How do you know when you're dealing with a narcissist? While most of us are guilty of some of the following behaviours at one time or another, a pathological narcissist tends to dwell habitually in several of the following personas, while remaining largely unaware of (or unconcerned with) how his or her actions affect others.

1. Conversation Hoarder. The narcissist loves to talk about him or herself and doesn't give you a chance to take part in a two-way conversation. You struggle to have your views and feelings heard. When you do get a word in, if it's not in agreement with the narcissist, your comments are likely to be corrected, dismissed, or ignored.

"My father's favourite responses to my views were: 'but...,' 'actually...,' and 'there's more to it than this...' He always has to feel like he knows better."— Anonymous

2. Conversation Interrupter. While many people have the poor communication habit of interrupting others, the narcissist interrupts and quickly switches the focus back to herself. He shows little genuine interest in you.

3. Rule Breaker. The narcissist enjoys getting away with violating rules and social norms, such as cutting in line, chronic under-tipping (some will overtip to show off), stealing office supplies, breaking multiple appointments, or disobeying traffic laws.

"I take pride in persuading people to give me exceptions to their rules"— Anonymous

4. Boundary Violator. Shows wanton disregard for other people's thoughts, feelings, possessions, and physical space. Oversteps and uses others without consideration or sensitivity. Borrows items or money without returning. Breaks promises and obligations repeatedly. Shows little remorse and blames the victim for one's lack of respect.

"It's your fault that I forgot because you didn't remind me"— Anonymous

5. False Image Projection. Many narcissists like to do things to impress others by making themselves look good externally. This "trophy" complex can exhibit itself physically, romantically, sexually, socially, religiously, financially, materially, professionally, academically, or culturally. In these situations, the narcissist uses people, objects, status, and accomplishments to represent the self, substituting for the perceived, inadequate "real" self. These grandstanding "merit badges" are often exaggerated. The underlying message of this type of display is: "I'm better than you!" or "Look at how special I am—I'm worthy of everyone's love, admiration, and acceptance!"

"I dyed my hair blond and enlarged my breasts to get men's attention—and to make other women jealous"— Anonymous

"My accomplishments are everything"— Anonymous executive

"I never want to be looked upon as poor. My fiancé and I each drive a Mercedes. The best man at our upcoming wedding also drives a Mercedes."— Anonymous

In a big way, these external symbols become pivotal parts of the narcissist's false identity, replacing the real and injured self.

6. Entitlement. Narcissists often expect preferential treatment from others. They expect others to cater (often instantly) to their needs, without being considerate in return. In their mindset, the world revolves around them.

7. Charmer. Narcissists can be very charismatic and persuasive. When they're interested in you (for their gratification), they make you feel very special and wanted. However, once they lose interest in you (most likely after they've gotten what they want, or became bored), they may drop you without a second thought. A narcissist can be very engaging and sociable, as long as you're fulfilling what she desires, and giving her all of your attention.

8. Grandiose Personality. Thinking of oneself as a hero or heroine, a prince or princess, or one of a kind special person. Some narcissists have an

exaggerated sense of self-importance, believing that others cannot live or survive without his or her magnificent contributions.

"I'm looking for a man who will treat my daughter and me like princesses"— Anonymous singles ad

"Once again I saved the day—without me, they're nothing"— Anonymous

9. Negative Emotions. Many narcissists enjoy spreading and arousing negative emotions to gain attention, feel powerful, and keep you insecure and off-balance. They are easily upset at any real or perceived slights or inattentiveness. They may throw a tantrum if you disagree with their views, or fail to meet their expectations. They are extremely sensitive to criticism and typically respond with the heated argument (fight) or cold detachment (flight). On the other hand, narcissists are often quick to judge, criticize, ridicule, and blame you. Some narcissists are emotionally abusive. By making you feel inferior, they boost their fragile ego and feel better about themselves.

"Some people try to be tall by cutting off the heads of others"— Paramhansa Yogananda.

10. Manipulation: Using Others as an Extension of Self. Making decisions for others to suit one's own needs. The narcissist may use his or her romantic partner, child, friend, or colleague to meet

unreasonable self-serving needs, fulfil unrealized dreams, or cover up self-perceived inadequacies and flaws.

"If my son doesn't grow up to be a professional baseball player, I'll disown him"— Anonymous father

"Aren't you beautiful? Aren't you beautiful? You're going to be just as pretty as mommy" — Anonymous mother

Another way narcissists manipulate is through guilt, such as proclaiming, "I've given you so much, and you're so ungrateful," or, "I'm a victim—you must help me, or you're not a good person." They hijack your emotions and beguile you to make unreasonable sacrifices.

CHAPTER 3
HOW TO PREVENT AND AVIOD NARCISSISTIC ABUSE

The Season of the Narcissistic Emotional Abuser

All things have a season. There was a season before the narcissistic emotional abuser in your life. There was or is a season of the narcissistic emotional abuser in your life. And surely, there is or can be the season after the narcissistic emotional abuser in your life. One season preparing the soil for the next season as is the natural progression of life.

It doesn't occur to you to question, "How on earth did I get into this mess?" before the narcissistic emotional abuser entered your life. No, you were probably asking yourself the question, most likely years before that question, something to the effect of, "Why did he/she/they do this to me?" That question wasn't about the abuse caused by the narcissistic emotional abuser with whom you fell in love as an adult. No, that question quite possibly would have been about the abuse caused by a different type of abuser in your life when you were but a child, many times a sexual abuser.

This is not to say the sexual abuser was not also a narcissist, as sexual abusers exhibit three of the minimum of five criteria needed to be "diagnosable." This is not to say that all those who find themselves having stories to tell of having been involved with a narcissistic emotional abuser have been victims of the trauma caused by childhood sexual abuse. Therein, however, exists the very strong possibility that someone did something to you in the early years of your life that prepared your "soil" to attract and be attracted to a narcissistic emotional abuser.

In the midst of being in the season of the narcissistic emotional abuser, you begin to realize that a change has begun to take place in the way you are thinking and the way you are talking. At the beginning of this season, when talking to those by your side experiencing near to the same emotional pain that you is experiencing due to your repeated return to the abuser, your conversations focused on what they, the narcissistic emotional abuser, was doing or more often not doing. Now, your focus is on you asking yourself, "How did I get in this crazy mess?" You begin to acknowledge your accomplishments and who you are or what you have gained in life. You begin to compare yourself to the others that you know exist in what you want to believe is an exclusive relationship.

In the midst of this season, you begin to do some soul searching. Your question of, "How did I get in this mess?" no longer is just a glib question. This q uestion miraculously begins to take on entire new energy. It wants an answer. It demands an answer. You are the owner of the question, and you hold the key to give you the answer.

The journey of finding your answer, be forewarned, is not an easy or painless journey. Assuredly you will go through life on some sort of another journey if not on the one searching for your answer. You have the choice to run towards or run away from your answer. In the running towards your answer, you have the chance to eventually find peace and healing. In the running away from your answer you take the chance of continuing to experience emotional abuse in your life and yet another.

How to Handle Narcissistic Abuse

We're all capable of abuse when we're frustrated or hurt. We may be guilty of criticizing, judging, withholding, and controlling, but some abusers, including narcissists, take abuse to a different level. Narcissistic Abuse can be physical, mental, emotional, sexual, financial, and spiritual. Some types of emotional abuse are not easy to spot, including manipulation. It can include emotional blackmail, using threats and intimidation to exercise control. Narcissists are masters of verbal abuse and manipulation. They can go so far as to make you doubt your perceptions, called gas lighting.

The Motivation for Narcissistic Abuse

Remember that narcissistic personality disorder (NPD) and abuse exist on a continuum, ranging from silence to violence. Rarely will a narcissist take responsibility for his or her behaviour. Generally, they deny their actions and augment the abuse by blaming the victim. Particularly, malignant narcissists aren't bothered by guilt. They can be sadistic and take pleasure in inflicting pain. They can be so competitive and unprincipled that they engage in anti-social behaviour. Don't confuse narcissism with an anti-social personality disorder.

The objective of narcissistic abuse is power. They act with the intent to diminish or even hurt other people. The most important thing to remember about intentional abuse is that it's designed to dominate you. Abusers' goals are to increase their control and authority while creating doubt, shame, and dependency in their victims. They want to feel superior to avoid hidden feelings of inferiority. Understanding this can empower you. Like all bullies, despite their defences of rage, arrogance, and self-inflation, they suffer from shame. Appearing weak and humiliated is their biggest fear.

Knowing this, it's essential not to take personally the words and actions of an abuser. This enables you to confront narcissistic abuse.

Mistakes in Dealing with Abuse

When you forget an abuser's motives, you may naturally react in some of these ineffective ways:

1. Appeasement. If you placate to avoid conflict and anger, it empowers the abuser, who sees it as weakness and an opportunity to exert more control.

2. Pleading. This also shows weakness, which narcissists despise in themselves and others. They may react dismissively with contempt or disgust.

3. Withdrawal. This is a good temporary tactic to collect your thoughts and emotions but it is not an effective strategy to deal with abuse.

4. Arguing and Fighting. Arguing over the facts wastes your energy. Most abusers aren't interested in the facts, but only in justifying their position and being right. Verbal arguments can quickly escalate to fights that drain and damage you. Nothing is gained. You lose and can end up feeling more victimized, hurt, and hopeless.

5. Explaining and Defending. Anything beyond a simple denial of a false accusation leaves you open to more abuse. When you address the content of what is being said and explain and defend your position, you endorse an abuser's right to judge, approve, or abuse you. Your reaction sends this message: "You have power over my self-esteem. You have the right to approve or disapprove of me. You're entitled to be my judge."

6. Seeking Understanding. This can drive your behaviour if you desperately want to be understood. It's based on the false hope that a narcissist is interested in understanding you, while a narcissist is only interested in winning a conflict and having a superior position. Depending upon the degree of narcissism, sharing your feelings may also expose you to more hurt or manipulation. It's better to share your feelings with someone safe who cares about them.

7. Criticizing and Complaining. Although they may act tough, because abusers are insecure, inside they're fragile. They can dish it, but can't take it. Complaining or criticizing an abuser can provoke rage and vindictiveness.

8. Threats. Making threats can lead to retaliation or backfire if you don't carry them out. Never make a threat you're not ready to enforce. Boundaries with

direct consequences are more effective.

9. Denial. Don't fall into the trap of denial by excusing, minimizing, or rationalizing abuse. And don't fantasize that it will go away or improve at some future time. The longer it goes on, the more it grows, and the weaker you can become.

10. Self-Blame Don't blame yourself for an abuser's actions and try harder to be perfect. This is a delusion. You can't cause anyone to abuse you. You're only responsible for your behaviour. You will never be perfect enough for an abuser to stop their behaviour, which stems from their insecurities, not you.

Confronting Abuse Effectively

Allowing abuse damages your self-esteem. Thus, it's important to confront it. That doesn't mean to fight and argue. It means standing your ground and speaking up for yourself clearly and calmly and having boundaries to protect your mind, emotions, and body. Before you set boundaries, you must:

1. Know Your Rights. You must feel entitled to be treated with respect and that you have specific rights, such as the right to your feelings, the right not to have sex if you decline, a right to privacy, a right not to be yelled at, touched, or disrespected. If

you've been abused a long time (or as a child), your self- esteem likely has been diminished. You may no longer trust yourself or have confidence.

2. Be Assertive. This takes learning and practice to avoid being passive or aggressive. Try these short-term responses to dealing with verbal putdowns:

* I'll think about it.

* I'll never be the good enough wife (husband) that you hoped for

* I don't like it when you criticize me. Please stop." (Then walk away)

* That's your opinion. I disagree, (or) I don't see it that way.

* You're saying... " (Repeat what was said. Add, "Oh, I see.")

* I won't talk to you when you (describe abuse, e.g. "belittle me"). Then leave.

* Agree to the part that's true. "Yes, I burned the dinner." Ignore

You're a rotten cook.

* Humor - "You're very cute when you get annoyed.

3. Be Strategic. Know what you want specifically, what the narcissist wants, what your limits are, and where you have power in the relationship. You're dealing with someone highly defensive with a personality disorder. There are specific strategies to having an impact.

4. Set Boundaries. Boundaries are rules that govern the way you want to be treated. People will treat you the way you allow them to. You must know what your boundaries are before you can communicate them. This means getting in touch with your feelings, listening to your body, knowing your rights, and learning assertiveness. They must be explicit.

Don't hint or expect people to read your mind.

5. Have Consequences. After setting boundaries, if they're ignored, it's important to communicate and invoke consequences. These are not threats, but the actions you take to protect yourself or meet your needs.

6. Be Educative. Research shows that narcissists have neurological deficits that affect their interpersonal reactions. You're the best approach is to educate a narcissist like a child. Explain the impact of their behaviour and provide incentives and encouragement for different behaviour. This may involve communicating consequences. It req

uires planning what you're going to say without being emotional.

Narcissistic Individuals Target Your Greatest Fears and Weaknesses

Individuals with narcissistic personality disorder are uncannily intuitive. They 'read' people. The narcissistic personality relies on obtaining other people's attention and knows exactly which buttons to push to get 'energy', otherwise known as narcissistic supply - the drug that allows the narcissist to feel significant, and 'alive'.

A narcissistic personality wishes to secure energy and ensure a place to project his or her damaged and tormented self on to. The narcissist is conscienceless, he or she has no remorse in using your weakest links against you.

Because the narcissistic personality operates as a chameleon, he or she may change tactics from person to person and from relationship to relationship, depending on the individual he or she is dealing with.

Within a short amount of time, if the narcissist has decided to secure you as narcissistic supply, he or she will win your confidence by being extremely attentive in getting to know you.

The purpose of this is to build information. The narcissistic personality looks for vulnerabilities, weak links and insecurities, which he or she can play on down the track to confuse and abuse.

It may seem ludicrous that a person hurting you with your insecurities can manipulate you to stay hooked while they abuse you. People with narcissistic personality disorder use gas lighting and projection people with high levels of conscience because they hate to feel like they are 'wrong' and 'misunderstood', this grants the perfect psychological cocktail for the narcissist to operate abominably while his or her victim stays attached trying to prove integrity to the narcissist.

Trying to win clemency, validation and approval from an individual with a narcissistic personality disorder is a deadly game. The narcissistic personality knows where to hit you at your lowest mark, at you most vulnerable, raw and insecure place. This leaves you reeling in disbelief, horror and dismay over how a person who claims to love you, care for you and who regularly gushes adoration at you, could be capable of such an atrocity. All logic regarding looking after self (leaving) may be non-existent in the fighting for decency in the face of such emotional onslaughts and shock.

You may believe the details of what the narcissist attacks you with matter to him or her. The truth is they don't. The narcissistic personality is uninterested in the 'details' of arguments. The narcissist is simply looking for 'reactions' from you.

The narcissistic personality isn't interested in justice, truth or your integrity. The narcissist thrives off your pain and loves the fact that all of his or her inner torment can be projected on to you, and you become the crazy, hurt and deranged one.

The moral to this story is, absolutely get to know people's integrity and character before sharing all your deep, dark secrets. Additionally your approval of self, regardless of other's opinions, safeguards you against having to prove yourself fruitlessly, all the way to your demise, to a person who has no remorse or conscience.

7 Phases of Narcissistic Abuse (and How to Stop It No Matter Where You Are)

Phases of narcissistic abuse

There are stages of abuse used by the narcissistic individual. After all, narcissism is a mental illness, sometimes uncontrollable and debilitating. These stages make it extremely difficult to see the truth behind the behaviour of narcissistic abuse. Here's a secret, however. You can stop this narcissistic abuse during any of these stages.

The honeymoon phase

When you first enter a relationship with a narcissist, you will have no clue who they are. The narcissist will seem like your soul mate, the perfect partner. He will shower you with attention and gifts. He will compliment you on your beauty and personality. If you are a young adult, you will all head over heels for him. If you are an older adult who is unaware of this phase of narcissism, you may also be easily fooled.

The honeymoon phase is so skillfully crafted to fulfil the needs of the narcissist, that it will seem legitimate. For a moment, the narcissist will truly be in love and filling a deep void within. So, it's no wonder why the honeymoon phase can seem like a dream come true.

Solution: Remember, never give too much of yourself during good times. Yes, it is important to let your walls down with someone who truly cares about you, but be careful. There's nothing wrong with protecting your emotions and your mind by limiting how much you choose to give away.

The fading phase

Over time, the interest of the narcissist will fade. You will notice they aren't as attentive as before, and they even stop giving compliments. Soon, the narcissist will become distant, and you will find yourself becoming clingy. After all, you were once spoiled by the lavish treatment you received before, and it's hard to adapt to sudden changes. The closer you get, the more they will pull away.

Solution: Make sure you retain those interests you had before you met someone. Spend time with family and friends so that the fading phase will not damage you as much as it could. This treatment is wrong, but you don't have to become a victim by falling into its trap.

The emotional phase

By this time, emotions are heightened from the push and pull of the changes occurring the narcissistic abuse. The strength of the relationship has faded, and anger and loneliness begin to take its place. The narcissist grows even more distant leaving their mate confused and hurt. During the phase, the narcissist will continue to pull further away as you try harder to mend what's broken.

Solution: Stop! Right now, just stop trying to pull them closer. Let them grow as distant as they please, and they will notice how you aren't chasing them. This will further reveal who they are. I guarantee they will accuse you of being the one who grew distant. This blame game will prove their serious mental illness to be true.

Anger and fighting phase

You may now start to make attempts to mend the relationship by confronting the narcissist. Unfortunately, confrontation never works with this type of personality. Fighting will start, and then the silent treatment will be used to keep you from forcing the narcissist to look at the truth of their behaviour. Before long, this silent treatment will force you to be the one to apologize, leaving you back where you started, with no answers and feeling alone again.

Solution: This will be hard, but no matter how much the narcissist uses the silent treatment, do not give in. You will feel lonely and hurt, but you should remain strong.

Self-blame phase

Now, we are convinced the whole break down of the relationship is our fault. Our self-esteem starts to take a hit, and we become obsessed with trying to fix the problems. We lose ourselves to the narcissist as we try desperately to make them happy. They have already lost interest, and this effort is ignored. Now we start to think we are crazy and we wonder who the person is that we once loved.

Solution: When you start to blame yourself, make a list. List all the actions and words used by the narcissist. Then you will see that none of this breakdown was ever your doing.

The end game

Whether the narcissist ends the relationship or you do it, it will be a gift. Sometimes the narcissist, although they have lost interest in you, will keep you around for certain satisfaction that you do provide. Some narcissists will get rid of their mates as soon as their interest has faded. It varies from person to person.

If you feel you are being dragged along and there is no hope for release, you will have to end the relationship yourself. This will be difficult because your self-esteem has suffered so much. Sometimes the narcissist has convinced you that no one else would love you. This is a lie and a desperate ploy to keep someone by their side for distraction.

Solution: It's best to leave the relationship unless a serious effort has been done to get help.

The Trap

If you stay, there is a small chance that the narcissist will seek help. If they do not seek help, they will trap you in a cycle of rage and peace. What this means is the narcissist will grow furious about something in which you are to blame for, in their eyes. They will taunt you, call you names and accuse you of being the source of their unhappiness. Since this rage is so intimidating, you will give in and apologize for things that aren't your fault.

The rage will quiet, and the narcissist will go through the cycle of a few weeks of extremely good behaviour. He will compliment you again and spend time with you. This doesn't last, however, and after a few weeks, the rage will return.

Some people in this position find it worth the rage to get the peacetime efforts. This is a trick, a trap, and you should consider getting out of the ordeal for good.

Narcissistic abuse and why it happens

There is no set reason for narcissistic behaviour. Sometimes these traits can be partially genetic. Other times, they come from severe childhood trauma and abuse. Unfortunately, abuse can repeat itself in the form of narcissism because the adult survivor of the abuse has a void which cannot be filled easily by normal behaviour.

If you are dealing with a narcissist, whether it's a family member or a life partner, please seek support. It can be difficult protecting your sanity and health when dealing with an individual of this sort. It's important that you stay healthy and remember your worth.

CHAPTER 4
WHY NARCISSISTIC ABUSE SURVIVOR GETS ADDICTED

What Is Narcissistic Abuse?

Narcissists don't love themselves. They're driven by shame. It's the idealized image of themselves, which they convince themselves they embody, that they admire. But deep down, narcissists feel the gap between the façade they show the world and their shame-based self. They work hard to avoid feeling that shame. This gap is true for other codependents, as well, but a narcissist uses defence mechanisms that are destructive to relationships and cause pain and damage to their loved ones' self-esteem.

Many of the narcissist's coping mechanisms are abusive-hence the term, "narcissistic abuse." However, someone can be abusive, but not be a narcissist. Addicts and people with other mental illnesses, such as bipolar disorder and anti-social personality disorder (sociopath) and borderline personality disorders are also abusive, as are many codependents without a mental illness. Abuse is abuse, no matter what is the abuser's diagnosis. If you're a victim of abuse, the main challenges for you are:

- Identifying it;

- Building a support system; and

- Learning how to strengthen and protect yourself.

- What is Narcissistic Abuse

•   Abuse may be mental, physical, financial, spiritual, or sexual. Here are a few examples of abuse you may not have identified:

Verbal abuse: Includes belittling, bullying, accusing, blaming, shaming, demanding, ordering, threatening, criticizing, sarcasm, raging, opposing, undermining, interrupting, blocking, and name-calling. Note that many people occasionally make demands, use sarcasm, interrupt, oppose, criticize, blame, or block you. Consider the context, malice, and frequency of the behaviour before labelling it narcissistic abuse.

Manipulation: Generally, manipulation is an indirect influence on someone to behave in a way that furthers the goals of the manipulator. Often, it expresses covert aggression. Think of a "wolf in sheep's clothing." On the surface, the words seem harmless - even complimentary; but underneath you feel demeaned or sense a hostile intent. If you experienced manipulation growing up, you might not recognize it as such.

Emotional blackmail: Emotional blackmail may include threats, anger, warnings, intimidation, or punishment. It's a form of manipulation that provokes doubt in you. You feel a fear, obligation, and or guilt sometimes referred to as "FOG."

Gaslighting: Intentionally making you distrust your perceptions of reality or believe that you're mentally incompetent.

Competition: Competing and one-upping to always be on top, sometimes through unethical means. E.g. cheating in a game.

Negative contrasting: Unnecessarily making comparisons to negatively contrast you with the narcissist or other people.

Sabotage: Disruptive interference with your endeavours or relationships for revenge or personal advantage.

Exploitation and objectification: Using or taking advantage of you for personal ends without regard for your feelings or needs.

Lying: Persistent deception to avoid responsibility or to achieve the narcissist's ends.

Withholding: Withholding such things as money, sex, communication or affection from you.

Neglect: Ignoring the needs of a child for whom the abuser is responsible. Includes child endangerment; i.e., placing or leaving a child in a dangerous situation.

Privacy invasion: Ignoring your boundaries by looking through your things, phone, mail; denying your physical privacy or stalking or following you; ignoring privacy you've requested.

Character assassination or slander: Spreading malicious gossip or lies about you to other people.

Violence: This includes blocking your movement, pulling hair, throwing things, or destroying your property.

Financial abuse: Financial abuse might include controlling you through economic domination or draining your finances through extortion, theft, manipulation, or gambling, or by accruing debt in your name or selling your personal property.

Isolation: Isolating you from friends, family, or access to outside services and support through control, manipulation, verbal abuse, character assassination, or other means of abuse.

Narcissism and the severity of abuse exist on a continuum. It may range from ignoring your feelings to violent aggression. Typically, narcissists don't take responsibility for their behaviour and shift the blame to you or others; however, some do and are capable of feeling guilt and self-reflection.

Malignant Narcissism and Sociopath

Someone with more narcissistic traits who behaves in a malicious, hostile manner is considered to have "malignant narcissism." Malignant narcissists aren't bothered by guilt. They can be sadistic and take pleasure in inflicting pain. They can be so competitive and unprincipled that they engage in anti-social behaviour. Paranoia puts them in a defensive-attack mode as a means of self-protection.

Malignant narcissism can resemble sociopath. Sociopaths have malformed or damaged brains. They display narcissistic traits, but not all narcissists are sociopathic. Their motivations differ. Whereas narcissists prop up an ideal persona to be admired, sociopaths change who they are to achieve their self-serving agenda. They need to win at all costs and think nothing of breaking social norms and laws. They don't attach to people as narcissists do. Narcissists don't want to be abandoned. They're codependent on others' approval, but sociopaths can easily walk away from relationships that don't serve them. Although some narcissists will occasionally plot to obtain their objectives, they're usually more reactive than sociopaths, who coldly calculate their plans.

Get Help

If you're in a relationship with a narcissist, it's important to get outside support to understand clearly what's going on, to rebuild your self-esteem and confidence, and to learn to communicate effectively and set boundaries.

Narcissistic Abuse Survivors Defenseless Against Ignorant Judgment

When people hear that I have chosen to have no contact with my highly toxic, aged mother and father they always tell me how sorry they feel for my parents. I can only assume that in me they see a happy, well-adjusted adult woman and must decide that I have chosen to afflict some sort of maliciously intended punishment on my poor defenceless parents. They cannot possibly understand how violated I feel hearing them defend the very people who nearly destroyed my life; people who would continue to wreak havoc in it if I chose to allow it.

The judgment handed down by the ignorant strikes a raw nerve and immediately put me on the defensive. Cases of appalling abusive actions from my supposedly old, frail, innocent parents, some old some new, come spewing out of my mouth one after another in an attempt to justify my position. My breath is wasted. My stance is never validated. I always end up looking cold-blooded and hard-hearted when in truth I am anything but.

I am a strong, confident woman. I have learned to love myself despite all I have been through. Perhaps it is that air of confidence that causes some to side against me. It must be because everything I stand for in my life demonstrates my compassionate, loving nature, yet all of that seemingly goes right out the window in the eyes of people who do not understand Narcissistic Personality Disorder abuse.

I know that I am not alone in this experience. Due to the covert nature of narcissistic abuse, it is one of the perpetual tragedies many survivors of NPD parents endure. The victim is often seen as the perpetrator and the perpetrator seen as the victim. Even when we find the courage to stop the abuse we can never redeem ourselves in the minds of the judgmental ignoramus, professional or otherwise.

As NPD abuse survivors our healing must come entirely from our courageous resolve. The Narcissistic Personality Disorder parent will never validate our feelings, verify our memories, or allow us our pain. Our friends, co-workers and acquaintances who cannot possibly understand what we go through often say the wrong thing, making us feel even worse. The only possibility of support is an alliance with siblings who have shared our experiences and have likewise abandoned their denial.

I am very fortunate. It took a few years, but my sisters both embraced the truth. We can emotionally support each other and have formed an ironclad alliance against our toxic parents, but that is uncommon. More often than not, siblings side with parents who are adept at exploiting their victimization and rallying sympathizers around them, alienating their recovering brother or sister even further.

NPD survivors must have a solid support system to keep them from self-destruction. Rationality does not exist in dealings with those who have Narcissistic Personality Disorder. Rational minds cannot make sense of NPD irrational behaviour, though that does not stop us from trying to rationalize the confusion we experience. It is that effort that makes us feel as if we are the crazy ones.

It takes a great deal of validation to convince us that we are not crazy. That is why I strongly recommend survivors work with a professional therapist, psychologist or counsellor who is highly skilled in working with Narcissistic Personality Disorder abuse until they feel strong and confident enough to stand on their own-however long that takes. That is the formula for success in completely overcoming the pain-for confidently moving forward in our lives.

There will always be issues throughout our lives that challenge us as NPD abuse survivors. Though I counsel other survivors and extensively write, speak and am highly knowledgeable about Narcissistic Personality Disorder, I am not immune to its ugly assaults. However, as a result of the work, I have done I am confident and skilled enough to get through them. The more healing work we do, the stronger we get and the easier those challenges are to deal with.

You have survived one of the most insidious forms of child abuse. Though often invisible, the abuse was real; your pain is real. But never choose to be a victim of your past. Reclaim your power. Start today.

7 Signs You've Arrived as a Survivor of Narcissistic Abuse

Recovering from narcissistic and emotional abuse can seem like an ordeal of the most grievous kind.

You may have endured months of struggle and suffering without knowing if you're making any progress because the pull to go back remains strong. You miss the moments under your abuser's sway because, in your traumatized mind, cognitive dissonance and memories of so-called "good times" cloud your objectivity.

How do you know where you stand on your road to recovery? Victory isn't always in-your-face. Arriving as a survivor of narcissistic abuse comes in waves, even ripples, but if you experience the following seven signs, you can feel gratified knowing that healing is within your reach.

1) You've begun to appreciate that self-care is something you need to participate in consistently.

Not only because you are healing from emotional abuse, but because healthy people, in general, understand the importance of putting on their oxygen mask before they can help others.

Life can be stressful enough without the added obstacle of toxic abuse. It only stands to reason that if you're healing from narcissistic abuse, your body and mind require extreme self-care. This might include reducing social engagements, staying off of the internet, saying "no" to friends and family, taking a nap when you feel exhausted, and making time to do meditations.

You resist the urge to make excuses as to why you can't take care of yourself, realizing that even single mothers can work self-care into their schedules. If you are a single mother, you deliberately get a babysitter on occasion to take yourself out. You do guide meditations at night. Your journal and do mirror work. If a friend asks you to visit and you don't have the energy, you respectfully decline. You take the initiative to be a little "selfish" because you understand the need to do so after putting out other people's fires for too long.

2) You do what it takes to protect your mental and physical space.

You no longer acquiesce to things that intrude on your privacy and peace of mind.

Most narcissists and other Cluster-B disordered individuals pull out all the stops when trying to hook a previous source of supply back into their realm of crazy. They pretend to have changed, to want to be friends (especially for the "sake of the kids"), to be just another normal person going through a typical breakup or divorce. They may go so far as to tell you their relationship problems with their new partner.

Arriving as a survivor means you no longer want, nor tolerate, any of those things. You want peace and autonomy so badly that you are willing to go complete No Contact and resolve not to let them into your home anymore. You don't leave yourself open to any of their tomfoolery, and instead, put up all necessary boundaries to protect your new sense of peace.

3) You no longer care about how your Ex will react to your decisions.

You don't worry whether your life choices will make your Ex angry or make life "inconvenient" for them. You understand that true fulfilment means honouring your dreams, desires, and ambitions regardless of how your ex may respond. As long as you abide by any court orders in place, you know that your future is in your own hands.

4) You may start to notice that some of your other relationships have been a big energy and time drain, and you resolve to do something about them.

You've gotten into the habit of honouring yourself and releasing that which doesn't serve your highest good. Consequently, you've become more sensitive to other relationships in which you feel taken advantage of. This doesn't mean that you would dump a friend in need, but rather that you've started noticing your relationship 'climates'. In the same way that a long-term weather pattern creates a climate in a particular region, if the climate of any of your relationships has proven – over time – that you typically feel put upon and used, then those are the ones that you now consider releasing.

5) You're more concerned about what you're doing with your life than what your Ex is doing with theirs.

You no longer obsess about your Ex with their new supply or the fact that they seem so happy because you've come to understand that your Ex is destined to repeat the same cycle of abuse with anyone they are with at any given time.

6) You no longer focus on problems, but on solutions.

You realize that you have the power to conquer and change your circumstances, rather than remain defenceless against whatever stunts your Ex might be playing.

You understand that for every action, there is an eq ual and opposite reaction. If you need to delete an email you've had for years because your Ex emails you from different accounts, you delete it. If you need to file a restraining order because your Ex is stalking and harassing you, you drive to the courthouse and file it. If you see the need to change your cell phone number and insist that they call you on your landline, you do so. If your Ex sends you unwanted gifts and flowers, you mark them "return to sender" or refuse the delivery. You fight the good fight to protect your newfound freedom.

7) You no longer consider what happened to you a punishment, but rather an eye-opener because you understand that it happened so you could heal the wounds you've carried since childhood.

You've arrived as a survivor from narcissistic abuse because you no longer look to your Ex for approval or appreciation, knowing that even the appearance of those things comes with a high price. You accept that there are people whose behaviour is disturbingly damaging, but you no longer open yourself up to it. Instead, you respond appropriately, with full awareness of why it's necessary to do so.

You've arrived as a survivor because you no longer tolerate anything that discounts your value – from anyone – for you've become your own best friend and advocate.

Forgive or Not Forgive Narcissistic Abuser?

Should Narcissistic Abusers Be Held Accountable for Their Actions?

Many recovering victims of narcissistic abuse struggle with the dilemma of whether or not to hold the narcissist accountable for his behaviour. We learn in our recovery that narcissism is a personality disorder and wonder, "Isn't having a personality disorder the same thing as having a mental illness? And if so, how can we hold a mentally ill person responsible for their actions?"

One reason we find ourselves in this conundrum is that for many years we have been trained by the narcissist to first sacrifice our own needs for theirs. So it stands to reason, given our brainwashing and our typically gentle forgiving natures that we overlook our suffering and wonder if narcissists are to be pitied for their lack of self-control.

And where does forgiveness fit in? Can and should we forgive them for their actions if we believe they cannot control them? What if we believe that they can control their behaviour but find it difficult to do so? And should we forgive them if we believe that they are in complete control of their behaviours?

There are two schools of thought on the culpability of the narcissist. I'll first talk about the less popular of the two.

Some say that the narcissist does what he does without conscious regard; that he does not premeditate his campaign of abuse. And when he is functioning on a conscious level, he is unable to predict the outcomes of his actions or control his behaviour.

This theory may be true in part but is not substantiated as a whole, though both theories do agree that the narcissist lacks impulse control. And they both maintain that because he lacks impulse control, he is not entirely responsible for his actions.

That is where the schools of thought differ. One believes that he is entirely at the mercy of his disorder; the other believes that he is partially at the mercy of it.

The second school of thought is that the decisions that propel the narcissist into action are unconsciously experienced, but that the narcissist is in complete control of how and when he will act them out. This theory maintains that he knows what is right and what is wrong, that he can anticipate the results of his actions, and that he is fully aware of the penalty others will pay for his choices. So the decision of whether or not to act on his compulsions is made consciously and calculatingly.

The problem for the narcissist is that suppressing his compulsions is not an option he is willing to take. And why should he? He doesn't care about anyone but himself.

As far as the narcissist is concerned, people only exist as sources of his narcissistic supply; sources of adoration, admiration, and attention. One person doesn't mean any more to him than another does. People are dispensable and interchangeable; they are merely a means to an end. So if one person doesn't give him what he wants, he disposes of them like trash and moves onto another source of supply.

The narcissist satisfies his never-ending hunger for attention at the expense of anyone naïve enough, dependent enough, or willing enough to feed him. He is an addict who will stoop to any level to get his fix. Since he cannot empathize, he does not have to experience the implications of what he does to others. He may know that you are hurting, but he can't feel your pain.

Narcissists are consumed by inner turmoil, conflict and fear. And what do they fear the most? They fear to lose their narcissistic supply; the supply they get from us. Acting out on their compulsions like parasites is how they alleviate the pressure and anxiety that restlessly stirs inside them. And they don't have a conscience regarding their treatment of others. They don't care about or feel responsible for whoever must be sacrificed or expended to fulfil their needs.

Narcissists may lack empathy, but they do not lack emotion. They are highly sensitive, though they only experience that sensitivity as it relates to them. And they do not experience emotion the way other people do. They have a false self; a powerful defence mechanism that keeps them from having to deeply feel their emotions. It keeps them from feeling responsible for anything that goes on in their lives.

They do feel pity, but only as it relates to their self and their interests. Because they have a false sense of grandiosity, they feel forever victimized. They see life as being unfair to them; they feel like they never get all they deserve. They believe that everyone owes them all the time.

But should we feel sorry for someone who is ruled by their fears and suffers a great deal emotionally? The answer is no... we should not. Who among us does not have emotional pain and feel fear? And haven't we suffered a great deal of pain and fear at the hands of the narcissist? We are the casualties of their behaviour; not the other way around.

The degree to which any human being suffers is directly related to how much he allows these common human emotions to impact his everyday life. The narcissist cowers and victimizes others in the face of his pain and fear. We do not. We draw on our inner strength and courage in the face of our pain and fear.

So narcissists have a personality disorder, but are they mentally ill innocents who know not what they do? Think about it this way. How many times have you witnessed the two faces of your narcissist? How many times have you seen him behave entirely different, with different people, under the same circumstances? How many times have you seen him control his behaviour when others are there to witness it, and then completely go off on you when no one is there to see it happen? The fact that he only acts out only when he thinks he can get away with it demonstrates the existence of choice.

And how many times have you seen your narcissist pouring on the charm with someone they think is important, influential, famous, or wealthy? These people are the narcissist's ideal. It doesn't matter what the person's morals or ethics are. Their position in life is the only thing that attracts the narcissist who believes that because he is unique and special, he should only engage with other special, rich, or accomplished people. Narcissists are attracted to wealthy people, beautiful people, and successful people who they believe they can benefit from in some way or which will enhance their self-image by association.

The fact that narcissists can turn their charm on and off, just as they would a light switch, is further evidence demonstrating the existence of choice and while the narcissist can admire these people, he is also envious of them and what they have that he does not. That is because narcissists live in a state of constant envy.

Narcissists are envious of everyone. They envy the fact that others have feelings. They envy others' houses, education, marriages, children, station in life, careers. They especially envy the fact that others are happy.

Being around happy people exaggerates their sense of deprivation and their misery. Happiness in others provokes viciousness in narcissists. They will do almost anything to snuff the light out of someone who is happy, especially someone who they feel they have control over. If they can't safely lash out at their target, they will lie and badmouth them to others, or do a slow burn about it and then blame or take it out on someone close to them. Making themselves feel better by making other people feel worse, reinforces their sense of omnipotence. They make it clear that those close to them are only allowed to feel happy when they want them to.

Narcissists do not feel remorse for the abuse they inflict on those closest to them. The narcissist sees them as easy marks that he does not have to try to win over; extensions of himself. He just takes it for granted that they are there for him, safely and readily at his disposal, to abuse as he pleases and fulfils his narcissistic supply as needed.

Have you ever told your narcissist that he is hurting your feelings or expressed how badly he is making you feel? Have you ever asked him to stop treating you the way he does?

Anyone who loves and cares about you would take your feelings into consideration, but not so for the narcissist. He sees your vulnerability the same way a lion sees a young gazelle. It provokes his predatory urges even more.

It also adds fuel to his fire. He is appalled that you would question his actions. Any suggestion that you see anything he does as less than perfect enrages him if you have lived with a narcissist you understand how terrifying being the target of narcissistic rage can be.

Narcissistic rage is a defence mechanism the narcissist's false self employs to protect his fragile ego.

But it is also a control mechanism meant to erode your self-confidence, intimidate you, humiliate you, and disable you; all to keep you around so he can continue to feed off of you.

Though the rage may be difficult for someone with a narcissistic personality disorder to control, the motive used to keep you in line is deliberate. They are fully aware of what they are doing but simply do not care.

CHAPTER 5
TIPS FOR COPING IN RELATIONSHIP WITH NARCISSISTS

Are You in a Relationship With a Narcissist?

If you are in a relationship with a narcissist you're living in hell on earth. A narcissist is someone who constantly belittles you at the drop of a hat. A narcissist makes you feel like a peasant while he is the king of not only his domain but yours. You spend every waking moment catering to their every wish, while all your wishes never come true. A narcissist doesn't care about your wishes, hopes, dreams, feelings, judgment or needs. A narcissist only cares about their own, and so should you, or you will be sorry.

You may try to keep the peace, but with a narcissist, peace is impossible. They create standards you can never reach so that you will fail again and again, and it is up to them to dish out your punishment. And dish it out they will. Since you are all alone with your thoughts and feelings and are unable to verbalize them or exhibit them, you will feel like a robot, and a very lonely robot to boot. How did someone so promising and charming hide the fact that they are a narcissist? How did you not see this coming?

A narcissist is always different at the beginning of a relationship, way different. They come across as prince charming, sweep you off your feet and place you on this pedestal and treat you in a way you thought only happened in fairy tales. Once you have fallen under their spell, a narcissist then lets his facade crumble. Not to the outside world though. Just in your personal life. They maintain their image for all the world to see but allow you to see what is behind the mask, and it is what nightmares are made of.

A relationship with a narcissist is a one-way street. The street leads towards them, and away from you. When you are in a relationship with a narcissist, you must constantly cater to them and build and maintain their inflated ego and sense of self at the expense of your self-esteem, dignity, and ego. Compassion will rarely be given to you by a narcissist, but they expect and demand it from you.

The term "double standards" is perfect to describe a relationship with a narcissist. It is all about them and has nothing to do with you. They get the praise; you get the complains and reprimands. They have a say on everything, you are afraid to say anything and better keep your mouth shut. If they are not happy, you will not be allowed to be happy either. A narcissist doesn't care about your happiness; they are only concerned with their own.

Since narcissists are so in love with themselves, they cannot be capable of really loving you because they can never put you first. Sure, if you try and end things with a narcissist, they may go overboard to get you back. But is it really because they love you and will change? No, it is for their ego, they do not want to be abandoned. THEY can leave YOU, but you cannot leave THEM. So how do you know if you are involved with a narcissist as a friend, lover or family tie?

A narcissist has an over-inflated ego and thinks they are above others and look down on everyone else they deem not up to their standards. Because they are special, rules do not apply to them. To everyone else, yes, but to them, no. A narcissist has delusions of grandeur. They are not ordinary so why should they have an ordinary wife, ordinary kids and ordinary job or an ordinary house? That may be good enough for "other people" but not for them. They have a sense of entitlement like no one you have ever met before or since. They think other people are jealous of them or out to get them.

Narcissists feel you should be able to take criticism from them, and they will give it to you constantly. However, you cannot criticize them for ANYTHING. They will also twist your words and take things you said critically when you did not mean it that way. They will have temper tantrums when they are unhappy over any little thing.

Narcissists will keep you guessing. One day they act like all is wonderful and they adore you, the next day, they are as cold as ice and treat you like a stranger or an enemy. A narcissist cannot sympathize or empathize with anyone other than themselves. Other people's feelings, unless it is to get what something from them, are irrelevant.

What Makes You Vulnerable to a Narcissistic Partner

There is no "type" that a Narcissistic individual will look to partner up with. They might perceive you as someone who will make them look good, or feel good. If you respond to them in a certain way consistently to feed their need for Narcissistic supply, then this behaviour will draw them to you.

There are traits in you that you can self-examine to see if you have vulnerabilities that attract Narcissistic individuals to you.

1. Not knowing what to look for. A Narcissistic individual will usually look for those who see the very best in them. They will usually know how to be so "in tuned" with you. It doesn't mean that they are. If you are left thinking, this is too good to be true. They shower with you with love and attention. They seemed to almost "read your mind," especially in the beginning stages. This is, so you fall in love with them. When you don't recognize the early stages behaviour that a Narcissistic person displays, you will fall right into their hands. Better for you to get familiar with what those signs are, and slow things down from the beginning. Someone can only mask their behaviour for so long before their true colours

show.

2. You carry the burden for false responsibility in your family of origin. If you have never dealt with those issues that have hindered you from your family of origin, this is where you might fall vulnerable to someone with Narcissistic tendencies. A Narcissistic individual is happy to have you carry the burdens of your family, as well as their issues while not caring about what you've been through. It's better for you to confront and deal with issues you've been through, so you are not blindsided by being saddled with someone else's issues placed on you. You can't fix another person, nor can they fix you. You can choose to deal with your issues, so they don't continue to be problems that hinder your future relationships. You can also spot someone quicker who wants you to carry the responsibility for their issues, and avoid a toxic relationship much better when you deal with your issues first.

3. You are highly empathic. There's nothing wrong with being empathic. It's a wonderful skill you've developed. It's just when it's one-sided, then it is a problem. If you start noticing, you are always needed to listen when some sort of traumatic drama goes on, but when you need someone to listen to you, the other person is nowhere to be found. If this is an ongoing pattern, beware. Chances are it will stay this way if you say nothing or accept that this is

okay. You will find yourself in a one-sided relationship. It's also a sign you might be involved with someone with Narcissistic tendencies. Don't ignore those warning signs that something isn't right. Address it early on.

4. You don't express, or you choose to repress a lot of your own needs. It could be that you might be telling yourself that they need you so that you won't express a whole lot of your own needs. Like number 3, don't ignore this. If you try to rationalize that it's okay for now, it may be that you need to do some personal growth work. No healthy relationship is one-sided. Everyone does have needs from time to time. You might need someone to listen to you when you are stressed out or to go through a tough time. If you can't talk to that other person, it's time to visit why not.

5. It doesn't feel like a partnership; they want you to re-parent them. We all know someone or seen someone who's "let down their guard," only to find them acting out childishly. You might hear them say, 'you remind me of my mother or my father.' This isn't a good sign. It's likely that person is telling you that they have unhealed wounding from their mother and father and they want to re-create that parent-child relationship again to rework through their unresolved pain. It's not healthy to be in a parent-child relationship where you are the "re-

created parent." You'll have an adult child on your hands, not a peer-to-peer relationship. This is also someone who's not ready to be in a relationship with you.

Realize that when you choose to continue a relationship with a Narcissistic individual once you recognize all the symptoms, you will be left with very little in return. You will likely be struggling with frustration, feel like it's a one-sided relationship, and feel incredibly drained from it.

If you're looking for a relationship who will be a real partner to you, then don't choose to be in a relationship with a Narcissist. These individuals, unfortunately, won't be able to meet you in a healthy partnership. It's the early stages of dating where they turn on the charm the most. It's good to know the signs early enough and be aware of what makes you vulnerable to stop before you get too emotionally invested.

How to Deal with a Narcissistic Partner

Some narcissists are obnoxious, offensive and obstinate. Others, however, present as attractive, appealing, easy-going people. It's not until a confrontation occurs that their narcissism becomes obvious.

Summon up the courage to tell him (or her) that he's self-centered and he'll either continue doing whatever he was doing as if you hadn't said anything at all or he will become irate. "Me? Me? Self-centred? How do you think that makes ME feel?" Though all narcissists are not cut from the same cloth, they do have many traits in common. Here are the most typical ones:

1. Narcissists find it hard (if not impossible) to truly appreciate the validity of another's point of view. They imagine that others think and feel the same way they do. If they don't, something's wrong with them.

2. Narcissists need constant validation from the outside. Admire and respect them, and they do fine. Find fault with them and watch out! Grandiose narcissists will strike back venomously; closet narcissists will shrink back into their cave.

3. Narcissists often display a façade self-based on impressive and admirable traits. What's wrong with that? Nothing, if it weren't mere window dressing. Their façade self is fake, covering up a real self that's insecure and vulnerable.

4. Narcissists view others as extensions of themselves. The narcissist sets the standards of behaviour and does not tolerate opposition - especially if your viewpoint requires him to respond in ways he doesn't wish to.

5. Narcissists believe that they are entitled to special treatment. Whether it's a "stupid" law or a "dumb" demand, narcissists feel that they shouldn't have to go along with the pack and confirm. They believe they are of higher status; therefore why to adapt just to please someone else.

6. Narcissists use the money to help them feel special. Status items such as expensive clothes, cars, homes, dinners and trips are essential ways that a narcissist enhances his ego. Spending money, if you have it, is one thing; spending money, if you don't have it, is another. Regardless, a narcissist believes that he deserves the best. And easily fools himself into believing that the money will be there in the future, even if it's not there right now.

7. Narcissists may make a show of being generous by being big tippers or taking care of bills. Look closely, however, and you'll see that their generosity is based upon establishing a reputation for themselves as a VIP.

If you discover that you are living with a narcissist, what can you do to make your life easier?

It may seem weird to say "discover" that you're living with a narcissist, but it's true. Many people don't realize that their partner (or parent or adult child) is a narcissist, discovering it only after much time has elapsed. Why isn't it obvious at the very beginning?

Two reasons:

1. Narcissists are great masters of disguise, describing their behaviour in the best of terms, (i.e. I'm only doing it for you!) Hence, it may take a while for you to 'get' what's going on.

2. Though narcissism has a bad rep (egocentric, egotistical), narcissists also have positive traits. Indeed, they may be quite charismatic and charming. Hence, it may be hard to believe that narcissism is driving their behaviour.

Once you recognize that you are living with a narcissist, here are seven valuable tips for you to maintain your sanity and self-esteem.

1. Know What You Will Tolerate and What You Won't

Trust your judgment. If he (or she) is spending recklessly, know what you will tolerate and what you won't. That doesn't mean that all spending has to be done your way (unless you're two narcissists battling it out). But it does mean that you don't tolerate the narcissist's explanation for free-spending (i.e. Hey, you only live once.") And you take necessary steps (whether he likes it or not)to protect your financial future.

2. Bolster Your Self-Esteem

Do not expect your narcissist to build up your self-esteem when he has just helped tear it down. That is something you must do for yourself. Spend more time with people who think well of you. Get involved with pleasurable activities that bolster your ego. Be kind to yourself.

3. Know when You're being 'Gaslighted'.

When your narcissist says something, then later denies saying it or claims to have said something different, you can begin to doubt your sanity. Were you listening? Were you dreaming? Is she nuts? Am I nuts? What's going on here? Your narcissist may be doing this maliciously to throw you off balance. Or, she may simply be responding to her need of the moment, forgetting what she previously said.

4. Develop a Positive Support System

It may be hard, to be honest with others. You may feel embarrassed, especially if you've been covering for your narcissist for so long. Nevertheless, see if there's a trustworthy friend or family member with whom you can share what's going on. Also, consider seeking the help of a professional who will be able to offer you objective feedback.

5. Don't Tolerate Denigrating Emotional Outbursts

At times you will be upset with each other and need to let off steam. But "how" one lets off steam is vital. If you're being spoken to with disdain and disrespect, stop the action. Make the issue, HOW you are being treated. Express your disappointment. Demand an apology. And if necessary, walk away, letting it be known that you'll be happy to pick up where you left off when you're treated with respect.

6. Learn the Skills of Negotiation

Just because your narcissist wants something, doesn't mean she needs to get it. Just because she expresses herself forcefully, doesn't mean you fold. Everything is negotiable. You just need to know where your power lies. Then you need to convey it and enforce it. The skills of negotiation will empower you in many areas of life - today and in your future.

7. Accept that you are not going to do a total makeover of your narcissist's personality.

Nor should you want to. If your relationship is that bad, consider splitting. But, if there are redeeming traits, see if you can work together to create "family rules" of acceptable behaviour.

Living with a narcissist is not easy. But putting into practice these seven rules will make things more manageable for you.

Relationship Tips - How to Manage Love with a Narcissistic Individual

I am sure you think as overrated the cliche that 'love is blind' - but neuroscience, this prodigy child of science, unveils with an almost cruel satisfaction that some areas of our brains shut down when love comes upon us, blinding the ration from the smart choices we should make.

Brain scans of the people who were madly in love are very similar to the scans of the brains of people who were doing cocaine. There you have it - love is pretty much a drug itself. In a way, we are all drug dealers - the drug of choice being love and other emotional enhancers.

Love could be a wonderful happening if sometimes we wouldn't fall in love with the wrong person. If that person is a narcissist, your burden will reach heights worth of better causes. Either way, you need to learn how to cope with this situation.

According to the American Psychological Association, people with a narcissistic personality disorder display a chronic and pervasive pattern of grandiosity, need for admiration, and lack of empathy.

Narcissists have a grandiose sense of self-importance like they would have a special mission on this earth and they often have a 'king style' type of personality, while all the others should behave as humble servants of their wishes.

They always exaggerate their achievements and talents making everything in their power to gain everybody's attention and recognition. Most of the times they are arrogant and self-absorbed to fulfil their special destiny.

The narcissist will indulge in fantasies of tremendous power, success or beauty, being addicted to the attention and admiration that others manifest. You will find much snobbery between them which they do not deny it but rather be proud of it.

They see themselves as unique masterpieces - God himself obtained his PhD by creating them. Complicated rather than complex personalities, they will find it difficult to empathize with other people.

They can't go out of the perimeter of their personality, not understanding how people don't think the same as they do. That's why many times you may have the feeling of talking to a wall because no matter how deep you explain your point of view, most likely a narcissist will not understand it. A brick and iron wall.

They can't maintain too long relationships, most of the times because people around them give up on explaining themselves over and over again. Narcissist transform their partners in beggars - you will beg for understanding and some unconditional attention and most of the time you will celebrate only leftovers from the feast the narcissist indulged.

You will find many successful individuals with this syndrome because narcissism will drive them to achieve success and accumulate power to feed their self-admiration. Many success achievers has a dose of healthy narcissism - or self-confidence, but healthy narcissism or selfishness will not ask the world to reflect them their inflated self-image and ego.

A relationship with a narcissistic personality will req uire lots of energy and work because they are in constant need for outside support and approval. Once these needs are fulfilled, they feel powerful, but many times this need will be very hard to be satisfied. They are left feeling vulnerable and lonely - that's how they will explain their "cheating" behaviour.

The genesis of this personality disorder goes back in time to childhood. Most of the time they will be the single child in a family but even then they have been ignored, or the parents had very big expectations of perfection from the child.

The child will fiercely embark on this quest of winning the appreciation of his parents, leaving him with the incapacity to understand other people's needs, as his needs were not understood as a child.

How to detect a narcissist?

1. Be aware of people who advertise themselves too much. They will always want to be in the centre of attention. Being in search of constant approval and

admiration they will take over "the stage" and monopolize the discussion and action. They want to be the star in everyone's movie.

2. Lacking empathy toward other people needs. They can't give attention to other people because they are in constant need for that attention. Everyone is a slave and object to fulfil their demands. Narcissist wants all the love, all the attention, all the possessions for themselves - they will be jealous of other people's achievements and will find it hard to acknowledge their success.

3. They cannot take criticism - it appeals to their childhood memories, and they will reject it with all their power. If you commit the leze-majesty to criticize them, besides the fact that they will deny it, they will feel hurt and unloved. They will never accept responsibility for any wrongdoing and will be on a constant search for finding people to blame for their mistakes.

4. Many will be workaholics - being driven by the huge desire for achievement; they will put all their efforts toward achieving massive success.

It takes time to identify all these character treats as many are under the camouflage of good looking, highly successful people which will always be fascinating and attractive. They can be interesting personalities but very difficult to handle, almost impossible.

The bad news is that they cannot be changed. Read again: narcissist cannot be changed! Since they reject any form of criticism, even the constructive one, they cannot comprehend any wrongdoing and indulge in their self-proclaimed image of perfection. Many of them will have secret thoughts of being god -like and will be blind to any mistake they will do.

It is not recommended to give in to all their demands - you will only just reinforce their grandiose needs, and they will get the feeling that it is normal to have all their wishes fulfilled without them giving much in return.

How to cope with narcissistic partners?

Since they cannot be changed, you need to reevaluate your needs and long term goals for a relationship - it may be interesting for a while to be around such type of people but in the long run it gets exhausting, and anger and resentment will overshadow any feelings of love and tenderness.

1. Do not give in to their never stopping demands, keep your independence from this type of person - if, in any way you depend on them, they will blackmail you to make you give in to their desires.

2. Don't let yourself be infuriated by their lack of empathy or understanding - they are not capable of it. Showing them their incapacity will do nothing - they will blame you for everything that it doesn't work.

3. Finally, decide when enough is enough. A relationship with a narcissist can take you places where you do not want to be, can make you behave in ways you do not recognize yourself. It can undermine your self-esteem and will rob you of the attention you need to give to yourself trying to meet all their needs.

Many artistic personalities will be narcissistic and self-absorbed, ego-centred. The fascination with them will make many of you fall for them since their love will be just like their personality: irrational, instinctual, possessive and overwhelming. Which sometimes will unlock that crazy passionate behaviour within you - fun for a while but it will wear you down and leave you with nothing in the end.

Narcissists will be attached to those that satisfy their needs but will never treat them as partners but as followers. They need to lead and be in control constantly - they do not need equals but disciples or pleasers. The worst thing that can happen is when one narcissist meets someone with low self-esteem -

it will be the perfect victim and toy for them.

Stand up for yourself, do not give up on your needs and do not believe all their explanations - their constant need for admiration and approval will make them flirt with many from the opposite sex and not rarely even cheat to reaffirm their power of seduction.

Although they have a certain charisma and aura - probably the outrageous feeling of self-confidence will be their most magnetic treat, they come with a lot of work. Enjoy for as long as you feel that what keeps you together is more than what pushes you apart, but know when to leave as for the moment no treatment is available - besides brain surgery. Guess not, since they consider themselves so perfect.

Let them create if they are artists or achieve the success they want, while you move on and fulfil your emotional and human needs. Love stories can be beautiful without drama and self-proclaimed kings and gods around you.

How to Stop Obsessing Over a Narcissistic Relationship

Obsessing over a narcissistic relationship is stressful and tiring; leading you to feel down, frustrated or hopeless. Fixating over your painful experience can interfere with your life by keeping you from doing the things you want to do. A particularly helpful skill to stop compulsive thoughts of the abuse is learning to control your attention, the degree to which you are focused on the mistreatment, the more you are aware of it. This is not about denying your pain; it is attending to something else. Negative thoughts are ideas that we tell ourselves and are not always accurate reflections of reality.

When we take feelings too seriously, we let how we feel control all our decisions. While learning to focus on the things you have control over, you will empower yourself to end the destructive attachment. Letting go of your resentments (desire to hurt your partner) happens when you believe in your right to happiness. Sometimes we need time to ready ourselves to cope. Change your thinking about the abuse, and about yourself, so that you don't blame yourself, or believe things are hopeless. The following steps are ways to stop your obsessions.

I believe the first step below requires us to give up our desire for vengeance and letting go of a victim mentality. If you want revenge to let it be your success at creating a decent manageable life. Allowing your abuser to rent space in your head means they get to continue punishing you. Narcissists feel all-powerful when they think your life is miserable with them, and especially without them. Feel your anger and use your emotional pain to motivate change in your life.

Take responsibility for having chosen your abusive partner. Accept the lesson and learn from the relationship pain, so you don't repeat it. Ask yourself, "what is the gift" from this relationship?

Stop talking about your ex-partner to others; refuse to establish a victim identity. Create a state of well-being within you.

Spend time each morning focused on forgiving the narcissist for not being able to love you, so you can free your ego from the desire to hurt them. Move on to a new freedom.

Care enough about your well-being to stop the self-punishing thoughts. Refuse to build drama stories in your mind.

Practice hearing and feeling the critical voice in your head. Banish fear and guilt from your mind.

Acknowledge and observe the destructiveness of your compulsive thoughts and emotions.

Keep your thinking and feeling centred on good things, care about how you feel. Lower your dark curtain and emerge from the darkness.

Work as hard on accepting what is good in your life as you have the painful and the difficult. Learn to trust yourself by finding out what is right for you.

4 Relationship Tips to Help You Deal with Your Narcissistic Partner

Jennifer cannot believe how self-absorbed her boyfriend, Sam, is.

She used to be inspired by his confidence, but now it comes off as arrogance. Sam seems more than willing to talk about his life, his day at work and his accomplishments and dreams and unwilling to focus any attention on her.

Sometimes, Jennifer feels like Sam continues to date her just so that he has someone to talk about himself with.

Recently, she became aware of just how narcissistic Sam is when her grandmother-- whom she dearly loves-- died. This was a big deal for Jennifer, and she is still feeling a lot of sadness and grief. Other than a, "So sorry to hear the news" from Sam, Jennifer has received little to no support or comfort from him.

This makes her feel even more empty and sad.

Are you in a love relationship or marriage with someone who seems all caught up in him or herself ?

Maybe your partner comes off as arrogant and self-centred. Perhaps your mate can't seem to think or talk about anyone but himself or herself.

If so, you might wonder if your partner is narcissistic.

Being with a narcissistic partner can be painful. You might feel ignored, deficient in some way, irritated, angry and possibly even worried about this apparent personality flaw. You may wonder if your partner needs professional help.

It's true. There is an actual psychological condition called narcissism. It is defined as: "A pattern of traits and behaviours which signify infatuation and obsession with one's self to the exclusion of all others and the egotistic and ruthless pursuit of one's gratification, dominance and ambition."

However, people who appear to be narcissistic may have something else going on. They might not be narcissistic. There is often more to a relationship dynamic than what it appears. For example, your insecurities or fears may cause you to perceive your partner as more self-centred than he or she is.

This doesn't mean that you are wrong and your partner is right or that you don't have valid reasons for how you feel. Not!

What it does mean is that if you want to stay in this relationship and you'd like to experience some improvement around this issue, you're most likely going to need to re-evaluate the situation-- including your role in it.

If you're with a self-absorbed partner, remember these four relationship tips...

#1: Question the labels you're applying.

In the moment-- or in a series of regularly occurring moments-- it may seem obvious to you that your partner is narcissistic. We caution you about applying this label to your partner (or to anyone) without truly understanding what it means.

To throw around labels like this can have real and negative consequences.

By all means, identify what's true for you and how you feel. Figure out what about your partner's words or actions is upsetting to you. It is far more effective to recognize that you feel ignored, for example, than to merely call your partner narcissistic.

Labels CAN be useful if applied accurately and with an intention to better understand.

#2: Get clear about what you want and need.

Recognizing your wants and needs in your relationship is essential. For the moment, focus less on what you find upsetting about your partner's habits and, instead, look at what you truly want from this relationship.

Be specific. If you feel ignored, what would it look like for you to be acknowledged and feel special in your relationship? Take out a piece of paper and a pen and write down what types of activities, conversations and experiences you'd like to share with your partner. How do you want to feel when you are together?

This isn't a demand list for you to present to your partner. It is a way for you to get clear about what your priorities are when it comes to your relationship.

#3: Create agreements with your partner.

Use your list of wants and needs to create agreements with your partner. This is not about presenting ultimatums or making threats to leave (unless you are willing actually to leave).

An agreement needs to be cooperatively reached. Make your agreements specific and ones that each of you is honestly willing to follow through with.

For example, if you feel ignored by your partner, come up with some tangible and meaningful ways that you two can make a connection-- whether it's at home, during the workday, at a party or in some other manner.

Another example of an agreement might be that you you're partner, you or both of you meet with a professional counsellor or coach who can help.

#4: Make decisions about what's in YOUR best interests.

Know that you get to decide what is in your best interests. A relationship is about two people coming together and honestly communicating about needs, but you are the one who ultimately chooses whether or not it's wise for you to stay in the relationship.

If your partner truly is narcissistic and refuses to do anything about it, you might decide that it is unwise for you to stay in this relationship.

Even if the "narcissist" label does not apply to your partner, you might decide that there are no indications that the improvements you seek are going to happen. You may choose to end the relationship because you believe this is an undesirable and possibly unhealthy relationship for you.

What I urge you to remember is that you get to choose. After questioning your beliefs about your partner and yourself, honestly assess whether this is the relationship you want to be in right now.

In Love with a Narcissist? Here's Some Great Relationship Advice for You!

Are you in love with someone who makes you feel like you're on a never-ending roller coaster? Is your husband, wife, boyfriend or girlfriend a bit melodramatic, constantly wanting to be at the centre of attention, a bit manipulative and acting like a spoiled brat? Are you asking yourself, is my relationship over? Then you are probably in a very tough spot -- you are in love with a narcissist. Don't go looking for breakup advice yet. Here are some classic symptoms of a narcissist, and how you can best stay in a relationship with one.

Characteristics of a Narcissist

- Often believing that they're better than others, they express disdain for others who they feel are inferior;

- They are preoccupied with power, success and attractiveness, and believe that others are jealous of them;

- They monopolize conversations and come across as conceited, boastful, or haughty;

- They exaggerate their achievements yet set unrealistic goals;

- They want constant praise and admiration;

- Appearing tough-minded, yet they are easily hurt and rejected;

- They are inconsiderate of other people's emotions and feelings;

- They often take advantage of others to the point of being exploitative.

How to Relate to a Narcissist

If you are in love with a narcissist, no doubt you have been a target of their explosive, obsessive behaviour. It is a difficult position to be in, and it's certainly easy to ask yourself if they are worth it, or when is a relationship over? As previously mentioned, it's not necessary to seek breakup advice. Here is how you can handle a narcissist.

First, give them options. Beneath their tantrums and blow-ups, narcissistic people fear being left out of the loop. What they want is to be always in control. Knowing this fact, you don't want to go to battle with them about decisions. Instead, make them feel respected and in control by offering them options to choose from, rather than bypassing their opinions and making decisions on your own. Always give them the chance to participate.

Second, have you noticed that your partner gets easily agitated when frustrated? Don't they love drama and seem to love the chaos even more? When there's a problem, direct their attention to the solution, not the details of the problem. Let them know what the challenge is, and go straight to the possible solutions. Again, this will direct their focus on the options, rather than getting them worked up about the problem! Want to make them happy? Let them grab the credit for choosing the right solution. Make them think it was their idea in the first place. If you feel uncomfortable about doing this, try it and see how the rewards you reap justify giving them the credit. People will understand - don't worry!

Lastly, go along with the ride. Now that you understand that narcissists lack empathy don't expect them to give you a lot of sympathies when you tell them your feelings, and don't expect a lot of praise from them either. Take them for who they are, and remember that they love power and truly believe they are special and unique. Since they live for attention and admiration, just praise them for their good qualities and show your delight when they do something to show their love for you.

Living with a narcissist is a mixed bag, and sometimes you might feel under-appreciated, overwhelmed, or frustrated by the relationship. But equipped with the right tools and skills, you can make it work. For more great advice about relationships, breakups and making up, please visit my website. You won't be disappointed!

CHAPTER 6
HEALING AND RECOVERING FROM NARCISSISM AND EMOTIONAL ABUSE

Discover Your Level of Narcissism

All of us have some characteristics and behaviours that fall into the category of narcissism. Narcissism is on a continuum from mild, occasional, and subtle to the more ubiquitous, obvious or extreme behaviours of a Narcissistic Personality Disorder. Since narcissism is likely a part of everyone's ego wounded self, it is helpful to your personal growth and development to be aware of your level of narcissism.

Be honest with yourself - but not judgmental - regarding the presence and intensity of the following characteristics:

I generally take others' rejecting, critical, harsh, shut-down, or diminishing behaviour personally. I tell myself that when others choose to behave in uncaring ways toward me, it is my fault - it is about me not being good enough or me doing something wrong. I make others' choices - to be open or closed, loving or unloving - about me.

I frequently judge and shame myself, trying to get myself to do things "right" so that I can have control over getting others' love, attention or approval. Getting others' love, attention and approval are vital to me.

I make others responsible for my worth, value, sense of aliveness and fullness. Others have to be kind, loving, approving of me, or sexually attracted to me, for me to feel that I'm okay. When others ignore me or are not attracted to me, I feel unworthy, depressed or empty inside.

I have a hard time having compassion for myself, so I expect others to have compassion for me when I feel anxious, depressed, angry, shamed or guilty, rather than taking responsibility for my feelings. If others lack compassion for me or criticize me, I turn things around onto them and blame them.

I lack empathy and compassion for the feelings of others, especially when I've behaved in ways that may be hurtful to others. I have a hard time recognizing or identifying with the feelings and needs of others.

When someone offers me valuable information about myself or 'tough love', I see it as an attack, rather than as a gift, and I generally attack back.

The DSM IV - The Diagnostic and Statistical Manual of Mental Disorders, states about people suffering from a Narcissistic Personality Disorder:

"Vulnerability in self-esteem makes individuals with Narcissistic Personality Disorder very sensitive to "injury" from criticism or defeat. Although they may not show it outwardly, criticism may haunt these individuals and may leave them feeling humiliated, degraded, hollow and empty. They may react with disdain, rage, or defiant counterattack. Such experience may lead to social withdrawal or an appearance of humility. Interpersonal relations are typically impaired due to problems derived from entitlement, the need for admiration, and the relative disregard for the sensitivities of others."

When in conflict with someone, or when someone behaves in a way I don't like, I often focus on getting them to deal with what they are doing, rather than focus on what I'm doing. I make them responsible for my choices and feelings, and I believe things will get better if I can get them to change.

I feel entitled to get what I want from others - whether it's money, sex, attention or approval. Others 'owe' me.

I often try to get away with things, such as not having to follow the rules or the law, and I'm indignant when I'm called to the carpet.

I see myself as special and entitled to do what I want, even if it's harmful to others.

I believe I should get credit for what I do and I should be recognized as superior, even if I do a mediocre job.

I am so unique and special that only other unique and special people can understand me. It is beneath me to associate with people who are not as special as I am. While some think I am arrogant, it is only because I'm truly so unique and special.

Because I'm so special, I have the right to demand what I want from others, and to manipulate others - with my charm, brilliance, anger or blame - into giving me what I want.

Again, all of us have some of these characteristics, and it is important to learn about them, rather than judge ourselves for them.

Narcissism can be healed. You can learn to define your worth, to give yourself the love and compassion you need to feel full inside, and to share love with others.

Healing From A Relationship With A Narcissist

Many of us have been there.

You met the person of your dreams - charming, intelligent, romantic, attentive, incredible chemistry and a great lover. You might have been told how wonderful you are, how this was the first time your lover had ever felt this way and had this level of connection, and you felt truly seen for the first time.

Perhaps there was a nagging unease that all this was happening too fast - that he or she couldn't possibly feel this way about you without knowing you better. But you were swept off your feet and finally decided to open your heart.

The confusion may have started then, as your lover pulled away and became critical. Or, it might have started after you married, and you found yourself with a partner different than the person you fell in love with.

Whether your relationship was two months or two years or two decades, it was likely tumultuous, confusing and painful. And if you were married and then divorced, it might have been more painful or even frightening.

There is much healing for you to do if you were in love with a narcissist.

The Process of Healing From Your Narcissistic Partner

1) First, you need to be very compassionate with yourself and let yourself grieve for the huge loss of what you had hoped for. It might seem easier to judge yourself for the big mistakes you believe you made, but self-judgment will keep you stuck. There is no possibility of healing when you judge yourself.

Each time the grief comes up, embrace it with kindness and caring toward yourself. Even though you know it's better to have ended this relationship; it's hard to let go of the intensity of a relationship with a narcissist. It's hard to imagine a future relationship that isn't boring compared to the intensity you've been experiencing.

2) Once some of the grief has subsided, then it's time to go inward and explore why you were vulnerable to this person. Was your partner giving you what you were not giving to yourself? Was your partner seeing you and valuing you in the way you need to be seeing and valuing yourself? Did you ignore some red flags because you so wanted it all to be true?

Did you make excuses for your partner to avoid facing the truth? Did you give yourself up to try to have control over getting your partner to be loving to you again? What did you sacrifice to keep the relationship - your integrity, your financial security, your time with family and friends, your time for yourself, your inner knowing?

It's vitally important to be honest with yourself so that you don't end up feeling like a victim, and so that you have less of a chance of repeating this in a future relationship.

During this time of self-reflection, it's very important to get support. You might want to join a 12-Step CODA group, go into therapy/ facilitation, and join a support group.

3) Educate yourself about narcissism. There are numerous books, websites and articles devoted to understanding narcissism. Since I'm certain that you don't want to repeat this, you need to do all you can to learn about what happened. You need to become sensitive to the numerous red flags so that you can pick them up very early in a subsequent relationship. I have also written several books on empathy and emotional intelligence that could be of great help to you.

One of my clients shared that she had met a man six years ago, dated him a few times, and then they remained distant friends. Recently, when she was in his town, they saw each other, and she was very attracted to him. He came on strong, inviting her to join him on an upcoming European vacation. She felt uneasy, but a day later texted him to see if he wanted to have dinner with her. He never responded to the invitation. It took her only 24 hours to recognize these two red flags of narcissism - coming on strong and then disappearing. She was pleased that she found this out so soon! Instead of beating herself up for being attracted to another narcissist, she congratulated herself for staying open to the truth.

Since narcissists are often very attractive, any of us can become attracted. But whether or not we will pursue it depends on how much Inner Bonding work we have done.

Recovery From Narcissistic Abuse - To Get Your Life Back On Track

Narcissism or Narcissistic Personality Disorder (NPD) is a mental disorder that involves a persistent pattern of grandiosity. The person with this disorder constantly wants to be admired, is obsessed and infatuated with himself. The narcissistic individual also lacks compassion and empathy; is ruthless, egotistical, seeking dominance and gratification. To deal with and to live with a narcissistic can leave someone very traumatized due to the emotional abuse the narcissistic partner has caused. If you were married to a narcissist, you might find that it is difficult to escape from that relationship. If you do escape, your recovery will be long and painful. No matter how difficult the road to recovery is, you have to get through it so that your life will be back on track again.

• You have to know what the qualities of a narcissistic person are. It would include a frequent display of jealousy, infidelity, control, lying, and insecurity, verbal and even physical abuse. If these behaviours are not excused and are often tolerated, it would seem to the narcissistic person that they are acceptable. If you were successful in leaving a narcissistic partner or spouse, he would certainly lure you back again. As much as you love this person, you have to be firm in letting him know that his narcissistic behaviour may only be resolved with the help of a professional. He must seek professional assistance to correct his abusive personality, or he will not change. Being manipulated and believing that your ex will change on his own accord will only bring you back to a miserable and painful life.

• In recovering, you also need to realize that you are your complete person. When you decided to be in a relationship or marry a narcissistic person, you may have already developed a dependency on that person. He may have captured your heart with his attentive, generous and suave personality. This then resulted in your emotional dependency on him that eventually turned out as something for you to regret. Once escaped from the binding relationship with a narcissist, do your best to regain your emotional independence. It will help you to be firm and able to stand again on your own. Learn to love and accept your self-worth. Set your standards for whoever will soon come into your life. Do not accept anyone whose attributes are less than the standards you have set and you know you rightfully deserve.

• You may also look for groups and organizations where you can be a part of. These groups offer help and an opportunity to communicate and interact with other people who have suffered and endured narcissistic relationships. These are the people whom you need to be with, together you can inspire one another and help one another obtain complete recovery and freedom from your experience.

Emotional Abuse - 8 Steps to Recovery

Do you remember the day your partner left you for someone new? That sick sinking feeling in your gut that you just weren't good enough? You tried so hard, and in the end, she was gone and with someone new.

At first, the silence was deafening, and you were so lonely, so very lonely. How could she be in love with you one day and love with someone else the next? You called. You texted. You just needed answers, but never got any response. You wanted a second chance to prove you could be better, but after a while, this passed, too, and you thought you were going to finally make it through the heartache.

You decide you don't want anything more to do with her and stop trying to contact her. BUT, now all those emotions are flooding back, and you just want to cry out in frustration after getting ANOTHER text, call or email from your ex. She hasn't heard from you in a while and misses you. She wants to get together, and so you do. She never really explains why she cheated or why she came back. She's just back, and you are on cloud nine... for a few months. Then the same thing happens again.

And here you are again, alone and still in love with the same person who "claimed" the breakup was your fault, that you weren't good enough. She's again ignoring your calls and texts wanting an explanation for why she walked out? The same person who was just posting all over Facebook about the "new" love in her life? And just like before, once you start to come out of the fog and start thinking it's over, all of a sudden, she wants you back? Do you feel trapped in a never-ending cycle of abuse, like a washing machine - rinse, spin, repeat, rinse, spin, repeat.

When you are together, does she make you feel like you are walking on eggshells, praying you don't do anything to upset her? Do you ignore or avoid calling her out on the hurtful things she says or does because you fear that every argument is your last? Does she constantly put you down and make you feel inferior to her? Have you stopped speaking to family and friends since you two have been together?

Wasn't this the same person who called you her soul mate? Do you remember she talked about her ex when you first got together? How crazy and jealous her ex was, and how glad she was to have found you. She told you that you were her soul mate.

Do you fall for her lies again, thinking you can recapture the early period of your relationship, when she was good and caring and kind? I don't like being the bearer of bad news, but I have to tell you, you're in relationship hell, stuck on a roller coaster, and to save yourself, you have to get away from this narcopath, who is nothing more than an emotional vampire.

Here's some hard-learned information. When you are desperately texting and calling to get "closure" by having your questions answered, you are feeding her energy. She thrives on this behaviour from you. It makes her feel powerful. She loves telling her new flame and all her friends how crazy psycho you are now. But, when you finally realize it's over, and stop calling and texting, guess what? She's not getting that supply of energy she is addicted to so much, and she thinks she's about to lose a great source of supply, so she starts calling and texting you. KNOW THIS: No normal person truly in love does this sort of thing. She is hovering - a term used to describe a narcopath who feels like you may be slipping away from her death grip.

It's imperative that you have no contact with this person. Even when she plays on your guilt or uses shame to trick you into "just talking to her", don't fall for it. Make yourself think like she thinks when you are dealing with her. She has no conscience or q ualms about hurting you, so you take on the same attitude. It will continue, and the no contact may very well send her into a narcissistic rage. It doesn't matter what she does, stick to no contact.

In recovering from the emotional and verbal abuse of your former partner, here are eight steps you need to take to prepare yourself not to break the no contact rule:

1. Recognize that your love for this person is REAL. Ignoring this fact only sets you up for more abuse;

2. Recognize that this person lied to you, tricked you into falling in love. Think about it for a second. Had you met the person you are with now, would you have gone on a second date? Hell, no. It was an act, only an act. A narcopath is incapable of experiencing real emotion like love, empathy, compassion, guilt, etc. The only emotion I believe they feel is anger, and I'm sure you've seen the irrational rage common with narcopaths;

3. Accept the fact you will never get the answers to the burning questions you have;

4. Accept that the dream she promised was a lie;

5. Accept the fact that you can only change yourself, you cannot change her, and despite promises of change she always makes to get you to come back, she will not change;

6. Once you have internalized the first four steps, then you are ready to commit yourself to have absolutely no contact with her whatsoever. If you have children together, then limit the contact to ONLY discussions about the children;

7. Find a therapist to talk to. If you aren't comfortable talking to anyone face-to-face, then join a members-only site that offers advice and counselling; and finally

8. Find activities that help you restore your self-worth, your self-confidence and your joy. Colour therapy is an excellent activity for opening up your mind to new ideas and focusing on colouring puts you in a positive state of mind. EBT is good if you understand how it's done.

Best Tips to Recover From Narcissistic Abuse

How to heal from emotional abuse starts by recognizing that you have a problem. Even if you have already severed ties from an abusive relationship, it doesn't mean that everything will just go back to being alright.

There is an invisible energy stream that still exists between you and your previous abusive partner. It prevents you from being able to move forward with your life as you still unconsciously carry the emotional burden caused by the narcissist. You need to actively work from separating yourself in mind and soul to be able to break free from it. You will soon learn how as you continue to read along.

It is very helpful to regard yourself as a survivor and a winner instead of a victim. It immediately empowers you and gives you back control of your life. Here are some tips on how to heal from emotional abuse:

Understand that it's not your fault

Once you can find comfort in the fact that it's not your fault, you will begin to realize that you are not the cause of negative experiences you have gone through as opposed to what your abuser made you believe.

Confide in a close friend or relative

The people you trust will be able to provide you with the love and support at this critical time of healing. Talking about what you have gone through will help you better understand and accept your experience of abuse.

Discover coping tools

Find out what helps you express your emotions, release anger or grief. Writing in a journal, composing poems or songs, painting, any sport or playing a musical instrument can help you cope and let out your feelings. It will aid you in taking your mind off the pain you suffered and replace it with good and happy memories.

Take care of yourself

Learn to look after yourself first before taking care of others. Believe that you are worthy of respect, love and acceptance just like everybody else. Take pride in your unique qualities and improve on your weaknesses. You have to have faith in yourself first before other people do.

CODEPENDENCY CYCLE RECOVERY

Be Codependent No More and Recover Your Self-Esteem NOW, Cure Your Soul from Emotional Abuse - Stop Being Manipulated and Controlled by Narcissists and Sociopaths

By

DANIEL ANDERSON

By reading this document, the reader agrees that under no circumstances is the author responsible for any losses, direct or indirect, which are incurred as a result of the use of information contained within this document, including, but not limited to, — errors, omissions, or inaccuracies.

TABLE OF CONTENT

CHAPTER 1
UNDERSTANDING CODEPENDENCY

What Is Codependency?

Codependence (or codependency) is usually defined as a behavior where an individual exhibits too much, and often inappropriate, caring for persons who depend on him or her. Another term associated with being "codependent" is enabling. In other words, being codependent is enabling the destructive behavior of an individual close to you to continue. It can also mean an individual may rely on the emotions and opinions of others around them to determine how they feel about themselves.

There are many things to consider before labeling yourself an enabler or codependent. No one should consider him or herself an enabler or codependent without first honestly reviewing their situation and environment. Being compassionate, sympathetic or empathetic to a suffering individual's predicament does not necessarily mean you are an enabler or a codependent. If you, by chance, are allowing an active alcoholic to live in your house free of charge while you pay the bills and this has gone on for a while now, well, you may be codependent. The reason being is you are enabling them to continue their destructive behaviors toward themselves and you. Taking little to none of the appropriate action to help a sick individual get well is a good sign of co-dependence.

One drawback many codependents experience is self-identification. If the destructive behavior has gone on for years, they may find themselves subconsciously sabotaging the sick individual's chances of getting better. A common fear is, "If they get better, what will happen to me? I won't be needed anymore." The disease of alcoholism and drug addiction is sometimes called a family disease because of all the people it affects. To some degree, everyone who lives with or is close to an active alcoholic or drug addict is sick. Years of destructive and sporadic behaviors of the alcoholic or drug addict will make a sick person out of anyone. Nearly no one is immune, employers, friends, coworkers, and especially the immediate family members.

Another situation for a codependent may be the result of being raised by an active alcoholic or drug addict. Usually what happens for the codependent in this scenario is they are overwhelming dependent on the actions, emotions, and opinions of others (such as a parent) to identify who they are. They are, in a sense, grown to believe they are incapable of living a successful life and usually suffer from extremely low self-esteem and possibly depression or other psychological disorders.

Codependent then implies that one is dependent psychologically on one who is dependent on a substance, behavior or another thing.

Codependents are those amongst us who worry obsessively about others. Most codependents were emotionally abused as children. They were made to feel psychologically invisible, and very often suffered various forms of abuse, including physical, sexual, verbal or psychological. The consistent theme amongst codependents is that they can think for others, but not for themselves.

Codependents pair off in relationships. It is not possible to have a codependent relationship with one who is not codependent. Noncodependents do not appreciate feeling smothered, overly relied upon for their partner's sense of satisfaction, and do not enjoy empty praise.

Codependents tend to whine and complain rather than act on their behalf. They complain about how sorry they feel for themselves and wallow on sounding as if they prefer the world see them as the martyrs they falsely believe that they are.

On a deep unconscious level, codependents are manipulators who are seeking a sense of validation from others. They manipulate others by their insatiable need to please others. In the pleasing of others, the codependent is in search of a return. The return is the notion that the object of their attention now 'owes' them. The object of the codependents attention is seen as a source of a much-needed sense of self.

Codependents do not cope well. Because they do not understand how to nurture their self, and because their childhood wounds are very deep, codependents are blind to the idea that their intentions are skewed and manipulative. Because in their minds they view themselves as being one who is giving, they are unable to see the error of their manipulative ways.

Codependents are flustered souls, who ultimately wind up feeling exasperated. Nothing that they thought might help them feel loved has worked. They have smothered others to the point of draining the ones that they loved, and wind up blaming others for their inability to love the codependent no matter how hard the codependent tries to love them.

One solution for someone who is suffering from codependency and would like to learn how to live without it is to attend some type of group support meetings. There, an individual can find freedom from the years of negative programming they experienced as a child, teenager or adult.

Understanding Codependency

The term codependency was originally coined by researchers studying the dynamics of alcohol addiction in families. It became clear to those who worked with alcoholics and their families that there was a very unhealthy two-way dependency created when a family member was addicted to alcohol.

Since then the term codependency has been expanded and used to describe almost any type of relationship where the dependent partner may be physically and psychologically dependent or addicted to a substance or may have chronic emotional, physical or financial problems.

The codependent partner tries to control the relationship. To keep the relationship from changing the codependent partner takes charge of the dependent partner by making excuses, hiding destructive behaviors, pitying him/her and generally enabling the dysfunctional pattern to continue.

A codependent person is someone who often shows excessive or even inappropriate caring for the dependent person. Both partners "need" each other in an unhealthy, symbiotic way.

Codependent people will often come from families where their personal needs were secondary to the needs of the family. The family may have been dealing with an addiction or some other difficult chronic problem. Codependents are somehow made to feel responsible for other family members who depend on them in an unhealthy way. They learn to repress their feelings and serve mainly to comfort and care for someone else.

As adults, codependent people are at greater risk to form relationships with others who are needy or emotionally unavailable. The familiar feeling of denying one's own emotions for the sake of someone else's is a strong pull towards repeating the early family dynamic.

Once they enter into a relationship codependents will feel that their controlling behavior is in the best interest of the family. They are convinced that the survival of the family depends on their taking control. Unfortunately, they are often doomed to feel unfulfilled and dissatisfied with the relationship and themselves.

The codependent is, in essence, living his/her life through another. The sense of personal identity, of actually discovering who you are, is sacrificed unwittingly for a compulsive and repetitive learned behavior. The feeling of being consumed by another's needs often leads to depression.

Loss of self occurs when I need your approval and lose the opportunity to think my thoughts and to feel my feelings. I start to live the eternal life instead of internal life. I become outer-directed and not inner-directed, and over time the space inside becomes less and less. I feel less than, and my self-esteem is diminished. I look to you to define me, to direct me, to approve of me, to fix me and, lose more and more of me until I feel empty. What develops is the false self, and that is codependency.

When I focus on getting your approval, I lose the approval of self, which is the power that self-esteem gives me. In losing my power, I lose me. I lose my voice. I lose me.

Loss of self occurs when I am focused on fixing, helping, understanding, caretaking you and not on caring about me. For me to not lose self, I need to care about you, not for you. My job is to care about me. I need to feel with you, not for you. You are responsible for feeling your feelings not me. I need to be responsible to you as my parent, spouse, child, or friend, not be responsible for you. I am responsible for me and to you and, you are responsible for you and to me. If we can do this in a relationship than both of us, have the opportunity to mature and to develop a sense of self.

Loss of self occurs when I say "no" when I mean, "yes" and when I say, "yes" when I mean "no." Of course, this sounds confusing, and the codependent often does feel confused, indecisive, and rattled. One can understand why! It is a lifetime of guessing what somebody else needs and wants and over time, the codependent forgets who he or she is. The sense of self is not developed. The individual does learn what he or she needs, wants, feels and the struggle of discovery is absent. Gradually, initially, however, bit by bit, little by little, year by year, the erosion occurs. It is not even the erosion; instead, it is the not building of self, so a double loss is occurring. You miss the journey. Giving out and not putting in is a bad investment whether it is about finances or relationships.

Loss of self is learned helplessness. Reinforced codependent behaviors do not serve me well, nor do they serve others well. Codependent relationship dynamics create and foster dependency for both individuals. It is a no-win dynamic. It is not about individual or relationship building. I cannot give up me and think there can be we. An "I" is needed for a "We" to exist.

Loss of self creates a victim mentality — a victim who cannot see how he or she has built his or her prison. Denial, anger, shame, guilt, passivity, fear, and sadness and often depression, are the bars of this prison. The wounded child and critical parent are present, and the adult ego state has yet to be built.

Loss of self affects the family members and friends of the codependent. Often, the codependent moves from one crisis to the next and others suffer. Denial is a core symptom for the loss of self. Codependent thinking is if I do not see it, acknowledge it, believe it, then it does not exist.

- Are you codependent? Do you have loss of self?

- Do I care for you instead of about you?

- Do I own responsibility for you and not to you?

- Do I need your approval and do not know my mind?

- Do I think for you and do not know my thoughts?

- Do I have appropriate emotional boundaries with you?

- Do I practice emotional detachment with you?

- Do I feel and act like a victim in relationships?

- Do I have low self-esteem?

- Do I repress feelings and have a wall of denial around me and in my relationships?

Codependency is real. It exists within self and relationships. Loss of self occurs as we have just described and it is destructive to self and others. A closing thought is when there is not enough of me for me; surely there cannot be enough of me to share with you. Codependency kills. Codependency is a loss of self. If after reading this article, you see yourself as codependent then reach out for help.

Codependency - Who Am I without Others?

When you find yourself obsessed with someone, walking on eggshells to keep someone you care about from leaving or trying to figure out how to keep someone safe from themselves, you may be experiencing signs of codependency. Codependency is an uneasy kind of love where one's true feelings and needs become secondary to someone else's. It often results in unhappiness, frustration, and exhaustion instead of closeness and understanding.

What is the difference between codependency and just caring a lot about someone? I define codependency as the habit of avoiding oneself by focusing on another person. When one has a codependent relationship, healthy love, respect and trust are compromised. If a codependent pattern has gone too far, establishing an important relationship on better footing may seem almost impossible.

Codependency is often a pattern that develops over time, so it can be hard to see. It is also reinforced by occasional payoffs - both on the conscious and unconscious levels. Conscious payoffs may include feeling needed and useful. And you need not feel alone, even when you are because that other person is on your mind. Other conscious payoffs may include the experiences of infatuation or drama, which can give rise to feelings of romance or excitement that one might be afraid would otherwise pass them by.

Unconscious roots of codependency run deeper. Sometimes, people develop codependency as a life-long strategy of handling fear and trauma by focusing on others. In some families, about the only positive attention a child gets is when they are useful and undemanding. As adults, these people often end up caretaking others beyond what is useful to either person. A person who is frequently criticized and judged at any age can become vulnerable to believing that they are not worthy of their support and attention. These are just a few of codependency's causes.

Ultimately, the worst thing about codependency is that it puts you in the backseat of your own life.

To be in the backseat of one's own life means that one's natural talents and abilities may not be fully realized or even recognized. Because codependency is draining, codependent people may find that they do not have the energy or confidence they need to carry out personal goals, including finding the kind of love they deserve. The habit of focusing too much on others means that ultimately, a person will miss taking charge of the only thing anyone can take charge of - their own life.

If you think you may have codependent leanings, you are not alone. If you feel stuck in codependent patterns with someone you care about, there is a silver lining: because codependency is a habitual state, it can be changed. Although this self-stifling pattern may not dissolve overnight, there are many tools available if you are serious about freeing yourself from it.

First, it is very important that you find supportive people that you can trust to help you break the codependency habit. To try to break this kind of habit just by reading about it is like trying to learn to swim without getting into the water. Find supportive friends and family with whom to talk. Also, it can be helpful to work with a therapist who understands codependency to develop a greater understanding of not only what you want to change but how you plan to get there. You may also want to attend group therapy, or try 12-step groups like Co-dependents Anonymous (CoDA) or Al-Anon. Groups like these can be motivating because you will find people there who are already working on issues similar to yours.

Here are some other tools to help you to free yourself of codependency:

* Keep a journal. Write about what you are grateful for, what you want out of your life, and what is stopping you. Self-focus is easier when you can see your thoughts on paper.

* Pleasing yourself has its reward. Remember what activities or hobbies you like and do them - even if no one else in your life wants to do them with you.

 * Become more aware of your inner world. Take time from your day to contemplate and meditate. If you remember your dreams at night, write them down.

 * Take a relationship inventory. Who in your current life makes a better or a worse person out of you when you are with them? You don't have to be someone's friend just because they want you to be. Seek out people who help you to grow inwardly.

 * Stop "enabling" others. If someone you are helping is not improving, check in with yourself. How do you feel - are you worried or resentful? Are you "help" really helping?

 * Avoid the payoffs of codependency, such as approval for doing more than your share, or getting sucked into drama and infatuation. These are inner enemies. Note what feelings different people and places bring up for you.

 * When you find you are obsessed, take time and space away from the person or thing you are obsessed with. Setting interpersonal boundaries can help to put your focus back on yourself. Generally, others will respect you more for it as well.

 * Develop a sense of spirituality. This can be as simple as appreciating nature, focusing on a hobby or talking to a wise person. Developing a concept of having a higher power within yourself that has answers for you is also helpful.

The most important tool in all of this is that you think well of yourself. This may feel awkward or even like you are just pretending at first. It is critically important to making progress. One of the most heartbreaking things is to watch a codependent person trying so hard to fix things, only to fail and then turn on themselves. People can treat themselves much more harshly than anyone else would. Codependency and low-self-esteem go hand in hand so let go of that inner voice that says you can't change. The beginning of recovery can be just as simple as allowing oneself to begin to see what is good and true about oneself.

Codependency - Being Dependent on Other's Dependency

You take care of others; you help, you go out of your way for...but when do you cross the line from being a compassionate friend or partner or family member to being "codependent"? There may not be a simple test or a clear marker, but if you consistently put someone else's needs first, to the detriment of your own, you may be codependent with your friend or partner, etc. This pattern may be an example of enabling - your behavior helps maintain someone else's destructive or dependent behavior.

A simple example of enabling might be your calling in sick for your husband when he is too hungover to go to work. Codependency may be a justification for allowing yourself to be mistreated based on your low self-esteem - your sense that you don't deserve better. On one end of the continuum, examples might be remaining in a relationship that doesn't support you or your personal growth, while on end, codependency might mean not being able to leave a relationship, even when you are being abused emotionally and physically.

Codependency involves behaviors that go above and beyond normal caretaking behaviors, or the everyday kind of self-sacrificing that happens within relationships. Some examples that are common in people who struggle with codependency include:

Denial patterns, such as having difficulty identifying your feelings, or minimizing how you feel;

Low self-esteem patterns, such as judging yourself harshly and believing you are never good enough or feeling unable to ask others for help;

Compliance patterns, such as compromising your values and integrity to avoid rejection, or staying in harmful situations for too long; and

Control patterns, which include believing that others are incapable of taking care of themselves, or need to be needed to have a relationship with others.

It is important to note that there are criticisms of the label "codependent." For example, caring for an individual with an addiction is not necessarily synonymous with pathology. To name the caregiver as a codependent responsible for the endurance of their partner's negative behaviors can pathologize caring behavior. You may only require assertiveness skills and the ability to place responsibility for negative behaviors on the other person. Also, when this idea is pathologized, the codependent person may swing from an extreme of excessive sacrifice to an extreme of excessive assertiveness or selfishness and an aversion to empathy, which is a positive human capacity. A healthy approach would be to develop a sense of balanced and healthy assertiveness, which still leaves room for caring and helping.

Tendencies and behaviors that can be identified as codependent frequently emerge from a childhood in a dysfunctional family; perhaps one or both parents were alcoholic or had some other profound problems, so these patterns have deep roots. For this reason, codependency may show up in a wide range of your relationships including work relationships and friendships. Some people find 12-step groups such as Al-Anon/Alateen or Codependents Anonymous helpful, although some people do not. Therapy can be a useful tool to help you understand the complexities associated with these patterns and to help you balance your own needs against those of others.

Codependence in Your Life

People that are codependent have grown up in homes in which their parents relied too heavily on each other for emotional support. They watched in disgust as their parents cheated on each other and mistreated each other in other ways. They stayed together long past the point when they should have called it quits. From this experience, the child learned that they were incapable of making it as a healthy and independent adult. The codependent unconsciously think they can't make it without a mate, they are worthless without a mate, and that they are not good enough, along with a host of other negative thoughts. Consciously, they may vow not to become their parents.

The codependent and their love relationships

These people are drawn to relationships that start hot and heavy. Because of their strong need to bond with another individual, they often get seriously involved early on in the relationship. Their mate, who is usually also a codependent, is always available, loving, and affectionate in the beginning. This is a dream come true for the codependent who constantly craves attention. This is until they begin to feel suffocated by their mate's possessive and jealous personality. They take up all their free time and isolate them from their friends and family. Their mate may demand too much not only emotionally, but also financially and mentally as well. The codependent thinks they are in love, although they soon become miserable, lonely, and depressed. To other people, it may appear that this couple is in love because of the amount of time they spend together and the length of time the relationship can continue. If they should split apart, they soon get back together. Healthy men can be attracted to the dependent personality. However, they are just as quickly turned off by their clingy personality and disappear, or they may stick around to take advantage of their generous ways.

Codependents and their interaction with family and friends

But, they tend to be very self-absorbed. They ignore other people's wants and needs to get what they want and need. They are short-term thinkers who constantly seek instant gratification. The codependent doesn't mean to hurt anyone. But, they are often too involved with holding on to their waning relationship to give their family and friends the love and attention they deserve. Their family will always be here, they may be thinking, but they may secretly know their relationship will not be. It is also a possibility that they are too ashamed of who they have become within their relationship to show their face. If the codependent is not involved in a love relationship, they may behave similarly with their family and friends. They may keep too close of an eye on their children and prevent them from hanging out with their friends. They may seem to be mean, but they are desperate not to be alone. When hanging out with their friends, the codependent may get upset when their friends invite someone else along. They can also be too loyal to their friends.

When the codependent tries to become more independent

Once the codependent tries to stand on their own two feet, their mate may become afraid that they will get left behind. Desperate to hold on, they may become violent, verbally abusive, and manipulative. Sometimes codependents halt their growth because they are afraid they will outgrow there mate or because they are afraid to start over.

Codependents at work

It can be hard for the codependent to function at work due to their constantly changing emotions. And, because of the tumultuous nature of their relationship, they often have to quit coming to work or call out often due to family emergencies. Without an attachment, they are very capable of doing a good job at work and making wise decisions. However, they tend to allow themselves to be mistreated by their coworkers and supervisors and they may neglect to ask for raises or promotions because of their self-esteem issues.

Codependence: The Flip Side to Narcissism

The flip side to Narcissism is Codependence. Some codependent traits include A lack of self-direction; looking for reassurance, encouragement or approval before you take on a task or set out to achieve a goal for yourself, often seeking this from people the least likely to give you this support. You feel responsible for other people's feelings or bad moods. You expect your loved ones to guess or interpret your needs when you are upset rather than communicate them directly.

The most common cause of Codependency is growing up with a childish parent. Codependency traits may begin when a child is expected to become caretaker to an emotionally demanding or needy parent where they were made responsible for keeping their parent(s) happy. If either of your parents were irresponsible, childish, an alcoholic, a gambler, unfaithful or abusive, you may have learned Codependency to survive. You may have been made to feel special for taking care of them and being treated more like an adult than a child, but this was at the expense of your own emotional needs and development.

This role may have won you a special favor, but probably felt very uncomfortable. A child's needs and personality have little room for expression or growth in this kind of relationship. You also may have learned some unhealthy ideas about happiness and personal goals.

If you have Codependent tendencies, narcissistic behavior will be extremely confusing and hurtful for you to live with. You probably grew up working hard to please people and confusing this for love. A person who once loved you, but is now irresponsible and points to you as the cause of their problems inflicts an incredible amount of confusion and emotional pain.

But you don't have to stay Codependent forever! There are strategies and tools to start you on having healthier, happier and more satisfying relationships.

Codependency and How It Affects Individuals

A common definition of codependency usually comprises the kind that often affects romantic relationships. One partner will do everything he or she can to please his or her partner, while the spouse takes advantage of these actions to the point of getting the codependent partner bend over backward, sacrificing his or her health, emotion, and income. If left neglected, the codependent partner may grow other dreadful side effects, such as anxiety state, PTSD, depressive disorders, or suicidal tendency. Another definition of codependency involves controlling codependents. Controlling codependents feel they must control the lives of others by dictating their every move. Typical signs of controlling codependents include determining for the other spouse where to go, what to eat, or what to put on. Often he or she will not allow the partner to visit family and friends.

Controlling codependents usually feel that they must manage everything because their partner wouldn't be able to function without them. While the definition of codependency frequently falls under romantic relationships, the fact of the matter is that you may also notice it in platonic relationships also. Quite often the relationships between parents and child are codependent as well. A common example of this includes parents who always sacrifice for their child's every choice to the point where it compromises their health or sanity. As stated by the definition of codependency, these intuitions often stem from childhood abuse in dysfunctional families. Once their parents exhibit neglect or cruelty, children learn to try and predict what their parents choose. This is a defense process that can significantly affect relationships when they grow up. If the definition of codependency sounds familiar, it's time to consider getting help. Institutions such as Codependents Anonymous are excellent for aiding you through this distressing situation. Their twelve phase program allows you to test yourself and your relationship toward others in a manner that will help you to learn why you behave the way you do. Counseling and group therapy are other alternatives you can think about. The truth of the matter is that you don't need to live through these problems alone. By getting help and overcoming your codependency, you will be doing your part to live a healthier, fuller life. Learn more today!

CHAPTER 2
CHARACTERISTICS AND SYMPTOMS OF CODEPENDENT PEOPLE

Are You Codependent?

Do you wonder if you are Codependent? Do you regularly sacrifice your opinions, needs or wants, and then feel resentful? Do you feel guilty saying no and resentful when you don't? Are you controlled by, or try to control someone else, whom your thoughts and feelings revolve around, as in the Barry Manilow song, "I'm glad when you're glad, sad when you're sad?" Are you afraid of speaking up? Resentment, guilt, control, and fear are the hallmarks of codependency; a term once used only to describe the enabler of an alcoholic is now more generally applied to an unhealthy dependency.

Melody Beattie in Codependent No More describes a codependent as: "A person who has let someone else's behavior affect him or her and is obsessed with controlling other people's behavior." John Bradshaw, author of Healing the Shame that Binds You, says, "Internalized shame is the core of codependency." Expert and author of numerous books, Earnie Larsen define it as: "Self-defeating, learned behaviors or character defects that result in a diminished capacity to initiate, or participate in, loving relationships." In Facing Codependence, Pia Melody writes, "Two key areas of a person's life reflect codependence: the relationship with the self and relationship with others."

The seeds of codependence are in childhood, when a child has no choice but to accommodate a parent who is controlling, selfish, depressed, addicted, or abusive. Such children don't get the sense that their wants or needs matter. The family may be one of addiction or neglect, where children take on parental responsibilities and lose touch with themselves in the process. On the other hand, a family may seem perfect. The parents give their children the best of everything, but they expect perfection or adhere to rigid rules and beliefs, leaving no room for individuality and self-expression to flourish.

Codependents usually do all the giving in relationships. Caring and helping others is fine, but if it's at the expense of oneself, or if you don't believe you have a choice - that it would be selfish not to, or you'd risk losing the relationship - then care to take is not just a behavior, it's an identity and source of self-worth. Alice has a big heart and a string of failed relationships. When she likes a man, she gives more than she gets. She helps her them with whatever their problem is. The men take her for granted or feel smothered and eventually leave.

Codependents learn in childhood to attune to the needs and moods of a parent, so much so that they usually don't know what they want or need. Others' needs, desires, and definition of reality take precedence over their own. Sometimes, they don't even know what they think or feel and have difficulty describing themselves. When asked, they shift to talking about family members or their job.

A codependent conversation sounds like this:

Him: "Where would you like to eat?"

Her: "What do you feel like?"

Him: "Whatever you want."

Her: "Do you feel like Chinese?"

Him: "Do you? Would you like Italian?"

You get the picture. Neither person will assert a position. No one will take responsibility for a choice. Maybe, one doesn't want to dine out and rather watch a TV show, but doesn't want to disappoint the other, or is ashamed to admit they can't afford it. Other times, neither knows what he or she wants. Sometimes, an argument starts. It's impossible to problem-solve or compromise if you don't take a position. Issues and feelings are avoided, problems don't get resolved, and resentment builds.

Codependents frequently become obsessed with another person. Their thoughts, motives, and actions begin to revolve around someone else instead of their feelings and goals. Cindy was preoccupied with Nick's health. She oversaw his diet, managed the marketing, and gave him nutrition articles, oblivious to her own health problems.

Codependents may try to control others' feelings and reactions with gifts or flattery, like "buttering up" to be loved, to get what they want, or to keep the peace. They give with an expectation, and when it's not fulfilled, they are not only hurt but also resentful and feel owed. Healthy giving is for the pure joy of it. Because their boundaries weren't respected as children, codependents don't set functional limits with themselves and others. They may be overly invested in someone else's problem or work long hours on the job to the detriment of their family or themselves. They never say no. They may have been taught that it's selfish or "un-Christian" to assert their will, and don't notice that someone else doesn't mind using up their time and resources. Jane was an accomplished landscape designer, but underbid her projects and spent many uncompensated hours with customers who gabbed away or changed their minds. She was always running behind and resented that she felt constantly pulled by her customers' demands. To her, charging more and setting boundaries was unthinkable.

In an organization, a codependent works harder for less and maybe the "go to" person who'll take the unwanted assignments. Another may be a martyr at home, never asking for help and never heeding her own needs for rest and rejuvenation. Both get satisfaction in being needed and relied upon, but eventually at a price. These women believe they won't be valued if they don't do extra work. Underneath they fear to lose a client, job, or relationship.

Sometimes, one partner appears more needy and dependent, because he or she is possessive, jealous, calls frequently, or constantly seeks reassurance and attention. However, the other partner is also codependent by allowing him or herself to be controlled by these unreasonable demands.

Low-self-esteem is characteristic of codependence. Childhood experiences and messages imprint feelings of being unlovable or unworthy. Codependents are hard on themselves. They push and judge themselves, and often are high-achievers and perfectionists. This sets them up to be in an abusive relationship or one where their needs are not met. They'll tolerate it even despite being attractive, smart, or successful at work because underneath they believe they don't deserve better.

Pointers of Codependency

Codependency usually comes about as your response to another person's chemical dependency. It revolves around your relationships with the people in your life. It involves the effects these people have on you. You, in turn, then try to affect them and their behaviors. As you begin to see them spiraling out of control, you end up trying to control their behavior.

The soul of codependency lays in you, though, not the other person. It is a silent war you begin within yourself. Usually, it develops from low self-esteem. The codependent person does not feel worthy. It is a dysfunctional relationship with the self. Because you live a dysfunctional relationship internally, it manifests externally to others. You don't love yourself, and you don't trust yourself either. You tend to be out of balance and out of harmony. You may feel disconnected. You tend to live life in a reactor mode and give your power over to outside sources.

Chemical dependency is recognized as a disease. Codependency may not be recognized in the same means, but it can make you sick and will not help you or your loved one start on the road to recovery. Codependency is a progressive state. As things around you get steadily worse, your reactions to those things become more intense. In the back of your mind, you may think you are helping the other person. You may have the best intentions. As you see it, they are destroying themselves. You don't realize that the characteristics

334

you portray as a response to their behavior not only sabotage your relationship with that person but sabotage yourself.

Codependents feel obligated to offer unwanted advice to help the other person solve what you see as their problems. You feel responsible for the other person. Somewhere wrapped up in that process you are trying to please others. You want them to see you as necessary in their lives. You want them to see how essential you are to their well being. You will even abandon your routine to help the other person.

When your help is either brushed off or not effective the way, you thought it would be you become angry. You blame others for the spot you are in. You blame others for making you feel the way you do. You feel unappreciated, used and you become a victim. Over time you learn how to endure it. You live with the anxiety, the hurt, and the anger.

If these signs sound familiar, there is a help. Once you have determined that these feelings and tendencies in no way help you or the other person, you must focus on correcting your inclination towards codependency. First, accept that we all are responsible for our feelings and actions. Do not be afraid to let the other person live their life, to live with the consequences they create. Love the person and be there for them, but do not try to control or manipulate the outcome of their behavior. It may be hard at first, but they too have a lesson to learn that you will not always be there to bail them out of their bad choices.

Second, realize that you are worthy of being loved. Don't center your life on other people thinking that you don't deserve happiness too. Stop looking at relationships to provide you all your good feelings. Look within you and start loving yourself. Then others around you will see the radiance you exhibit and will gravitate toward you.

Third, begin to focus on your own life. You have probably let it slide to the wayside. Look for your happiness within yourself, not outside towards others. Think about your passions and what makes you happy. Then start to concentrate on the steps you can take to start living a joyful life.

You may be codependent, but know that you are a strong people. You have just mistakenly focused your attention toward the wrong thing. You have the power to change and to start recovery. That will let you be who you are while letting the other person be who they are.

Symptoms of Codependency

The term codependency has been around for almost four decades. Although it originally applied to spouses of alcoholics, first called co-alcoholics, research revealed that the characteristics of codependents were much more prevalent in the general population than had been imagined. They found that if you were raised in a dysfunctional family or had an ill parent, it's likely that you're codependent. Don't feel bad if that includes you. Most families in America are dysfunctional, so that covers just about everyone, you're in the majority! They also found that codependent symptoms got worse if untreated, but the good news was that they were reversible.

Here's a list of symptoms. You needn't have all of them to qualify as codependent.

Low self-esteem

Not feeling that you're good enough or comparing yourself to others is a sign of low self-esteem. The tricky thing about self-esteem is that some people think highly of themselves, but it's only a camouflage for really feeling unlovable or inadequate. Underneath, usually hidden from consciousness, are feelings of shame. Some of the things that go along with low self-esteem are guilt feelings and perfectionism. If everything is perfect, you don't feel bad about yourself.

People pleasing

It's fine to want to please someone you care about, but codependents usually don't think they have a choice. Saying "No" causes them anxiety. Some codependents have a hard time saying "No" to anyone. They go out of their way and sacrifice their own needs to accommodate other people.

Poor Boundaries

Boundaries are sort of an imaginary line between you and others. It divides up what's yours and somebody else's, and that applies not only to your body, money, and belongings but also to your feelings, thoughts, and needs. That's especially where codependents get into trouble. They have blurry or weak boundaries between themselves and others. They feel responsible for other people's feelings and problems or blame their own on someone else.

Some codependents have rigid boundaries. They are closed off and withdrawn, making it hard for other people to get close to them. Sometimes, people flip back and forth between having weak boundaries and rigid ones.

Reactivity

A consequence of poor boundaries is that you react to everyone's thoughts and feelings. If someone says something you disagree with, you either believe it or become defensive. You absorb their words because there's no boundary. With a boundary, you'd realize it was just their opinion and not a reflection of you and not feel threatened by disagreements.

Caretaking

Another effect of poor boundaries is that if someone else has a problem, you want to help them to the point that you give up yourself. It's natural to feel empathy and sympathy for someone, but codependents start putting other people ahead of themselves. They need to help and might feel rejected if another person doesn't want help. Moreover, they keep trying to help and fix the other person, even when that person isn't taking their advice.

Control

Control helps codependents feel safe and secure. Everyone needs some control over events in their life. You wouldn't want to live in constant uncertainty and chaos, but for codependents, control limits their ability to take risks and share their feelings. Sometimes they have an addiction that either helps them loosen up, like alcoholism, or helps them hold their feelings down, like workaholism so that they don't feel out of control.

Codependents also need to control those close to them, because they need other people to behave in a certain way to feel okay. People pleasing and caretaking can be used to control and manipulate people. Alternatively, codependents are bossy and tell you what you should or shouldn't do. This is a violation of someone else's boundary.

Dysfunctional communication

Codependents have trouble when it comes to communicating their thoughts, feelings, and needs. Of course, if you don't know what you think, feel or need, this becomes a problem. Other times, you know, but you won't own up to your truth. You're afraid to be truthful because you don't want to upset someone else. Instead of saying, "I don't like that," you might pretend that it's okay or tell someone what to do. Communication becom es dishonest and confusing when you try to manipulate the other person out of fear.

Obsessions

Codependents tend to spend their time thinking about other people or relationships. This is caused by their dependency and anxieties and fears. They can also become obsessed when they think they've made or might make a "mistake."

Sometimes you can lapse into a fantasy about how you'd like things to be or about someone you love as a way to avoid the pain of the present. This is one way to stay in denial, discussed below, but it keeps you from living your life.

Dependency

Codependents need other people to like them to feel okay about themselves, and they're afraid of being rejected or abandoned - even if they can function on their own. Others need to always be in a relationship because they feel depressed or lonely when they're by themselves for too long. This trait makes it hard for them to end a relationship, even when the relationship is painful or abusive. They end up feeling trapped.

Denial

One of the problems people face in getting help for codependency is that they're in denial about it, meaning that they don't face their problem. Usually, they think the problem is someone else or the situation. They either keep complaining or trying to fix the other person, or go from one relationship or job to another and never own up the fact that they have a problem.

Codependents also deny their feelings and needs. Often, they don't know what they're feeling and are instead focused on what others are feeling. The same thing goes for their needs. They pay attention to other people's needs and not their own. They might be in denial of their need for space and autonomy. Although some codependents seem needy, others act like they're self-sufficient when it comes to needing help. They won't reach out and have trouble receiving. They are in denial of their vulnerability and need for love and intimacy.

Problems with intimacy

By this, I'm not referring to sex, although sexual dysfunction is often a reflection of an intimacy problem. I'm talking about being open and close with someone in an intimate relationship. Because of the shame and weak boundaries, you might fear that you'll be judged, rejected, or left. On the other hand, you may fear smothered in a relationship and losing your autonomy. You might deny your need for closeness and feel that your partner wants too much of your time; your partner complains that you're unavailable, but he or she denies his or her need for separateness.

Painful emotions

Codependency creates stress and leads to painful emotions. Shame and low self-esteem create anxiety and fear about:

- Being Judged

- Being rejected or abandoned

- Making mistakes

- Being a failure

- Being close and feeling trapped

- Being alone

The other symptoms lead to feelings of anger and resentment, depression, hopelessness, and despair. When the feelings are too much, you can feel numb.

3 Ways to Spot the Damaging Symptoms of Codependency

If you're worried that you might be suffering from codependency, there are a couple of major things to consider when deciding if the concern is warranted. First, ask yourself whether your relationship is based on an addiction-a habit that interferes with your everyday life. It may be surprising, but at its core, codependency is an "addiction" to love and relationships. Codependents frequently lose sleep, have poor eating habits, and an unhealthy social and work life. These symptoms of codependency develop because the addict is too concerned with making his or her partner happy or worrying about the latest conflict. Second, do you have an unequal stake in your relationship when compared to your partner? Codependents tend to make major life sacrifices and are much more devoted to the relationship than their partners are.

Finally, codependents often had awful relationships growing up. This includes rejections and betrayals from many kinds of relationships, even their parents. They see poor relationships as their own fault and grow desperate for love. Look back and see whether you had healthy friendships and family ties growing up. As childhood is such a vulnerable time, it's when negative experiences have the most prolonged effects, which can evolve into symptoms of codependency.

Here are a few more things to think about before checking our codependency quiz:

1. Do you avoid major conflicts by giving in to your partners will?

2. Do you try to control everything and everyone?

3. Do you wish there were an easier way out of your relationship?

4. Are you jealous and possessive?

5. Do you always have to have things perfect and in order?

6. Is it common for you to be insecure in your relationships, including past romances and friendships?

If you have many of these symptoms of codependency, then it's worth exploring whether or not you truly have a problem. Don't despair, though; there is hope for you. Codependency is a very common addiction, and many people deal with it daily.

There are many negative side effects of codependency symptoms. Codependency can lower your self-esteem. Ask yourself whether you value yourself as a person. Codependents often lack a proper sense of self-worth. If your self-esteem suffers, especially in the company of your partner, it's a strong sign of codependency. Beyond damage to your mental health, codependency can also damage relationships. Even though it may seem like your relationships would be safer since you're controlling things to try and make people happy, you're undermining it. Good relationships develop through genuine interaction, which sometimes involves conflict, and this is perfectly healthy and normal. Even though conflict can be troublesome initially, it allows the relationships to grow and strengthen over time.

Symptoms of codependency can lead to emotional crutches we use to struggle along while pretending nothing is wrong. Unfortunately, ignoring a problem doesn't make it go away. Abuse and emotional distress are common in these situations. If you suspect you have symptoms of codependency, a good first step is to further educate yourself about this addiction and come to terms with it. There are many terrific resources out there to help you with this and get you on the road to healing.

Codependency - Identifying Its Causes and Effects

Codependency is a condition brought on by growing up in a dysfunctional family and promoted by our culture. Children whose parents are unable to be fully present with them because they are unable to be fully present to themselves and each other, can be deeply affected. You grow up without seeing how to love with openness and spontaneity, as well as discipline. You gradually turn off your ability to be fully alive. You learn distorted ways to protect yourself from abuse (i.e., core beliefs and coping patterns) that interfere with intimacy.

This process can take place subtly, much like water eroding a rock little by little. Eventually, you adapt by burying your heart and denying that you need your parents' love in the way you do.

Here are some doubts and concerns of clients which reflect the harm that codependency can cause in one's life:

-Did my parents love me? Care for me? If they loved me, why didn't they treat me with more dignity and caring? Why were they so distant, so self-absorbed and sometimes even abusive and violent?

I got burned growing up. My family hurt me so much. Why should I give anyone else a chance to hurt me again?

-I feel drained and my helping others is never enough. I can't fix the problem, and people just get mad at me for interfering.

-Is being intimate something I can learn or am I doomed to feel alone even when I am with others?

-Is it possible to have a good relationship? Sometimes I feel I give my heart, but they want my soul. Recognize energy drainers.

These statements may sound familiar to you. You may have heard them said or said them yourself. They reflect what I call the "Dilemma of Love."

The AMA has recognized codependency as a disease, meaning it has an onset, a progression, and a finality. When you try to take care of unhealthy parents and protect your family system, you have no time to be a child or learn, in age-appropriate ways, how to be an adult. Your feelings and needs are frequently suppressed as they are too threatening. Your emotional growth becomes stunted. Subtly, you learn to play your role, follow the rules, doing what is expected of you. You feel you have to act this way to help your parents and family. Usually, on an unconscious level, you believe that if you truly love your family, you will keep trying to save it. As you continue to abandon yourself, you fall prey to the disease of codependency.

In her book, "Choicemaking," Sharon Wegscheider-Cruse calls codependency...

"... a specific condition characterized by preoccupation and extreme dependence (emotionally, socially and sometimes physically) on a person or object. Eventually, this dependence on another person becomes a pathological condition that affects the codependent in all other relationships." Anne Wilson Schaef has identified this same pathological condition in our society as a whole. She looks at how a society can operate as a dysfunctional system just as a family can.

Codependency now refers to people who are afflicted by their addictive process. They may come from families in which there were no noticeable addictions. Everything may have looked fine on the surface, but the parents were emotionally unavailable to the children and each other. Because addiction is built into our society, most people, regardless of their family background, need to recover from some form of addictiveness.

The prefix "co" in the term codependency means "about" an addictive process. It reflects the reality, recognized by clinicians that a family of addictive disorders exists that includes alcoholism, drug addiction, gambling, sex addiction, and compulsive spending as well as compulsive deprivations such as anorexia nervosa, sexual anorexia, compulsive saving and hoarding, and some phobic responses. The most important new insight of all is that the compulsive deprivation of one substance or behavior often balances the excess of another in the same person.

You can become addicted to substances, people, ideas, activities, behaviors or anything that takes away the pain of reality and gives you a sense of personal identity. The addictive process is the same regardless of the addiction. Therefore, to free your heart and become fully alive it is necessary to heal on two levels: to arrest your addictions, as well as to heal your underlying disease of codependency.

As with any other disease, if you do not seek help, your codependency will progress. As you fall prey to addictions and continually live from a false self, you will eventually break down under strain. Untreated codependency invariably leads to stress-related complications, physical illness, depression, anxiety and eventually death. Fortunately, although it is a chronic and fatal disease, it is also treatable.

It is especially challenging to treat because it can be subtle and insidious. You may have a successful career and look all together on the outside, but feel tense and uneasy on the inside. This can make it difficult for you to seek help. You may not be able to make sense of the way you feel, and you may not see a cause for your pain. Codependents often say, "Everything's fine in my life. I'm married; I've got a family and great kids. I should be happy, but I feel so empty."

It is important for you to understand that you are not at fault for having this illness. It was passed on to you through the generations whether you wanted it or not.

It is possible to suffer from this even if your parents were not emotionally unavailable. This "late onset codependency" appears even if you come from a relatively healthy family but stay with an untreated partner, you find yourself caught up in the abuse cycle of a dysfunctional relationship. This means your partner lives by dysfunctional rules, and you can develop codependent symptoms as an adult. This leaves you vulnerable to developing some degree of codependency. It is not a black or white situation. It is on a continuum.

As with any issue, your responsibility begins once you are aware you may have this illness and begin to research how to treat your problems. At this point, you can begin to recover your power and choose the kind of life you want. There is so much hope today and as I have said, working with a knowledgeable coach/counselor can bring you the freedom to be who you want to be

Recognizing Codependent Behavior

Codependency is a disorder that develops over time. Dysfunctional childhood patterns that interfere with the person's ability to form healthy relationships lie dormant for many years; the problem only surfaces once the person begins to experience adult relationships.

Codependents do not usually recognize that their behavior is unhealthy, and so they go from one unsatisfying toxic relationship to another. These relationships always end in heartbreak without the codependent ever understanding the primary role he or she played in its demise.

Codependents fear vulnerability. They feel undeserving, not worthy of having others meet their needs, so they put themselves in the role of perpetual caregiver. They believe that they must earn love to get it; fear that if they do not measure up to others' expectations, they will be abandoned. Their fear of others' being angry with them and rejecting them largely determines all their actions and reactions within the relationship.

Codependents often they feel like they do not deserve a better relationship than they already have. They fear giving up the false security it provides them, therefore resign themselves to always settling for second best. At the same time that they are feeling these insecurities, codependents may become angry because they are also feeling used and unappreciated by those they are trying desperately to help. When they do attempt to stand up for themselves, they feel guilty because they are taking rather than giving. They become trapped in a maze of heartbreaking confusion and disappointment.

The codependent person does not know that love is not supposed to be painful. I grew up in a drama-laden, angry home where my parents fought constantly. What was so confusing is that they often told my sisters and me how much they loved each other. That made a deep impression on my young psyche; somewhere along the line that twisted message translated into "love hurts." I grew up believing that true love was supposed to be painful; all my adult relationships reflected that way of thinking. Every one of them was drama-laden and traumatic. Crazy as it seems, even as I think back from a healthy perspective, I thought that pain proved the depth of a couple's love and commitment to each other.

Codependents believe that they have to have another person in their lives to survive. What they do not realize is that they have an addiction and the object of their affection is their drug. They believe to the core of their being that what they feel is deep love and that their behavior is loving, but they do not love healthily. What they perceive as love is, in fact, parasitic neediness.

The codependent person must learn to get his emotional needs met without making others dependent on them. He must also learn to give up his job as a people pleaser. The healing process reinforces that taking care of his own needs before the needs of others does not make him a selfish person.

Codependent behaviors prevent us from finding peace and happiness with the most important person in our lives-ourselves. Codependency is a mental health issue that can only be healed if it is recognized. Recovery is about learning to establish healthy boundaries in all areas of life.

Though codependency is an addiction, it is one can be fully recovered from. Once recognized it takes lots of time, patience, and support to heal from. It also takes honest reflection and great determination, but all efforts are worth it.

Great freedom and serenity come with healing. No longer codependent, the person can easily embrace positive feelings like love, happiness, and fulfillment. She can give when she wants to; not out of insecurity or the expectation of others.

Many people enjoy helping and caring for others. The thing to remember in all our relationships is that there should always be balance and compromise.

CHAPTER 3
PROBLEMS AND RISKS ASSOCIATED WITH CODEPENDENTS AND THEIR RELATIONSHIPS

Codependency - A Crippling Relationship Problem

Dependency problems are one of the biggest issues many relationships face. It can take many different forms, from alcoholism to drug reliance to less overtly dangerous problems, like adrenaline addiction or chronic adultery. Fortunately, modern science and medicine may be able to treat many such dependencies, and addicts of all types can start on the road to recovery. Relationships can survive these problems.

What they may not be able to survive is dependency enabled by codependency. Codependency is an emotional disorder so severe that some experts classify it as a psychological disease. A codependent is a person who is emotionally controlled by someone who has a dependency issue. Some recovery programs refer to these people as enablers, people who encourage the dependent's addictions by making excuses for the behavior, fixing the problems caused by the dependent's addictions, or otherwise relieving that person of the consequences of his or her actions.

It can be almost impossible for an addict to get better when a codependent is throwing up a smokescreen around them. But it's important to understand that a codependent often doesn't engage in this behavior consciously. Rather, they may do it without realizing. Sometimes, they do realize what they're doing but are unable to control it, even going so far as to feel extreme guilt over their actions and expressing a desire to change.

The cause of codependency usually lies in a lack of inherent self-esteem and self-worth in the codependent. He or she looks outward for feelings of adequacy and acceptance, and the relationship with the dependent is vital to establishing his or her worth as a human being. The relationship, therefore, becomes something of a self-sustaining circle: the dependent's addiction is encouraged by the codependent, and the codependent's self-worth is propped up by the dependent. For many people, this is a difficult, even impossible, cycle to break. But neither person can see real development and growth while the unhealthy relationship exists.

It's also important to realize that codependency is not always enabled by a dependency. All that's required is someone with low enough self-worth to look elsewhere for feelings of adequacy and acceptance. If your partner exhibits signs of secretiveness, jealousy, enabling, self-pity, and shame, he or she might be suffering from this dangerous psychological disorder. You should convince him or her to seek medical attention immediately.

Codependency: Effect of Self-Esteem on Relationships

Research has well-established the link between good self-esteem and relationship satisfaction. Self-esteem not only affects how we think about ourselves but also how much love we're able to receive and how we treat others, especially in intimate relationships.

A person's initial level of self-esteem before the relationship predicts partners' common relationship satisfaction. More specifically, although happiness generally declines slightly over time, this isn't true for people who enter a relationship with higher levels of self-esteem. But the steepest decline is for people whose self-esteem was lower, to begin with. Frequently, those relationships don't last. Even though communication skills, emotionality, and stress all influence a relationship, a person's experience and personality traits affect how these issues are managed and therefore have the greatest bearing on its outcome.

How Self-Esteem Affects Relationships

Self-esteem suffers when you grow up in a dysfunctional family. Often you don't have a voice. Your opinions and desires aren't taken seriously. Parents usually have low self-esteem and are unhappy with each other. They neither have nor model good relationship skills, including cooperation, healthy boundaries, assertiveness, and conflict resolution. They may be abusive, or just indifferent, preoccupied, controlling, interfering, manipulative, or inconsistent. Their children's feelings and personality traits and needs tend to be shamed. As a result, a child feels emotionally abandoned and concludes that he or she is at fault-not good enough to be acceptable to both parents. This is how toxic shame becomes internalized. Children feel insecure, anxious, and angry. They don't feel safe to be, to trust, and to like themselves. They grow up codependent with low self-esteem and learn to hide their feelings, walk on eggshells, withdraw, and try to please or become aggressive.

Attachment style reflects self-esteem

As a result of their insecurity, shame, and impaired self-esteem, children develop an attachment style that, to varying degrees, is anxious or avoidant. They develop anxious and avoidant attachment styles and behave like pursuers and distances described in "The Dance of Intimacy". At the extreme ends, some individuals cannot tolerate either being alone or too close; either one creates intolerable pain.

Anxiety can lead you to sacrifice your needs and please and accommodate your partner. Due to basic insecurity, you're preoccupied with the relationship and highly attuned to your partner, worrying that he or she wants less closeness. But because you don't get your needs met, you become unhappy. Adding to this, you take things personally with a negative twist, projecting negative outcomes. Low self-esteem makes you hide your truth so as not to "make waves," which compromises real intimacy. You may also be jealous of your partner's attention to others and call or text frequently, even when asked not to. By repeated attempts to seek reassurance, you unintentionally push your partner away even further. Both of you end up unhappy.

Avoiders, as the term implies, avoid closeness and intimacy through distancing behaviors, such as flirting, making unilateral decisions, addiction, ignoring their partner, or dismissing his or her feelings and needs. This creates tension in the relationship, usually voiced by the anxious partner. Because avoiders are hypervigilant about their partner's attempts to control or limit their autonomy in any way, they then distance themselves even more. Neither style contributes to satisfying relationships.

Communication reveals self-esteem

Dysfunctional families lack good communication skills that intimate relationships require. Not only are they important to any relationship, but they also reflect self-esteem. They involve speaking, honestly, concisely, and assertively, and the ability to listen, as well. They require that you know and can communicate your needs, wants, and feelings, including the ability to set boundaries. The more intimate the relationship, the more important and more difficult practicing these skills becomes.

Codependents generally have problems with assertiveness. At the same time, they deny their feelings and needs, because they were shamed or ignored in their childhood. They also consciously suppress what they think and feel so as not to anger or alienate their partner and risk criticism or emotional abandonment. Instead, they rely on mindreading, asking questions, caretaking, blaming, lying, criticizing, avoiding problems or ignoring or controlling their partner. They learn these strategies from the dysfunctional communication witnessed in their families growing up. But these behaviors are problematic in themselves and can lead to escalating conflict, characterized by attacks, blame, and withdrawal. Walls get erected that block openness, closeness, and happiness. Sometimes, a partner seeks closeness with a third person, threatening the stability of the relationship.

Boundaries protect self-esteem

Dysfunctional families have dysfunctional boundaries, which get handed down through parents' behavior and example. They may be controlling, invasive, disrespectful, use their children for their own needs, or project their feelings onto them. This undermines children's self-esteem. As adults, they too, have dysfunctional boundaries. They have trouble accepting other people's differences or allowing others' space, particularly in intimate relationships. Without boundaries, they can't say no or protect themselves when necessary and take personally what others say. They tend to feel responsible for others' stated or imagined feelings, needs, and actions, to which they react, contributing to escalating conflict. Their partner feels that he or she can't express themselves without triggering a defensive reaction.

Intimacy requires self-esteem

We all have needs for both separateness and individuality as well as for being close and connected. Autonomy requires self-esteem - both necessary in relationships. It's an ability to stand on your own and trust and motivate yourself. But when you don't like yourself, you're in miserable company spending time alone. It takes courage to communicate assertively in an intimate relationship-courage that comes with self-acceptance, which enables you to value and honor your feelings and needs and risk criticism or rejection in voicing them. This also means you feel deserving of love and are comfortable receiving it. You wouldn't waste your time pursuing someone unavailable or push away someone who loved you and met your needs.

Solutions

Healing toxic shame from childhood takes working with a skilled therapist; however, shame can be diminished, self-esteem raised, and attachment style changed by altering the way you interact with yourself and others. Self-Esteem is learned. Sharing at 12-Step meetings is also very beneficial. Learning assertiveness also raises self-esteem.

Couples therapy is an ideal way to achieve greater relationship satisfaction. When one partner refuses to participate, it's nonetheless helpful if one willing partner does. Research confirms that the improved self-esteem of one partner increases relationship satisfaction for both. Often, when only one person enters therapy, the relationship changes for the better and happiness increases for the couple. If not, the client's mood improves, and he or she is more able to accept the status quo or leave the relationship.

2 Biggest Codependent Traps You Might Be Falling Into

The two biggest traps codependents get themselves into are:

- **Codependents depend on another's approval and acceptance**

- **Codependents forgive before rehab is completed**

Co-dependency is a way of avoiding one's own life by taking on the problems of another. Codependents tend to avoid their own lives by trying to solve the problems of other people.

A codependent person would feel trapped or obligated to stay in a relationship no matter what damage was committed to themselves or others by an abusive partner. Abuse means financial, emotional, physical or sexual abuse.

The easiest place to observe codependency is in relationships where one or both members are abusing drugs, sex or money. One of the partners will feel compelled to remain in the relationship and support the other.

1. Why Do They Depend On Abusers?

A co-dependent's emotional need to help and gain acceptance from an abusive relationship seems illogical at first. An easier way to see why a person would tolerate all the damage and disturbance a loved one creates has to do with survival.

Codependency is about ensuring another life no matter what. It's like a codependent took on another's life and is trying to continue their lives. Ex: person gets into financial trouble due to cocaine abuse, reckless living, etc. and the co-dependent pays the mortgage, car payments or worse the drug dealers at the door.

Love or obligation to the abusive person is the major justification. Sometimes the abusive person uses coercion, threats, and extortion to demand support. If support isn't given, emotional pleas, upsets, and threats of leaving the relationship are used. Ex: making a supportive person feel guilty if they don't comply with demands for money or support.

Often sympathy for the abuser is used to plead for forgiveness of wrong doings. Apologies and pleadings for forgiveness will be made. Often these pleas are made until the abuser gets what they want. Then they lay off. Promises will be made that won't be kept.

2. Co-dependents Forgive Instead of Rehabilitate

Although the damage has happened before, a codependent will eventually forgive the abuser. Love, emotional outpourings, sex or other 'payoffs' are given by the abuser as a reward or payment for receiving forgiveness.

The need for a codependent for acceptance of the abuser, the promises and emotions are craved by a codependent. A codependent will sometimes use these forgiveness times as opportunities to gain a false upper hand and control over the relationship.

The Codependent needs the abuser or addict to be helpless, in jeopardy, victimized, in trouble, needing help, vulnerable, for the codependent to feel valued or important! Often a codependent will only help enough to keep a person alive but not enough to change their course of destruction.

Ex: pay off the person's debts with only a promise of the abuser to go to an effective rehab. The drug abuser promises but doesn't fulfill their promise. The codependent uses this bad experience to justify them continuing to pay off debts etc. and never get the true addict help.

Admit you've been drawn into a destructive cycle of codependency that is destructive and only leads to eventual disappointment and you'll begin to see the hook. Just because it looks like drug abuser has the problem, doesn't mean you aren't also wearing the problem for them, feeding fuel to their downward drive.

Codependency is a trap. One way to end codependency is to learn about professional intervention support who will help you break your dependency on another. The goal is getting complete rehabilitation.

Codependence: A Manifestation of the Adult Child Syndrome

Those who live with or are closely associated with those who are chemically or alcoholically dependent for their daily functioning can be considered "codependent," because they quickly become "dependent" with and through them. Although the primary person may be considered the one afflicted with the disease, the secondary one or ones, who are usually the children chronically exposed to his or her behavior, adopt a byproduct of it, struggling to keep it together and function as optimally and efficiently as they can in the world after childhood circumstances progressively pulled them apart. Liquor and other substances need not be present.

Indeed, para-alcoholism, an early term for codependence, implies that a person's actions are driven by the unresolved, painful emotions and fears he was forced to shelve to survive the unstable and sometimes detrimental effects of being raised by the alcoholic himself.

Origins, Definitions, and Manifestations of the Disease

The codependent seed is planted when a person turns his responsibility for his life and happiness to either his ego (false self) or others, becoming preoccupied with them to the extent that he temporarily rises above his pain and, in its extreme, can entirely forget who he even is, when he consistently mirrors someone else-in other words, if he looks out here to the other, he will not have to look in there to himself.

"Codependence, (a major manifestation of the adult child syndrome), is a disease of lost self-hood," according to Dr. Charles L. Whitfield in his book, "Co-Dependence: Healing the Human Condition" (Health Communications, 1991, p. 3). "It can mimic, be associated with, aggravate, and even lead to many of the physical, mental, emotional, or spiritual conditions that befall us in daily life.

"When we focus outside of ourselves, we lose touch with what is inside of us: beliefs, thoughts, feelings, decisions, choices, experiences, wants, needs, sensations, intuitions... These and more are part of an exquisite feedback system that we can call our inner life."

In short, a person can sever his connection with his consciousness and consciousness is who he is.

Like expecting a home appliance to operate without plugging it into an electric socket, a codependent may merge with and feed off of another to such an extent that he no longer believes he can function independently.

The origins of the malady are the same as those which cause the adult child syndrome.

"The hallmark of codependency is taking care of people who should have been taking care of you," according to

Dr. Susan Powers of the Caron Treatment Centers.

Instead of being self-centered and expecting to get their needs met, children from dysfunctional, alcoholic, or abusive homes are forced, at a very early age, to become other- or parent-centered, meeting their needs, attempting to resolve or fix their deficiencies, and sometimes making Herculean efforts to achieve their love in what may be considered an ultimate role reversal.

If this dynamic could be verbally expressed, the parent would say, "What I can't do, you're expected to do yourself, substituting you for me."

And this reality may well extend beyond themselves, since they are often forced to replace their parents during times that their younger siblings need for them, becoming surrogate mothers and fathers.

In essence, they disregard their own need for a parent and become one themselves. Instead of being nurtured, they cultivate codependence, since it places them on a path that will entail seeking it in others.

"Our experience shows that the codependent rupture, which creates an outward focus to gain love and affection, is created by a dysfunctional childhood... ," according to the "Adult Children of Alcoholics" textbook (World Service Organization, 2006, p. 60.) "The soul rupture is the abandonment by our parents or caregivers... (and) sets us up for a life of looking outward for love and safety that never comes."

This condition is only exacerbated by the same parents who neither support nor permit a child to express or heal his hurts-and may be met with denial or shame if he tries to do so-leaving him little choice but to stuff and swallow them, resulting in a repressed, but the mounting accumulation of unresolved negative emotions. After repeated squelching of a child's observations, feelings, and reactions, in essence, his reality-he progressively disconnects from his true self and denies his crucial inner cues. Unraveling, he is poised on the threshold that leads from into out-that is, toward others and away from himself, sparking the conflict between his once true and since replaced false self, which manifests itself as codependence.

Forced, additionally, to focus on his parent's moods, attitudes, and behaviors further plant the roots of this condition but become a necessary survival tactic for two primary reasons.

First and foremost, children assume responsibility for their parents' deficiencies and ill-treatment by justifying it, erroneously reasoning that their flaws, lack of worth, and general unlovability are the culprits for the withholds of their validation and acceptance, thus shifting the burden from the ones who should be carrying it to the one who should not.

Secondly, adopting a sixth sense concerning their parents' moods becomes a safety gauge and enables them to emotionally and physiologically prepare themselves for what has most likely become habitual and even cyclical negative confrontations of verbal and physical abuse.

As episodes of "expected abnormalcy," they add insurmountable layers of trauma to the original but no longer remembered one. Unable, then or now, to use the body's fight or flight survival mechanisms, yet still drowned in a flood of stress hormones (cortisol) and elevated energy, they have no choice but to tuck themselves into the inner child protective sanctuary they created at a very young age as the only realizable "solution" to the parental-threatened and -inflicted danger, enduring, tolerating, and downright surviving the unfair power play and "punishment" they may believe is being administered because of "deserved discipline."

Like signals, a mere frown on or cringe of a parent's face may prime the child for the episodes he knows will assuredly follow. So thick can the tension in the air become at these times, that he can probably cut it with a knife?

Part of the wounding, which reduces a person's sense of self and esteem and increases his feeling of emptiness, occurs as a result of projective identification. Volatility charged, yet unable to get to the center of or bore through his emotional pain, a parent may project, like a movie on to a screen, parts of himself on to another, such as his vulnerable, captive child, until that child takes on and identifies with the projection.

Releasing and relieving himself, the sender, (the parent) does not have to own or even take responsibility for his negative feelings. If the recipient (the child) ultimately acts them out after repeated projected implanting, whose emotions now mount into uncontainable proportions, the sender may berate or belittle him for them, in an ultimate out-of-persona dynamic, which transfers emotions from one to the other.

"If we have unhealthy boundaries, we are like sponges that absorb the painful, conflicted material of others sent from their inner life," wrote Whitfield in "Co-Dependence: Healing the Human Condition" (Health Communications, 1991, p. 93). "It is not ours, yet we soak it up.

"(This only causes) the true self to go into hiding to protect itself from the overwhelming pain of mistreatment, abuse, lack of being affirmed and mirrored healthily, and the double and other negative messages from toxic others around it," he noted.

These incidents become breeding grounds for both the adult child syndrome and its codependent manifestation.

"The adult child syndrome is somewhat interchangeable with the diagnosis of codependence," according to the "Adult Children of Alcoholics" textbook (World Service Organization, 2006, pp. 6-7). "There are many definitions for codependence; however, the consensus is that codependent people tend to focus on the wants and needs of others rather than their own. By doing so, the codependent or adult child can avoid his or her feelings of low self-worth... A codependent focuses on others

372

and their problems to such an extent that the codependent's life is often adversely affected."

Part of a codependent's breeding occurs because a child needs his parents for his emotional and psychological development, yet he often dips into a dry well when he connects with them to achieve this goal, emerging dissatisfied, unfulfilled, and almost stung by the negative, rejecting energy. He may implement several strategies to attain what he vitally needs, but will often fail since his parents themselves never received what he seeks because of their own dysfunctional or incomplete childhoods.

If they could be considered profit-and-loss statements, they would most likely show an emotional deficit and, eventually, so, too, will the child, prompting his ultimate outward- and other- focus.

Bombarded with parental blame and shame, a child can quickly believe that he causes others' negative or detrimental actions by his sheer existence as if he were a negatively influencing entity and may carry both this belief and its burden for most of his life.

"As children, we took responsibility for our parents' anger, rage, blame, or pitifulness...," according to the "Adult Children of Alcoholics" textbook (World Service Organization, 2006, p. 7). "This mistaken perception, born in childhood, is the root of our codependent behavior as adults."

Dr. Charles L. Whitfield uncovers an even deeper cause.

"The cause of codependence is a wounding of the true self to such an extent that, to survive, it had to go into hiding most of the time, with the subsequent running of its life by the false or codependent self," he wrote in "Co-Dependence: Healing the Human Condition" (Health Communications, 1991, p. 22). "It is thus a disease of lost self-hood."

"... The child's vulnerable true self... is wounded so often that to protect (it), it defensively submerges (splits off) deep within the unconscious part of the psyche," he also noted (p. 27).

This split, one of the many detriments of codependence, arrests this development, as his inner child remains mired in the initial trauma that necessitated its creation. Although his chronological age may advance, his emotional and psychological progress remains suspended, creating the adult child. His body and physical statue may suggest the first part of this "adult" designation to others, but his reactions may more closel y approximate the second "child" part of it.

Conflicted, he may engage in an internal battle he does not entirely understand, as his adult side wishes and needs to function at an age-appropriate level, but his child half clings to the sting of his unresolved harm, seeking sanctuary and safety. He is unable to satisfy both.

People naturally seek relief from pain and addictions and compulsions, the second manifestation of codependence, is one of the methods they employ, especially since they lack any understanding about their affliction. Because they spark the brain's reward system, however, they only provide temporary, fleeting fixes, not solutions.

Exacerbating this dilemma is the fact that they flow from a false sense of self, which itself can only be mollified, quelled, or deceptively filled by these means.

Since their childhood circumstances were both familiar and normal to them, they subconsciously may also attract, now as adult children, those with similar upbringings using sixth-sense intuitions or identifications, creating a third codependent manifestation.

"... On (an even) deeper level," according to Whitefield in "Co-Dependence: Healing the Human Condition" (Health Communications, 1991, p. 54), "they may also be drawn to one another in a search to heal their unfinished business and, perhaps more importantly, their lost self."

Nevertheless, inter-relating with others who themselves function from the deficit-dug holes in their souls, they only re-create the childhood dynamics they experienced with their parents, substituting their partners for them and suffering a secondary form of wounding over and above the primary one sustained in childhood. In effect, they become another link in the intergenerational chain.

Even if they encounter whole, loving people, who can provide the needed acceptance and validation they crave, they are unable to accept it, since they do not function from the true self that otherwise could-nor, in the event, do they even believe that they deserve it. It bounces off of them like an image on a mirror, only creating yet a fourth byproduct of codependence.

Aside from the codependent foundation laid in childhood by dysfunctional parents, who themselves were wounded and caused the adult child syndrome upon which its codependent aspect was based, the condition is far more prevalent in society than may at first be apparent. Continually, but sometimes subtly modeled, it can almost be considered contagious.

Identifying Codependence:

One of the frustrating aspects of codependence is that it either wears a disguise or remains altogether hidden, prompting the behavioral modifications and almost-scripted roles of those who suffer from it, such as rescuer, people-pleaser, perfectionist, overachiever, victim, martyr, lost child, comedian, mascot, bully, and even abuser, that deludes others to the fact that it is present. The motivation for such behavior is not always immediately apparent.

Nevertheless, there are several traits which characterize codependence.

Sparked by the need to protect the traumatized inner child and to arise, in part, from disordered relationships, it results, first and foremost, in the creation of the false self, which replaces the genuine, intrinsic one, and becomes the root of all other addictions and compulsions. The emptier a person feels inside, the more he seeks to fill that void outside.

"Codependence is not only the most common addiction," according to Whitefield in "Co-Dependence: Healing the Human Condition" (Health Communications, 1991, pp. 5-6), "it is the base out of which all our other addictions and compulsions emerge. Underneath nearly every addiction and compulsion lies codependence. And what runs them is twofold: a sense of shame that our true self is somehow defective or inadequate, combined with the innate and healthy drive of our true self that does not realize and (cannot) express itself. The addiction, compulsion, or disorder becomes the manifestation of the erroneous notion that something outside ourselves can make us happy and fulfilled."

And underlying codependence is a shame and a deep belief that the person is inadequate, incomplete, and flawed.

Avoiding his negative feelings and painful past, he becomes externally and other-focused, yet is unable to genuinely connect with them, with himself, or with a Higher Power of his understanding through the false or pseudo-self, he was forced to create. This has the opposite or repelling effect.

His boundaries, another aspect of the disease, may be distorted, undefined, and extend beyond himself.

Finally, as a defense, codependence is learned, acquired, progressive, and inextricably tied to the adult child syndrome, since the false self serves as the link between the two.

Codependence and the Brain:

Codependence is both additive and breeds addictions. People's actions are usually motivated by rewards and, in this case, the reward is the temporary disconnection from their painful pasts by focusing on others and the belief that doing so will bring them happiness and fulfillment, as they attempt to avoid their emptiness and negative self-feelings.

Although they feel flawed because of their upbringing, the real flaw is that an external source can fill and replace an internal one. The more they look toward others, the more they deny and disconnect from their own needs, wants, and deficits.

"This love deficit condemns us to existence of addiction, para-alcoholism, codependence, or seeking some other outward source to heal an inward feeling of being unwanted or defective," according to the "Adult Children of Alcoholics" textbook (World Service Organization, 2006, p. 438).

Although certain strategies can temporarily relieve their adverse condition, such as avoiding, depending, obsessing, and compelling, excessive reliance upon them, as ultimately occurs with codependence, exaggerates them and elevates them to addiction levels, transforming their "benefits" into deficits. Doing so is not a solution, since it fails to address the underlying reason for it and only ends up creating what can be considered a byproduct problem.

The more a person seeks gratification to rise above his unresolved past, the more he reinforces the neuropathway to pleasure in his brain, cementing the belief that this "other-person" addiction can provide satisfaction through external means-so much so, in fact, that the moment his "fix" is removed or is even threatened to be removed, he crashes and falls back into his pit of pain.

Like all addictions, however, it affects not to end there: indeed, the brain eventually creates a tolerance for them, demanding ever greater quantities, frequencies, and intensities to satisfy him, until he becomes that proverbial binary star, orbiting around others, unable to function without them, as he becomes nothing more than his mirror image.

"Just as we develop a tolerance to the effects of chemicals, we develop a tolerance to the effects of our behaviors... ," according to Sharon Wegscheider-Cruse and Joseph Cruse in their book, "Understanding Codependency: The Science Behind it and How to Break the Cycle" (Health Communications, 2012, p. 33). "This vicious, one-way circle is a trap that ends in depression, isolation, institutions, and sometimes death."

Excessive psychological and emotional reliance on others is, in essence, an exaggeration of normal personality traits and can ultimately disable a person, culminating in the disease of codependence. The way the body can quickly become dependent upon mood-altering chemicals, it can equally become physically dependent upon behaviors to the point that compulsions serve as his armament.

"The disease of codependency can be seen as a personal struggle with a variety of compulsive disorders," Wegscheider-Cruse and Cruse wrote (Ibid, p. 131). "People... have lived in a condition of denial, distorted feelings, and compulsive behaviors, and as a result, they have developed low self-worth, deep shame, inadequacy, and anger."

But the codependent erroneously believes two mistruths. One is that he is intrinsically flawed and the other is that someone outside of himself can fill what he already possesses inside of himself.

Recovery

Problems can be painful, but can often point to solutions -or, at the very least, that they need to be sought.

"Rather than being simply an escape from reality," wrote Whitfield in "Co-Dependence: Healing the Human Condition" (Health Communications, 1991, p. 98), "codependence is also a search. It starts as a search for happiness and fulfillment outside ourselves. After repeated frustration, it ultimately becomes a search for inner wholeness and completion."

Unless recovery is undertaken, usually through therapy and twelve-step program venues, and understanding is achieved, the mistreatment, dysfunction, and abuse that causes a person's early wound and transforms him into an adult child will only perpetuate, suppressing, paralyzing, or altogether removing the tenets of positive emotions, trust, and love needed for healthy human life and increasing the chances of its byproduct, codependence, by placing him on the fruitless path of looking outside of himself for fulfillment until it reaches addiction levels.

"Recovery involves re-accepting and honoring your individuality," according to Dr. Susan Powers of the Caron Treatment Centers.

You are you, as created, and not the image of what others will have you be attained using unhealthy attachments.

Desensitizing traumas, resolving core issues, and progressively regaining trust leads to the gentle recovering of your true or authentic self, enabling it to express itself and provide the internal fulfillment that was always present, but was distorted and deflated through childhood wounding.

Narcissists are also Codependents

Writers often distinguish narcissists and codependents as opposites, but surprisingly, though their outward behavior may differ, they share many psychological traits. Narcissists exhibit core codependent symptoms of shame, denial, control, dependency (unconscious), and dysfunctional communication and boundaries, all leading to intimacy problems. One study showed a significant correlation between narcissism and codependency. Although most narcissists can be classified as codependent, the reverse isn't true - most codependents aren't narcissists. They don't exhibit common traits of exploitation, entitlement, and lack of empathy.

Dependency

Codependency is a disorder of a "lost self." Codependents have lost their connection to their innate self. Instead, their thinking and behavior revolve around a person, substance, or process. Narcissists also suffer from a lack of connection to their true self. In its place, they're identified with their ideal self. Their inner deprivation and lack of connection to their real self make them dependent on others for validation. Consequently, like other codependents, their self-image, thinking, and behavior is other-oriented to stabilize and validate their self-esteem and fragile ego.

Ironically, despite declared high self-regard, narcissists crave recognition from others and have an insatiable need to be admired - to get their "narcissistic supply." This makes them as dependent on recognition from others as an addict is on their addiction.

Shame

Shame is at the core of codependency and addiction. It stems from growing up in a dysfunctional family. Narcissists' inflated self-opinion is commonly mistaken for self-love. However, exaggerated self-flattery and arrogance merely assuage unconscious,

internalized shame that is common among codependents.

Children develop different ways of coping with the anxiety, insecurity, and hostility that they experience growing up in dysfunctional families. Internalized shame can result despite parents' good intentions and lack of overt abuse. To feel safe, children adopt coping patterns that give arise to an ideal self. One strategy is to accommodate other people and seek their love, affection, and approval. Another is to seek recognition, mastery, and domination over others. Stereotypical codependents fall into the first category, and narcissists the second. They seek power and control of their environment to get their needs met. Their pursuit of prestige, superiority, and power help them to avoid feeling inferior, vulnerable, needy, and helpless at all costs.

These ideals are natural human needs; however, for codependents and narcissists, they're compulsive and thus neurotic. Additionally, the more a person pursues their ideal self, the further they depart from their real self, which only increases their insecurity, false self, and sense of shame. (For more about these patterns and how shame and codependency co-emerge in childhood, see Conquering Shame and Codependency.)

Denial

Denial is a core symptom of codependency. Codependents are generally in denial of their codependency and often their feelings and many needs. Similarly, narcissists deny feelings, particularly those that express vulnerability. Many won't admit to feelings of inadequacy, even to themselves. They disown and often project onto others feel that they consider "weak," such as longing, sadness, loneliness, powerlessness, guilt, fear, and variations of them. Anger makes them feel powerful. Rage, arrogance, envy, and contempt are defenses to underlying shame.

Codependents deny their needs, especially emotional needs, which were neglected or shamed growing up. Some codependents act self-sufficient and readily put others needs first. Other codependents are demanding of people to satisfy their needs. Narcissists also deny emotional needs. They won't admit that they're demanding and needy, because having needs makes them feel dependent and weak. They judge as needy.

Although narcissists don't usually put the needs of others first, some narcissists are people-pleasers and can be very generous. In addition to securing the attachment of those they depend on, often their motive is for recognition or to feel superior or grandiose because they're able to aid people they consider inferior. Like other codependents, they may feel exploited by and resentful toward the people they help.

Many narcissists hide behind a facade of self-sufficiency and aloofness when it comes to needs for emotional closeness, support, grieving, nurturing, and intimacy. The quest of power protects them from experiencing the humiliation of feeling weak, sad, afraid, or wanting or needing anyone-ultimately, to avoid rejection and feeling shame. Only the threat of abandonment reveals how dependent they truly are.

Dysfunctional Boundaries

Like other codependents, narcissists have unhealthy boundaries, because theirs weren't respected growing up. They don't experience other people as separate but as extensions of themselves. As a result, they project thoughts and feelings onto others and blame them for their shortcomings and mistakes, all of which they cannot tolerate in themselves. Additionally, the lack of boundaries makes them thin-skinned, highly reactive, and defensive and causes them to take everything personally.

Most codependents share these patterns of blame, reactivity, defensiveness, and taking things personally. The behavior and degree or direction of feelings might vary, but the underlying process is similar. For example, many codependents react with self-criticism, self-blame, or withdrawal, while others react with aggression and criticism or blame of someone else. Both behaviors are reactions to shame and demonstrate dysfunctional boundaries. (In some cases, confrontation or withdrawal might be an appropriate response, but not if it's a habitual, compulsive reaction.)

Dysfunctional Communication

Like other codependents, narcissists' communication is dysfunctional. They generally lack assertiveness skills. Their communication often consists of criticism, demands, labeling, and other forms of verbal abuse. On the other hand, some narcissists intellectualize, obfuscate, and are indirect. Like other codependents, they find it difficult to identify and clearly state their feelings. Although they may express opinions and take positions more easily than other codependents, they fre quently have trouble listening and are dogmatic and inflexible. These are signs of dysfunctional communication that evidence insecurity and lack of respect for the other person.

Control

Like other codependents, narcissists seek to control. Control over our environment helps us to feel safe. The greater our anxiety and insecurity, the greater is our need for control. When we're dependent on others for our security, happiness, and self-worth, what people think, say, and do become paramount to our sense of well-being and even safety. We'll try to control them directly or indirectly with people-pleasing, lies, or manipulation. If we're frightened or ashamed of our feelings, such as anger or grief, then we attempt to control our feelings. Other people's anger or grief will upset us, so that they must be avoided or controlled, too.

Intimacy

Finally, the combination of all these patterns makes intimacy challenging for narcissists and codependents, alike. Relationships can't thrive without clear boundaries that afford partners freedom and respect. They require that we're autonomous, have assertive communication skills, and self-esteem.

If you have a relationship with a narcissist, check out my book, Narcissist: Discover the true meaning of narcissism and how to avoid their mind games, guilt, and manipulation (Mastery Emotional Intelligence and Soft Skills Book 11).

CHAPTER 4
START LOVING YOURSELF AND STOP BEING CODPENDENT

Do You Know Who You Are?

The thoughts we have about ourselves are linked to all the feedback we get from a huge range of sources, take a moment and consider all the people who have had influence on how you think about yourself during your lifetime. My list would comprise of my parents, siblings, teachers, friends, colleagues, employers, previous partners, my children. We all have our ups and downs, moments when we feel fabulous and others when we don't. When we're feeling really good someone may have paid us an unexpected compliment, your partner may have brought you flowers for no reason, your child may have given you a hug just because... this good feeling was caused by an outside influence, but unfortunately this equation also works the other way around but with more punch it seems. If you're not feeling particularly good about yourself maybe a teacher/coach said you weren't good enough, your partner asks if you are going to get dressed for dinner when you are ready to go, your parents asked why you couldn't be more like them?

The interesting thing about this is that we hold onto the negative a lot longer than the positive, even though it makes us feel bad. The comments, for example from your teacher or parents, could have been made years ago, but the positive ones much more recently and yet still the negative comments override the positive ones. If we carry on holding on to negative statements and letting them impact how we feel about ourselves, we are setting ourselves up for misery and constant questioning of who we are and whether we are worth loving.

So you will need some time alone, without distraction, to get to know who you are, this is for no-one else's benefit but yours (at this stage, but we'll get to that).

Here's what I'd like you to write down;

• Your three core values, what are you not negotiable on?

• At least five strengths you have in abundance.

• Your weaknesses, we all have them, be honest with yourself.

• What makes you smile, feel calm, content, satisfied with your life.

• What makes you feel upset, anxious, sad, dissatisfied with your life.

It's not as easy as it sounds, is it? Have you written down what you expected or did taking the time and thinking thoroughly about yourself produce some surprises?

Healing requires that you admit the truth about yourself...

Firstly, your core values, the foundation for who you are and what you stand for. When you are running your life and relationships in line with these, you will feel calm, content and balanced because everything is working in harmony together. When we do or are asked to do something that is not in line with our core values we experience discomfort, anxiety, worry, and unhappiness. For example, your boss asks you to attend an important meeting when you know you have to be at your child's recital, if one of your core values is family, this situation will make you feel very unsettled, anxious and potentially upset. We have all made decisions at some point that have not been in line with our core values, but maybe we did not understand the reason behind the negative feelings we were experiencing at the time. The key thing to note here is knowledge is power, when we consciously know exactly what our core values are we know to remain calm, content and balanced in our life we must work in line with them.

Steps to Understanding and Accepting Who You Are

Sometimes we lack a realistic view and understanding of ourselves which can lead to feelings of being "lost" in our lives and depression. Understanding yourself helps you to accept yourself the way you are, and in turn, makes you a happier person. You cannot control everything in life, but if you understand yourself and make good choices based on who you are and knowing what you want out of life, you can begin to enjoy life to the fullest.

Here are a few steps to start you on the road of understanding yourself:

Step 1: Accept that you are unique and valuable in your special way, just as you are. We all matter to our close friends and family. You are very important both for yourself and to others.

Step 2: Now you need to dig deep to understand the real YOU, without any pretenses. Set time aside to do this exercise. Explore the way you really feel about yourself, you can start with answering a few questions like:

• What are the fears and beliefs that are holding you back?

• Are you living your life or are you just existing from day to day?

• What makes you truly happy?

• What are the things that you know you can do well?

- What is your self-talk? Negative? Positive?

- Do you treat yourself and others with respect?

- Do you take responsibility for your life or do you feel like a victim of your circumstances?

- What do you want out of life?

In understanding yourself as much as you can, you start to gain confidence in your strengths, and you will also recognize your weaknesses. Rather than shying away from your flaws, you could help yourself better by accepting them and working on them. Build an honest picture of who you truly are. Maybe you can ask close friends and family members, whose opinions you respect, to give you honest feedback on their perception of you and how you interact with them and respond to situations.

Step 3: Once you understand yourself, you can always work to better yourself, but it should be because of what you want to achieve in life and what you expect from yourself, not because you believe it to be what others want from, or expect from you. Remember there is no reason for you change who you are unless you feel it will be beneficial to you and move you in the direction of the way you ultimately want to live your life.

Understanding yourself means being comfortable with who you are and what you are. It also helps you realize your strengths and weaknesses so you can accept and embrace yourself - warts and all.

Love Yourself for Your Own Sake

The love for family and friends is second nature and often taken for granted. It isn't always easy, but there is a foundation that sustains relationships and holds them together through the hardest times. That base grows in the heart and builds on strength from within. Caring about others is what others expect from you, but you must love yourself to make that possible. Take an inner assessment of all that is good about yourself, and appreciate your value. It is the strongest force you possess.

Consider and Assess

Celebrating the good things in life is joy. Making it to the end of a hard day is part of the routine. Supporting loved ones in crisis is a call to duty. There is a soldier in the soul who rises to the best, handles the mundane and responds to the battle call. When too little attention is given to the emotional toll of dealing with everyday ups and downs, the soldier becomes weary. Coping is a survival mechanism, but living well involves more than simply getting through the day. Understand that your inner strength depends on your ability to know, appreciate and celebrate yourself.

Value and Admire

Taking stock of inner worth begins with understanding the inventory of what makes you special. The ability to empathize, an unselfish nature or an artistic touch are not unique traits. However, when channeled through your individuality, a common asset becomes your treasure. It deserves nurturing and sharing. Appreciate all that is good within you. Know that it is the essence of who you are and what you have to offer. Being told the importance of self-worth is as easy as reading a popular book or attending a self-help seminar. Truly believing in yourself only comes from realizing how very special you are.

Develop and Grow

A garden thrives on attention and care, and its beauty comes from its variety of colors and flowers. Develop an inner catalog of your best features, and indulge in cultivating them to their finest. Recognize the accomplishments that bring you the most satisfaction, and make them a part of your daily life. Volunteering once a month at a shelter is satisfying, but sharing your ability to give every day magnifies your generosity and the pleasure you receive from giving. A gift for painting or writing deserves more than a weekend of dabbling. Focus your creative imagination into unusual corners, such as daily problem solving or weekly planning. Celebrate your talents, recognize their power, and treat them with loving care. Always be your own best friend.

The value you place on yourself is a reflection of how well you understand yourself. Cherish the traits and strengths that bring you true fulfillment and sustain inner peace and joy. Nurture your natural abilities, appreciate them, and indulge them. When you take care of yourself first, your capacity to give, share and love become unlimited. Treasure the talents that give you pride and satisfy you. Set aside a little time each day to reflect on your positive attributes, and think about the best way to express your best. Appreciate how much better you are for simply knowing yourself better. Trust your courage, and celebrate how unique you are. No one can love you as well as you can love yourself.

Accept Who You Are

You look around and realize that you are not the same as other people. You may realize that someone else looks better than you. You may see that someone else has better clothes than you or is in better physical shape. Those differences occur because we are all different people. We were made differently, and we need to realize that we are different so that we can love each other's differences. If we were all the same, where would the fun be in that?

Having a positive attitude about life is easier said than done. Some people may have a negative attitude about life because of past experiences. Others may have a negative outlook because things in their lives never turn out their way. Those people might hate who they are and desire to be like someone else. They may give up hope and decide to end it all. Ending it all is a very bad thing to do because that person who ends it all could have been successful; he/she could have saved lives, yet took his/her own.

To increase self-esteem, and thereby prevent suicide, one must accept himself/herself. The first step in learning how to accept yourself is learning how privileged you are. Some people think their situation is the worst situation. However, through one perusal of the news, one might find out that his/her situation is nothing compared to other people around the world. Another way to start accepting who you are is by learning your history. Ask your mom or dad about your past. If they don't know, or if you cannot find out that information, try to find out information about your own history.

Learning your own history means learning the history of people of your ethnicity. Once you learn how people in your culture struggled and overcame struggles in history, you will accept who you are and start loving yourself.

If you don't like history, as many people don't, then focus on the present. Think of the struggle you're going through. For example, if you are a person who is overweight, search online for stories about people who used to be overweight, people who lost the weight. Maybe you could search for people who have stories about how they overcame their internal struggles. Real stories from present-day people are very helpful. While you read those stories, you learn that you're not alone. Other people feel the exact same way you feel. Don't despair, keep trying.

Once you have read the stories, start a goal list. A building is never built roof-down. Therefore, your first goals should be very, very short term. Start with something you can achieve in one minute. For example, make it a goal to read a joke every day. Jokes can be found online. They could be in the form of text, or pictures. You could look up funny pictures, cool short jokes, or you could look up videos of cats playing the piano. Make it a goal to have at least one minute where you laugh each day. After that, you could start a goal that takes an hour per day. Then move onto one that takes a day per week, then one that takes a week per month, then one that take a month per year. Before you know it, your goal to laugh a minute per day has changed into achieving joy throughout the whole year. And if you're joyful throughout the whole year, you will certainly be during the next, and the next.

All this seems easier said than done. However, if you start with a minute's goal and move up, true acceptance of your self is possible.

Self Esteem - 5 Ways to Feel Better about Who You Are

The definition of self-esteem is how you feel about yourself and how you think others feel about you. Do you feel that other people, especially those with influence in your life value, love, and accept you for who you are? If the answer is yes, then you probably have a normal to high self-esteem level. On the other hand, if you have low self-esteem, you may feel a low sense of self-worth and feel incapable of pleasing those around you.

An individual's self-esteem is directly related to his or her self-image. This is the mental picture that you have of yourself based on some factors like how you look, what you can do successfully, and the things that you are not so good at. Because these two are so closely related, as you grow over time and develop new interests and experience new things your self-image will change too. This affects your self esteem in either a negative or positive way.

First, it is important to understand that self-esteem is affected by how you see yourself and how others treat you. For children and even adults, critical parents, teachers, spouses, and bosses all have the power to negatively affect self-esteem. While you may not be able to control others, you can change the things that you think about yourself by first becoming more aware of them.

Take time to reflect on how you are thinking and even talking to yourself so to speak. If you find that you freq uently have a negative inner voice, this could be a large cause of low self-esteem.

The good news here is that your self-esteem is not set in stone. You can do some things to improve it:

1. Reverse Your Negative Thought Patterns

If you have discovered that you are your own worst critic, you need to begin to focus on the things that you like about yourself. At first, you might need to be very deliberate about this by writing positive aspects about yourself down in a journal.

2. Set Realistic Goals

Some individuals set standards and goals for themselves that only aim at perfection. And, since perfection cannot be achieved their self-esteem is damaged even further. Set small achievable goals for yourself. Don't forget to congratulate and even reward yourself as you meet your goals.

3. Improve Self Esteem With New Experiences

Try new things including hobbies, sports, and events just because you want to. As you experience success in these areas, your self-esteem will soar.

4. Make Exercise Part Of Your Daily Routine

Exercise will not only give you more energy and increased health; it also releases endorphins that contribute to positive self-esteem. Working out regularly is something you need to make a habit of, even if it is just a walk around the neighborhood.

5. Cut Yourself Some Slack

Some people with low self-esteem are so hard on themselves whenever they make a mistake that they are afraid to ever try something new. Teach yourself to see mistakes as a learning experience. See it as a chance to get better next time.

Self-esteem is important because it can affect every area of your life. Your relationships will thrive or suffer based on how you feel about yourself and how you think others feel about you. Maybe you have heard it said that if you want people to like, then you first have to like yourself. That is exactly how self-esteem works.

Learning to Love Who You Are

It's a true statement to say that we were all born selfish. But it's not a true statement to say that we all were born with the understanding of self-love. Most of us are not aware of just how much we don't love ourselves until we've experienced negative encounters with other people. Is it possible for a person to be selfish and not love who they are? Most definitely! Today, you see a lot of people that proclaim to have self-love, when in fact what you see are people that have had a growth spur in selfishness.

Webster's dictionary defines selfishness as "concerned excessively or exclusively with oneself; seeking or concentrating on one's own advantage, pleasure, or well -being without regard for others." Webster's also defines love as "an unselfish loyal and benevolent concern for the good of another; as the fatherly concern of God for humankind, brotherly concern for others. " Though many equate selfishness with self-love, by these definitions, clearly you can see that they are not!

Learning how to love and accept yourself means taking away all the conditions and mental limitations that would cause you to believe that you don't deserve to be loved or accepted. It may also require you to end unhealthy relationships that will perpetuate feelings of unworthiness and hopelessness. In general, you will have to evaluate those experiences both past and present to help you understand what may have prohibited you from developing in this area of your life.

Were you the product of a single parent home? Were you abused mentally, physically or sexually as a child? Were you bullied and humiliated before classmates in school? It's these types of experiences that will develop as a root in a person's life which ultimately bears fruits of selfishness, drug and alcohol addictions, and sexual misconduct.

The first step in learning how to love and accept yourself is to forgive yourself and others for what may have caused a lifetime of pain. Forgiveness is so important because this is where your freedom resides! Your freedom from hurt and pain lies in your ability to forgive those that have hurt you in any fashion. If you allow un-forgiveness to harbor in your heart, you also allow bitterness and brokenness to live there as well. You must forgive others and also forgive yourself for moving forward.

The second step is to observe your actions and reactions concerning life situations. You must learn to be aware of the why behind every decision you make concerning your life. We don't realize most of the time that what we do and how we react to life circumstances says a lot about how we feel about ourselves. Our decisions can shape our views of self and can block our development of self-love. Decisions can be both conscious and sub-conscious. We usually know why we are making a conscious decision to do something; therefore; it's the sub-conscious decisions that get us into trouble. This is why it is important to evaluate the why behind EVERY decision, so you can become more aware of your reasoning.

The third step is to understand that you are unique! There will never be anyone like you in all the years to come! There is something special about you and there is a reason and purpose for why God created you. You have a unique plan purposed for YOUR life. So many times we judge and compare ourselves to other people and this is a dishonor to you. There are certain things you were graced to do and other things you were not graced to do. When we try to cross over into areas that are not our gifts, this can cause a deep sense of dislike towards yourself because you feel that something is wrong with you. Stay in your lane! Don't try to do things that you know you don't have the grace to do.

Developing self-love and acceptance can be a lifelong process for many. But it doesn't have to be if you can identify those areas in your life that continually keep you from personal growth and make peace with them. Decide today that you will learn to love and accept who you are, regardless of your past. Your past can be a great teacher, or it can be a memoir of pain and mistakes that often revisits you leaving feelings of inadequacy. You're more than that! You just have to start believing that you are!

Six Tips for Loving the Fabulous Person You Are

Throughout my life, I've encountered scores of people who don't appear to love themselves. They say negative things about their appearance, their lack of success at work, not being a good parent or child, or not making the right choices in life. While it is true that we all grapple with issues related to any of these items, we should spend more time on itemizing and being grateful for our positive attributes and successes, and less time on what we feel is wrong with us, negative experiences, or perceived failures.

Make list of the things you like about yourself

These items could relate to your physical appearance, your emotional status, your mental acuity, the type of friend or parent you are, how you relate to people at work or any other positive attribute that comes to mind. Add to this list as you identify additional items you like about yourself. Keep this list in a place where you see it daily. It will remind you of your unique strengths, talents, skills, attributes, and gifts.

Make a second list of complements that you have received from family members, friends, coworkers, neighbors, and others.

Again, add to this list every time you receive a compliment if it is different from those already on your list. You will begin to see a pattern of the positive attributes that others see in you. Remember to keep this list in a place where you can review it daily. If you are experiencing difficulty in developing this list, ask people you trust what they love most about you.

Make time for yourself every day,

Even if it is just for 15 minutes. During this time, review your lists. They will remind you of what you and others like about you. This can be uplifting when you are having a rough day. Spending time with yourself can also allow an opportunity for you to examine issues, resolve problems, or recharge your batteries. By allowing yourself this special time, you are taking care of yourself, which is part of loving one's self.

Learn how to enjoy those times when you are alone.

Engage in activities that make you feel good and give you comfort, whether this is watching your favorite TV program, reading a good book, going out to your favorite restaurant, or taking a hot bubble bath. When you can be comfortable in being alone, doing those things you love most, you are showing yourself how much you value you. If you do not enjoy being alone, examine what is behind that. Assess why you need to constantly be around other people. What are you hiding from? What don't you want to face?

If you constantly berate yourself or can't understand how people can love you

You might want to consider counseling or therapy. Whether your issues come from childhood traumas or a series of negative experiences, it is never too late to put the past to rest and move on. We can't change the past, but we can shape our future. A counselor or therapist can help you to see how past experiences have resulted in current feelings and behaviors. Once you understand this and know that you can't change the past, you will be in a better position to move forward and begin exploring ways to appreciate you for the person you are and love yourself.

Spoil yourself, as you deserve it

Pamper yourself by doing what makes you feel good or loved. If it is spending a day at the spa, going on a vacation, or spending time with loved ones, set aside time to do it. Although I think you should spoil yourself daily, make sure you do this at least once a week. And don't feel guilty... you deserve it!

If you are experiencing difficulty in loving yourself, take time to develop a list of your strengths and attributes, take note of the compliments people give you, take time every day to relax and remember what makes you unique, learn how to enjoy your alone time, seek counseling or therapy if you need to work through past issues, and remember to spoil yourself, at least weekly if not every day. You are a loving person and are loved by more people than you can imagine. Learn how to love yourself... you are your most important asset!

Six Pillars of Self Esteem - Accept Yourself for Who You Are

The six pillars of self-esteem are a vital key to success. Self-acceptance is one of the six pillars of self-esteem. If you don't have a good level of self-esteem and self-acceptance then you will find that being successful is more difficult. Your interactions with people will not produce the results you want, you will suffer from poor motivation, and you will drift from day to day running the risk of not facing up to reality.

The six pillars of self-esteem include facing up to facts, being willing to stand up for ourselves, having a purpose, having integrity, and being responsible for our actions.

The last of the six pillars of self-esteem is self-acceptance - being willing to experience who we are even if we don't like what we see. Only a person with high self-esteem can accept themselves for who they truly are. If you want personal growth and personal success, you will need to be able to accept yourself as you are.

A failure of self-acceptance will cost you dearly

Being unwilling to accept yourself for what you can lead you to waste enormous amounts of time and energy trying to be something you are not. In the long run, this effort is usually wasted as you true self comes shining through -warts and all!

While you are busy rejecting our true self, you are increasing our levels of unhappiness, stress, and anxiety. If you have severe difficulty in accepting yourself, the mental consequences can be very serious indeed.

How to accept yourself?

Of the six pillars of self-esteem, self-acceptance is the one that is most closely associated with our past conditioning, and it is most deeply rooted in our very core. Improving your levels of self-acceptance can take time and patience. However, the rewards in terms of personal growth and personal success are very worthwhile.

Very often we have the most difficulty accepting our faults - we seem them as massive mountains when if we could see ourselves as others see us, they would just be tiny molehills. So one thing to do is to get the opinions of people who you trust, to be honest with you and who you know will help you.

On the flip side, if you are the person who does not have the six pillars of self-esteem firmly embedded in your makeup, it is very common to overlook many of your positive qualities in favor of beating yourself up about your weaknesses. Find some time to sit down quietly and think about the successes you've had throughout your life. Identify and write down all the positive qualities that have led to those successes.

Think about people you know well enough to recognize their good and bad sides. That should help you to realize that no one's perfect. If everyone were perfect, the world would be a very uninteresting place. You need some imperfections to highlight your best qualities

Provided your faults don't lead you to be dishonest, immoral, or cause harm to other people, accept that there's nothing wrong with them.

Where your faults have led you to make mistakes, don't beat yourself up endlessly for your perceived failure. Understand that there's no such thing as failure or mistakes; they are just learning experiences. If you can use them to move forward, you will be much better off.

Finally try at all times to make sure that all your actions are aligned with universal principles such as love, mutual respect, honesty, integrity... that way you don't have anything to feel bad about.

Working on the six pillars of self-esteem, which includes working on accepting yourself for what you are, both the good and the not so good is important for you to live a happy and fulfilled live, achieving personal growth and personal success. There are many keys to success that let you come to terms with yourself as you are.

Loving Yourself for Who You Are

One of the major underlying issues in the vast majority of health problems is having a lack of self-confidence. This, in turn, stems from not truly loving yourself for who you are. Women, especially, tend to fall prey to this notion. Because women feel a higher demand placed on them to look and act a certain way while at the same time competing with men for corporate positions and employment, they often are super critical of their body image. Often, when you compliment a woman, she won't take it seriously, thinking that surely you must not see her imperfections the way that she does.

Self-confidence doesn't come wrapped up in a neat package. Rather, it is something that must be learned and ingrained in you. You gain self-confidence by loving yourself and accepting all of your "faults" as being a part of your physical makeup. Sure, there are some things that you can change about yourself such as body image by working out and eating healthier, but other things you cannot do so much to change quite as easily. Even though it sounds sort of cliché, you truly have to love yourself. Part of that means respecting yourself before you can respect others. You cannot truly love other people if you don't love yourself first.

Stress and the demands of a job and a family can put a lot of pressure on you at times. This is why it is important to have other outlets to turn to to relieve stress. Many people, when they are faced with stressful situations put a lot of pressure on themselves. Often, they will be the first ones to blame themselves for things that are often out of their control and for which they had no part of. Having a support system of close friends and family is important when learning how to love and respect yourself. We all need someone to encourage us in times when we are feeling most vulnerable.

Learning how to live a good life is often difficult to do because there are many temptations out there which make it so. By being a good person and doing the right things, we can gain more confidence in ourselves. It is in times when we know that we are not doing the right things to help ourselves or other people that we feel the most guilty. Whenever we make decisions, we need to remind ourselves what is at stake. You need to live a life that you can be proud of. You want to be able to sleep soundly knowing that you made well-thought-out decisions which had positive outcomes.

All of this is part of being a better person. If someone else approaches you and asks you to do something unethical, whether it is a boss, colleague or friend, what will you decide to do? It is a matter of prioritizing what is important to you in your life as well as what you can live with at the end of the day. Learn to see people and situations for what they are worth. Don't sell yourself short, and learn to speak up for yourself. You'll do yourself a favor in the long run, not to mention the fact that you'll do so much more in terms of your personal development as a human being.

Discard Approval, Love and Accept Yourself

Let go of the need for approval and just be who you are and spread love and appreciation around you like there's no tomorrow.

Have you any idea how common it is for people to think about what others think of them?

To be concerned about what others might have thought of them yesterday when they said something that wasn't what everyone else thought? And if they really could do this thing they feel passionate about- what if people laugh at them, or thought they were. well, different?

The truth is that many do think these thoughts while thinking they are the only ones who think them... People are more hung up on what others think of them and haven't even had time to be worried about what you said at all.

The next time you find yourself consumed by thoughts like this; turn it all around and look at the other person as a person who has the very same concerns that you have. How could you give the other some comfort? What would you say to yourself if it was you, (which it is on a deeper level), that wondered if you had said something "stupid" or "wrong"? What would happen if you turned your attention away from your little self and put it instead on the other person and his/her well-being? And what if that other person did the same to you and thought of you first..?

Well, things would be very different between us humans.

Now comes the next step, and it sometimes makes people again think "What will they think of me if I said this or that to or about this person?" It has to change; the fact that it is easier to talk negatively behind someone's back than it is to openly say something positive to someone.

To give someone appreciation for no reason at all, a compliment or a word of encouragement can really scare people, and sometimes you might even get a strange look from someone if you do this openly, especially if you don't have any "reason" for being supportive and "nice." If we only knew how much it could mean to someone else to hear that we matter, or that which we do is appreciated.

Yesterday I listened to a seminar online, and I don't remember which brand or company it was, but it is a famous hair salon. Anyway; the story was that he, the owner, had had a customer who wanted a nice hairdo because she was going away later that evening, so while making her look more beautiful he also said many times that she is beautiful and so on; he gave her compliments and made her feel important. I don't remember the whole story, but the core message was, that the woman had planned to kill herself that evening, and went to the hairdresser to make herself beautiful before she killed herself, but that while being there she changed her mind because of this hairdresser who made her feel beautiful and important.

From that moment on; the hairdresser has trained all his employees to ask within themselves "how can I make your day better?" or something like that to all of their costumes. I thought it was a wonderful story.

Think about the effect a kind word can have! Let us be brave and give compliments and encouragement regardless of what others might think of us.

I have had times in my life when I have asked myself if what I do really has any meaning at all, times when I have felt discouragement, when suddenly I get an email from someone who has been touched by my words, or someone says to me that what I have done for them has helped them to see things differently and therefore helped them to take a step in the right direction.

That has been the sign I needed form God to continue what I do regardless of how things have seemed to evolve.

Today; do something similar for at least three people in your life. Tell them that they matter, tell them that you appreciate what they have done for you. Make them feel important. Or just smile to someone on the street and say "hello."

What I have done for years now is that I send a silent blessing to people I meet or see. When I walk by them, I say "God bless you" in my mind to them, I say "may your day be blessed with joy," "may you always be protected by the Angels" and so on.

I do this every day; it has become a habit, and sometimes I can feel and see they knew something happened, I can see in their eyes that they on some level "heard" and received the blessing. I can feel the love flowing between us, even if we have never seen each other before.

What if we all did that? Wouldn't it be wonderful? It can be done, and it's easy; because it all begins with You.

CHAPTER 5
HEALING AND RECOVERING FROM NARCISSISM AND EMOTIONAL ABUSE

Discover Your Level of Narcissism

All of us have some characteristics and behaviors that fall into the category of narcissism. Narcissism is on a continuum from mild, occasional, and subtle to the more ubiquitous, obvious or extreme behaviors of a Narcissistic Personality Disorder. Since narcissism is likely a part of everyone's ego wounded self, it is helpful to your personal growth and development to be aware of your level of narcissism.

Be honest with yourself - but not judgmental - regarding the presence and intensity of the following characteristics:

I generally take others' rejecting, critical, harsh, shut-down, or diminishing behaviour personally. I tell myself that when others choose to behave in uncaring ways toward me, it is my fault - it is about me not being good enough or me doing something wrong. I make others' choices - to be open or closed, loving or unloving - about me.

I frequently judge and shame myself, trying to get myself to do things "right" so that I can have control over getting others' love, attention or approval. Getting others' love, attention and approval are vital to me.

I make others responsible for my worth, value, sense of aliveness and fullness. Others have to be kind, loving, approving of me, or sexually attracted to me, for me to feel that I'm okay. When others ignore me or are not attracted to me, I feel unworthy, depressed or empty inside.

I have a hard time having compassion for myself, so I expect others to have compassion for me when I feel anxious, depressed, angry, shamed or guilty, rather than taking responsibility for my feelings. If others lack compassion for me or criticize me, I turn things around onto them and blame them.

I lack empathy and compassion for the feelings of others, especially when I've behaved in ways that may be hurtful to others. I have a hard time recognizing or identifying with the feelings and needs of others.

When someone offers me valuable information about myself or 'tough love', I see it as an attack, rather than as a gift, and I generally attack back.

The DSM IV - The Diagnostic and Statistical Manual of Mental Disorders, states about people suffering from a Narcissistic Personality Disorder:

"Vulnerability in self-esteem makes individuals with Narcissistic Personality Disorder very sensitive to "injury" from criticism or defeat. Although they may not show it outwardly, criticism may haunt these individuals and may leave them feeling humiliated, degraded, hollow and empty. They may react with disdain, rage, or defiant counterattack. Such experience may lead to social withdrawal or an appearance of humility. Interpersonal relations are typically impaired due to problems derived from entitlement, the need for admiration, and the relative disregard for the sensitivities of others."

When in conflict with someone, or when someone behaves in a way I don't like, I often focus on getting them to deal with what they are doing, rather than focus on what I'm doing. I make them responsible for my choices and feelings, and I believe things will get better if I can get them to change.

I feel entitled to get what I want from others - whether it's money, sex, attention or approval. Others 'owe' me.

I often try to get away with things, such as not having to follow the rules or the law, and I'm indignant when I'm called to the carpet.

I see myself as special and entitled to do what I want, even if it's harmful to others.

I believe I should get credit for what I do and I should be recognized as superior, even if I do a mediocre job.

I am so unique and special that only other unique and special people can understand me. It is beneath me to associate with people who are not as special as I am. While some think I am arrogant, it is only because I'm truly so unique and special.

Because I'm so special, I have the right to demand what I want from others, and to manipulate others - with my charm, brilliance, anger or blame - into giving me what I want.

Again, all of us have some of these characteristics, and it is important to learn about them, rather than judge ourselves for them.

Narcissism can be healed. You can learn to define your worth, to give yourself the love and compassion you need to feel full inside, and to share love with others.

Healing from A Relationship With A Narcissist

Many of us have been there.

You met the person of your dreams - charming, intelligent, romantic, attentive, incredible chemistry and a great lover. You might have been told how wonderful you are, how this was the first time your lover had ever felt this way and had this level of connection, and you felt truly seen for the first time.

Perhaps there was a nagging unease that all this was happening too fast - that he or she couldn't possibly feel this way about you without knowing you better. But you were swept off your feet and finally decided to open your heart.

The confusion may have started then, as your lover pulled away and became critical. Or, it might have started after you married, and you found yourself with a partner different than the person you fell in love with.

Whether your relationship was two months or two years or two decades, it was likely tumultuous, confusing and painful. And if you were married and then divorced, it might have been more painful or even frightening.

There is much healing for you to do if you were in love with a narcissist.

The Process of Healing From Your Narcissistic Partner

1) First, you need to be very compassionate with yourself and let yourself grieve for the huge loss of what you had hoped for. It might seem easier to judge yourself for the big mistakes you believe you made, but self-judgment will keep you stuck. There is no possibility of healing when you judge yourself.

Each time the grief comes up, embrace it with kindness and caring toward yourself. Even though you know it's better to have ended this relationship; it's hard to let go of the intensity of a relationship with a narcissist. It's hard to imagine a future relationship that isn't boring compared to the intensity you've been experiencing.

2) Once some of the grief has subsided, then it's time to go inward and explore why you were vulnerable to this person. Was your partner giving you what you were not giving to yourself? Was your partner seeing you and valuing you in the way you need to be seeing and valuing yourself? Did you ignore some red flags because you so wanted it all to be true?

Did you make excuses for your partner to avoid facing the truth? Did you give yourself up to try to have control over getting your partner to be loving to you again? What did you sacrifice to keep the relationship - your integrity, your financial security, your time with family and friends, your time for yourself, your inner knowing?

It's vitally important to be honest with yourself so that you don't end up feeling like a victim, and so that you have less of a chance of repeating this in a future relationship.

3) Educate yourself about narcissism. There are numerous books, websites and articles devoted to understanding narcissism. You can also buy my book on Narcissist. Since I'm certain that you don't want to repeat this, you need to do all you can to learn about what happened. You need to become sensitive to the numerous red flags so that you can pick them up very early in a subsequent relationship.

One of my clients shared that she had met a man six years ago, dated him a few times, and then they remained distant friends. Recently, when she was in his town, they saw each other, and she was very attracted to him. He came on strong, inviting her to join him on an upcoming European vacation. She felt uneasy, but a day later texted him to see if he wanted to have dinner with her. He never responded to the invitation. It took her only 24 hours to recognize these two red flags of narcissism - coming on strong and then disappearing. She was pleased that she found this out so soon! Instead of beating herself up for being attracted to another narcissist, she congratulated herself for staying open to the truth.

Since narcissists are often very attractive, any of us can become attracted. But whether or not we will pursue it depends on how much Inner Bonding work we have done.

Recovery from Narcissistic Abuse - To Get Your Life Back on Track

Narcissism or Narcissistic Personality Disorder (NPD) is a mental disorder that involves a persistent pattern of grandiosity. The person with this disorder constantly wants to be admired, is obsessed and infatuated with himself. The narcissistic individual also lacks compassion and empathy; is ruthless, egotistical, seeking dominance and gratification. To deal with and to live with a narcissistic can leave someone very traumatized due to the emotional abuse the narcissistic partner has caused. If you were married to a narcissist, you might find that it is difficult to escape from that relationship. If you do escape, your recovery will be long and painful. No matter how difficult the road to recovery is, you have to get through it so that your life will be back on track again.

• You have to know what the qualities of a narcissistic person are. It would include a frequent display of jealousy, infidelity, control, lying, and insecurity, verbal and even physical abuse. If these behaviours are not excused and are often tolerated, it would seem to the narcissistic person that they are acceptable. If you were successful in leaving a narcissistic partner or spouse, he would certainly lure you back again. As much as you love this person, you have to be firm in letting him know that his narcissistic behaviour may only be resolved with the help of a professional. He must seek professional assistance to correct his abusive personality, or he will not change. Being manipulated and believing that your ex will change on his own accord will only bring you back to a miserable and painful life.

• In recovering, you also need to realize that you are your complete person. When you decided to be in a relationship or marry a narcissistic person, you may have already developed a dependency on that person. He may have captured your heart with his attentive, generous and suave personality. This then resulted in your emotional dependency on him that eventually turned out as something for you to regret. Once escaped from the binding relationship with a narcissist, do your best to regain your emotional independence. It will help you to be firm and able to stand again on your own. Learn to love and accept your self-worth. Set your standards for whoever will soon come into your life. Do not accept anyone whose attributes are less than the standards you have set and you know you rightfully deserve.

• There are various materials that are now available online about dealing with narcissism. These resources will help you in understanding more about this disorder. Your gained knowledge will empower you and will make you realize what weaknesses have caused you to be captured in the narcissistic bait.

• You may also look for groups and organizations where you can be a part of. These groups offer help and an opportunity to communicate and interact with other people who have suffered and endured narcissistic relationships. These are the people whom you need to be with, together you can inspire one another and help one another obtain complete recovery and freedom from your experience.

Emotional Abuse - 8 Steps to Recovery

Do you remember the day your partner left you for someone new? That sick sinking feeling in your gut that you just weren't good enough? You tried so hard, and in the end, she was gone and with someone new.

At first, the silence was deafening, and you were so lonely, so very lonely. How could she be in love with you one day and love with someone else the next? You called. You texted. You just needed answers, but never got any response. You wanted a second chance to prove you could be better, but after a while, this passed, too, and you thought you were going to finally make it through the heartache.

You decide you don't want anything more to do with her and stop trying to contact her. BUT, now all those emotions are flooding back, and you just want to cry out in frustration after getting ANOTHER text, call or email from your ex. She hasn't heard from you in a while and misses you. She wants to get together, and so you do. She never really explains why she cheated or why she came back. She's just back, and you are on cloud nine... for a few months. Then the same thing happens again.

And here you are again, alone and still in love with the same person who "claimed" the breakup was your fault, that you weren't good enough. She's again ignoring your calls and texts wanting an explanation for why she walked out? The same person who was just posting all over Facebook about the "new" love in her life? And just like before, once you start to come out of the fog and start thinking it's over, all of a sudden, she wants you back? Do you feel trapped in a never-ending cycle of abuse, like a washing machine - rinse, spin, repeat, rinse, spin, repeat.

When you are together, does she make you feel like you are walking on eggshells, praying you don't do anything to upset her? Do you ignore or avoid calling her out on the hurtful things she says or does because you fear that every argument is your last? Does she constantly put you down and make you feel inferior to her? Have you stopped speaking to family and friends since you two have been together?

Wasn't this the same person who called you her soul mate? Do you remember she talked about her ex when you first got together? How crazy and jealous her ex was, and how glad she was to have found you. She told you that you were her soul mate.

Do you fall for her lies again, thinking you can recapture the early period of your relationship, when she was good and caring and kind? I don't like being the bearer of bad news, but I have to tell you, you're in relationship hell, stuck on a roller coaster, and to save yourself, you have to get away from this narcopath, who is nothing more than an emotional vampire.

Here's some hard-learned information. When you are desperately texting and calling to get "closure" by having your questions answered, you are feeding her energy. She thrives on this behaviour from you. It makes her feel powerful. She loves telling her new flame and all her friends how crazy psycho you are now. But, when you finally realize it's over, and stop calling and texting, guess what? She's not getting that supply of energy she is addicted to so much, and she thinks she's about to lose a great source of supply, so she starts calling and texting you. KNOW THIS: No normal person truly in love does this sort of thing. She is hovering - a term used to describe a narcopath who feels like you may be slipping away from her death grip.

It's imperative that you have no contact with this person. Even when she plays on your guilt or uses shame to trick you into "just talking to her", don't fall for it. Make yourself think like she thinks when you are dealing with her. She has no conscience or qualms about hurting you, so you take on the same attitude. It will continue, and the no contact may very well send her into a narcissistic rage. It doesn't matter what she does, stick to no contact.

In recovering from the emotional and verbal abuse of your former partner, here are eight steps you need to take to prepare yourself not to break the no contact rule:

1. Recognize that your love for this person is REAL. Ignoring this fact only sets you up for more abuse;

2. Recognize that this person lied to you, tricked you into falling in love. Think about it for a second. Had you met the person you are with now, would you have gone on a second date? Hell, no. It was an act, only an act. A narcopath is incapable of experiencing real emotion like

love, empathy, compassion, guilt, etc. The only emotion I believe they feel is anger, and I'm sure you've seen the irrational rage common with narcopaths;

3. Accept the fact you will never get the answers to the burning questions you have;

4. Accept that the dream she promised was a lie;

5. Accept the fact that you can only change yourself, you cannot change her, and despite promises of change she always makes to get you to come back, she will not change;

6. Once you have internalized the first four steps, then you are ready to commit yourself to have absolutely no contact with her whatsoever. If you have children together, then limit the contact to ONLY discussions about the children;

7. Find a therapist to talk to. If you aren't comfortable talking to anyone face-to-face, then join a members-only site that offers advice and counselling; and finally

8. Find activities that help you restore your self-worth, your self-confidence and your joy. Colour therapy is an excellent activity for opening up your mind to new ideas and focusing on colouring puts you in a positive state of mind. EBT is good if you understand how it's done.

Best Tips to Recover from Narcissistic Abuse

How to heal from emotional abuse starts by recognizing that you have a problem. Even if you have already severed ties from an abusive relationship, it doesn't mean that everything will just go back to being alright.

There is an invisible energy stream that still exists between you and your previous abusive partner. It prevents you from being able to move forward with your life as you still unconsciously carry the emotional burden caused by the narcissist. You need to actively work from separating yourself in mind and soul to be able to break free from it. You will soon learn how as you continue to read along.

It is very helpful to regard yourself as a survivor and a winner instead of a victim. It immediately empowers you and gives you back control of your life. Here are some tips on how to heal from emotional abuse:

Understand that it's not your fault

Once you can find comfort in the fact that it's not your fault, you will begin to realize that you are not the cause of negative experiences you have gone through as opposed to what your abuser made you believe.

Confide in a close friend or relative

The people you trust will be able to provide you with the love and support at this critical time of healing. Talking about what you have gone through will help you better understand and accept your experience of abuse.

Discover coping tools

Find out what helps you express your emotions, release anger or grief. Writing in a journal, composing poems or songs, painting, any sport or playing a musical instrument can help you cope and let out your feelings. It will aid you in taking your mind off the pain you suffered and replace it with good and happy memories.

Take care of yourself

Learn to look after yourself first before taking care of others. Believe that you are worthy of respect, love and acceptance just like everybody else. Take pride in your unique qualities and improve on your weaknesses. You have to have faith in yourself first before other people do

CHAPTER 6
OVERCOMING AND RECOVERING FROM CODEPENDENCY

Shedding Codependency - 3 Tips for Overcoming Codependent Tendencies

Codependency is a term that has been used primarily to describe some of the common characteristics and behaviors that occur in people who are closely involved with an addict. These traits, which include excessive levels of tolerance for damaging behavior from their addicted loved one, a tendency to try to "rescue" or save the addict from his or her behavior, extreme caretaking tendencies, and a sense of responsibility for the addict's choices can all fall under the heading of codependency. These same traits can be found in other relationship dynamics where one person is behaving in destructive ways, such as in abusive scenarios. Here is three tips for overcoming codependent tendencies:

1. Consider it a act of love to allow the person you are protecting, defending, or making excuses for to face responsibility for his or her actions. The fact is, by trying to control his or her behavior, by shielding him or her from consequences, you become part of the system that allows these behaviors to continue. Without consequences, your loved one has no motive to change.

2. Begin to take better care of yourself. Make a conscious effort to shift focus away from solving your partner's problems, and consider your own needs in terms of diet, vitamins and supplements, and exercise. Eat healthy, unprocessed, organic foods whenever possible. Take vitamins and supplements according to your naturopath or other health practitioner's recommendations. Fish oil and a food-based multivitamin are a good start for many people. Exercise according to your doctor's recommendations, ideally doing 45 minutes of cardiovascular exercise 5 times a week. These activities not only focus on you and improve health, but send your

mind the message that you are worth the effort and care.

3. Begin imagining your own life, your own dreams and aspirations, and spend regular time focused on that rather than focusing on what your loved one is doing. Allowing yourself to spend some time daydreaming and fantasizing about your ideal future in detail - how it will look, sounds, taste, feel, and smell - will increase your motivation and likelihood of seeing it manifest in reality.

Overcome Codependency - Discover the Freedom of Emotional Independence

Codependency has been defined in many different ways. Originally, it referred to the dynamic which is created when the support person of an alcoholic/addict becomes attached to being needed by that person and begins to unconsciously (or consciously) enable their destructive behavior, thereby maintaining the alcoholic's/addict's debilitation. Since then, codependency has begun to be defined more broadly. In order to fully understand what it means to be codependent, let's first define what it means to be emotionally independent.

Emotional independence is the ability to consistently meet your own needs. It means knowing how to pay attention to yourself, validate yourself, and provide yourself with a sense of self-worth. It is about fulfilling your own emotional needs rather than going outside yourself to have those needs met by other people. No one lives in a vacuum, so of course you are bound to receive attention, validation, etc. from the people you interact with, however, there is a vital distinction between receiving those gifts and being dependent upon them. Is having someone compliment you the icing on your cake, or is it your whole cake? Do you enjoy getting attention from the people you care about or do you need that attention to feel good about yourself?

Looking at emotional independence in this way, it becomes clear that emotional dependence, or codependency, does not exist as a specific label, but as a spectrum of interrelatedness. Therefore, codependency is herein defined as the degree to which you are reliant upon other people to meet your emotional needs. As you go along with book, consider what percentage of your emotional wellbeing you take care of in-house and what percentage you outsource. Is this a balance which is serving you or a lopsided arrangement which leaves you feeling needy and insatiable?

Changing yourself...

A vicious cycle:

The need for other people's recognition is a self-reinforcing cycle. Uncomfortable feelings arise (lonely, sad, empty, worthless, unlovable, etc.) and your first instinct is to do whatever is necessary to get rid of these "negative" emotions. Unable to supply yourself with the antidote to these feelings, you look to those around you to provide you with worth, fulfillment, love, or at least a distraction from the lack of those experiences. Each time you go outside yourself to get your emotional needs met, you are sending yourself some very strong messages.

Another people's attention is more valuable than mine. My own love is worthless. I am not capable of meeting my own needs. I will never feel whole on my own

These messages are internalized unconsciously and reinforce both the "negative" feelings you were experiencing originally, and the belief that you are dependent upon other people's attention/approval/validation, etc. The reliance upon other people's validation increases as the value you place on your own recognition plummets.

Breaking the cycle:

Breaking this cycle begins with becoming aware of your emotions.

When you have the urge to reach out to someone for emotional support, resist the temptation to react to that urge. Instead, turn your focus inward. What feelings are is you experiencing? What do you want to avoid by going outside yourself? Is what emotions does being alone bring up for you (lonely, afraid, bored, anxious, etc.)? Just sit with those feelings and try to allow them without judgment.

Notice the subtle reward of paying attention to yourself. Self-recognition is a much quieter experience than being recognized by others. It may be difficult to detect it's presence at first but look for it. You are breaking a habit, changing yourself, becoming more self-reliant. That is something to be proud of. Can you get in touch with that feeling?

Get in the practice of stopping and paying attention to yourself whenever you feel needy. Even if you later decide to seek out attention from someone else, you have taken the time to pay attention to yourself first. You has valued your own recognition. You are learning to validate yourself internally.

Changing your relationships...

We tend to be drawn to people who have a similar degree of emotional dependence to our own. If you rated yourself on the extreme end of the codependency spectrum, chances are, you have several people in your life who are in the same range. The "co" in codependency refers to the mutual emotional dependence people develop with one another. Both parties have become accustomed to needing to be need ed so when one person begins to be less needy, this can disrupt the relationship.

Set and maintain boundaries. This isn't just about learning to say "no" to doing people favors. It can also mean declining invitations, choosing to keep some aspects of yourself private, making unpopular choices, protecting yourself from the judgment or verbal abuse of others, etc. It is about valuing and asserting your own interests. This is not selfish, it is self-loving. It is not about saying "no" to others, it is about saying "yes" to yourself and honouring your needs.

When you create a boundary with someone, notice the sense of self-respect this brings. If you are not used to putting yourself first, you may also have feelings of guilt, shame, or self-judgment arise. See if you can dig beneath those feelings to the satisfaction of having taken care of yourself.

Cultivate an interest in yourself. Discover ways of connecting with you. Exploring a hobby, you have always wanted to pursue, taking a class you are interested in, journaling your thoughts and emotions, writing poetry or doing something creative, taking walks, photography, anything that you find fulfilling. You are learning new ways of bringing yourself a sense of worth and joy.

Prioritize your new, self-worth building activities. If a friend invites you to lunch but you had already been planning to go to your yoga class, it may be tempting to drop everything to enjoy your friend's company. The problem is, that sends those same destructive messages ("Other people's attention is more valuable than mine. Spending time with someone else is more fulfilling than pursuing my own interests. Spending time with someone else is more appealing than spending time with me"). Make your commitment to your new activities sacred. It is a promise you are making to yourself. Imagine what kind of a message you are sending yourself each time you keep that promise.

Codependency is a difficult habit to break, but it can be done. Emotional independence is freedom in the purest sense. You are a whole, fulfilled, joyful person all on your own. Since your mood and wellbeing are no longer dependent upon others, there is no need to manipulate, to pull on people for validation. You can be fully present and authentic. Emotional independence is a challenging path to follow, but the empowerment, freedom, and self -respect you will find on this journey will sustain and motivate you along the way.

Three Ways to Overcome Codependent Relationships

Of all relationships, codependent relationships are probably the least healthy ones. If you happen to be in one of these relationships, you should quickly figure out how to solve the issue of codependency or simply call it quits. Whether you are codependent or she is, if the problem is left unsolved, it's going to have negative consequences on you and her in the future. Below is three ways to overcome codependent relationships.

Therapy/Counseling

If you have the financial means, this is probably the best solution. Having professional help is the fastest and most effective way to finding out why has your relationship become codependent and what needs to be done for you and her to go back to those wonderful times you had at the beginning of the relationship. It is also important to note that professional help is unbiased compared to a relative or close friend. A more familiar person will think of what's best for you not for the couple while the professional will consider both parties' interest in the issue at hand.

Let Your Partner Know What's Wrong

Everyone has needs and those needs need to be satisfied. At some point not expressing your needs or feelings will lead to a bigger need of attention which will eventually lead to selfishness. Selfishness is one of the main symptoms in codependent relationships. One of the partners feels the other one should drive all their attention towards them which is not healthy for both partners. Talking about it is the easiest way out of it so don't hesitate to communicate your needs to your partner. After all, if she wasn't interested in making you happy then you need to ask yourself why she's with you.

Participate in Different Activities

This may sound controversial but believe it or not, some activities are better done alone. Usually things are better done in pairs but if it's making you and your partner uncomfortable it's time to switch it up a little. For example, training sessions, girls night out, boys night out, basically any activity you would do better without your partner around. Why? It'll give you the opportunity to meet new people and sometimes it's all it takes to make you or her realize how dependent you've become and how you or her need to change.

When it comes to relationships, drama is inevitable. You can't predict when something will go wrong in the beginning because you seem to be in heaven. However, if you end up in one of that bad relationship, there are very few options for you to choose. Should you try and resolve the issue or move on? One thing's for sure, if it's one of those codependent relationships, you may want to opt for a solution as soon as possible since it can only get worse from this point on.

Recovering from Codependency

Codependency underlies all addictions. The core symptom of "dependency" manifests as reliance on a person, substance, or process (i.e., activity, such as gambling or sex addiction). Instead of having a healthy relationship with yourself, you make something or someone else more important. Over time, your thoughts, feelings, and actions revolve around that other person, activity, or substance, and you increasingly abandon your relationship with yourself.

Recovery entails a 180-degree reversal of this pattern to reconnect with, honour, and act from your core self. Healing develops the following characteristics:

* You're authentic

* You're autonomous

* You're capable of intimacy

* Your values, thoughts, feelings, and actions become integrated and congruent

Change is not easy. It takes time and involves the following four steps:

1. Abstinence

Abstinence or sobriety is necessary to recover from codependency. The goal is to bring your attention back to yourself, to have an internal, rather than external, "locus of control." This means that your actions are primarily motivated by your values, needs, and feelings, not someone else's. You learn to meet those needs in healthy ways. Perfect abstinence or sobriety isn't necessary for progress, and it's impossible concerning codependency with people. You need and depend upon others and therefore give and compromise in relationships. Instead of abstinence, you learn to detach and not control, people-please, or obsess about others. You become more self-directed and autonomous.

If you're involved with an abuser or addict or grew up as the child of one, you may be afraid to displease your partner, and it can require great courage to break that pattern of conceding our power to someone else.

2. Awareness

It's said that denial is the hallmark of addiction. This is true whether you're an alcoholic or in love with one. Not only do codependents deny their addiction - whether to a drug, activity, or a person - they deny their feelings, and especially their needs, particularly emotional needs for nurturing and real intimacy.

You may have grown up in a family where you weren't nurtured, your opinions and feelings weren't respected, and your emotional needs weren't adequately met. Over time, rather than risk rejection or criticism, you learned to ignore your needs and feelings, believed that you be wrong. Some decided to become self-sufficient and find comfort in sex, food, drugs, or work.

All of this leads to low self-esteem. To reverse these destructive habits, you first must become aware of them. The most damaging obstacle to self-esteem is negative self-talk. Most people aren't aware of the internal voices that push and criticize them - their "Pusher," "Perfectionist," and "Critic."

3. Acceptance

Healing essentially involves self-acceptance. This is not only a step but a life-long journey. People come to therapy to change themselves, not realizing that the work is about accepting themselves. Ironically, before you can change, you have to accept the situation. As they say, "What you resist, persists."

In recovery, more about yourself is revealed that requires acceptance, and life itself presents limitations and losses to accept. This is maturity. Accepting reality opens the doors of possibility. Change then happens. New ideas and energy emerge that previously were stagnated from self-blame and fighting reality. For example, when you feel sad, lonely, or guilty, instead of making yourself feel worse, you have self-compassion, soothe yourself, and take steps to feel better.

Self-acceptance means that you don't have to please everyone for fear that they won't like you. You honour your needs and unpleasant feelings and are forgiving of yourself and others. This good-will toward yourself allows you to be self-reflective, without being self-critical. Your self-esteem and confidence grow, and consequently, you don't allow others to abuse you or tell you what to do. Instead of manipulating, you become more authentic and assertive and are capable of greater intimacy.

4. Action

Insight without action only gets you so far. To grow, self-awareness and self-acceptance must be accompanied by new behaviour. This involves taking risks and venturing outside your comfort one. It may involve speaking up, trying something new, going somewhere alone, or setting a boundary. It also means setting internal boundaries by keeping commitments to yourself or saying "no" to your Critic or other old habits you want to change. Instead of expecting others to meet all your needs and make you happy, you learn to take actions to meet them and do things that give you fulfilment and satisfaction in your life.

Each time you try out new behaviour or take a risk, you learn something new about yourself and your feelings and needs. You're creating a stronger sense of yourself, as well as self-confidence and self-esteem. This builds upon itself in a positive feedback loop vs the downward spiral of codependency, which creates more fear, depression, and low self-esteem.

Healing Codependency

Healing codependency does not mean curing codependency. Healing codependency is a process. Healing always begins by recognizing the problem. Knowledge is power, and that is true when we talk about Healing Codependency.

Let us continue the journey of understanding the process of Healing Codependency. Ask yourself these questions: Am I codependent? What does this mean? What codependent behaviours do I have? What does it cost me? These are essential questions as one begins the journey of healing and questions that need to be explored. I suggest you begin a journal and start recording your responses to these questions, allowing it to be your touchstone.

In addition to the journal, a group setting in the form of support groups facilitates the healing process. The community you live in may have some Codependency Support Groups. If not, perhaps try to find the name of a psychotherapist who specializes in addictions and understands codependency. I have found Al-Anon groups to be effective if there is not a Codependency Support Group.

Developing an understanding of the roots of your codependency can provide a foundation for your healing. Many codependents are adult children of alcoholics/addicts and come from dysfunctional families. The journey of healing is about the family of origin work as you discover the role and, the rules you were given and general dynamics from your first family. Most adult children from dysfunctional families remain in those roles, abide by those rules and, struggle with dynamics that are similar to those learned in their family of origins, repeating patterns with their significant other and their children today. However, please keep in mind that as wonderful as insight can be, insight alone will not heal your pain nor provide you with the healing necessary for changing codependent behaviours and patterns.

Learning emotional detachment will assist you in early recovery and be a mainstay throughout your recovery program. Detaching is about learning to balance self in relationship with others. It is the beginning of boundary work, which you will hear much about at support groups and in your recommended readings. Detaching allows your emotional reactivity to lower and an emotional space to open, creating the opportunity for less dependency in relationships. It will be in this new space that one can begin to develop a sense of "who am I?" Needs wants, and feelings can begin to be identified and communicated as you move toward less codependent relationships.

Communication skills, self-esteem building and improving how you manage stress will also be areas that will need to be addressed in your codependency recovery. These "tools" will assist in regaining one's sense of self that was lost in codependent relationships. Recovery is about regaining your power that was lost in the dynamics of codependent relationships. It is about feeling empowered to live one's life without the need of approval, the fear of abandonment, of being preoccupied with pleasing others, about caring too much, and in general over functioning in relationships. Recovery is claiming back self.

CPSIA information can be obtained
at www.ICGtesting.com
Printed in the USA
BVHW030412090722
641728BV00009B/683

9 781801 445979